Louise Schweitzer first worked as an advertising copywriter before a career in journalism, music and theatre criticism, and literary agency. Her education includes a diploma in Journalism and Advertising from London University, an O.U. Humanities degree, a Dip.Mus, Cambridge certificate of Language Teaching, a Music and Aesthetics MA and a Doctorate in Literature from Sussex University. She is an amateur musician, chorister and organist.

Once a bloodhound quarry, she is still a keen cross-country runner and long distance walker. Her book on the South Downs came out in June, 2012.

Louise Schweitzer has three adult children, two grandchildren, three step children, assorted in laws, six step grandchildren and a Rhodesian Ridgeback; she lives with her husband Reicke Schweitzer near the sea in east Sussex.

ONE WILD FLOWER

To my Dumas family who originally inspired a love of Nonsense, to my children Virginia, Alastair and Henrietta who grew up with it, to my husband Reicke who lives with it, and to Norman Vance who taught me how to put it into academic shape.

LOUISE SCHWEITZER

ONE WILD FLOWER

AUSTIN & MACAULEY
PUBLISHERS LTD.

A CIP catalogue record for this title is
available from the British Library.

ISBN 978 1 84963 146 4

www.austinmacauley.com

First Published (2012)
Austin & Macauley Publishers Ltd.
25 Canada Square
Canary Wharf
London
E14 5LB

Printed & Bound in Great Britain

With respect and admiration for Edward Lear, Lewis Carroll, and William Gilbert – all who published them, read them, remember them and still laugh.

INTRODUCTION

Walter de la Mare's picturesque description of Nonsense as the one wild flower[1] of Victorian literature provides the title for this book.[2] My aim is to examine this particular genus and uncover the reasons why it grew, blossomed and flourished between 1840 and 1875. What conditions were necessary for this brief, unique flowering of inspired lunacy? What may we understand by it, and why has it survived? Has it been cut and dried into canonic acceptability: has our response to the implicit anarchy of the uncultivated altered over time? Constant revision of criteria makes the canon a shifting thing – veterans of the first Salon de Refusés in 1874[3] might gasp and stretch their eyes as watery lilies or sunlit cathedrals fetch millions of pounds at international auction. Impressionists are now as firmly part of the canon as Beethoven or Stravinsky, two examples of artists whose novelty and violence initially prompted critical outrage but whom posterity soon learned to love and admire. Counter-cultural movements born in resistance to the norm appear throughout history as artists by their very natures are outsiders, constantly balancing the need to survive against either a quest for the new or a revival of the forgotten. In turn, they may become part of what they reacted against, promoted by critics, fellow-artists, or chance (Thoré-Burger's[4] 'rediscovery' of Vermeer in 1866 is a case in point.) Nonsense and the canon are interdependent: Nonsense cannot dictate taste or fashion, but follows them in an eccentric slipstream. It accepts the hospitality of the norm but behaves in a profoundly disrespectful fashion.

Flowering shoots of Victorian Nonsense curled themselves around art, architecture, photography and stained glass. They grew up in the new media of newspapers, comic journals and children's books. They tangled themselves up in religion, but they survived politics. Nonsense was acted in public, recited in private, sung around the piano, or read by the fireside. It was pleached along contemporary concerns of gender, nationalism, class and language and

---

[1] Horticultural metaphors for poetry are well established: John Sparrow defined Betjeman's verses as 'the forsythia in the Banbury Road' (Introduction to Betjeman *Collected Poems*, John Murray, 1979, pxiii); Arthur Quiller Couch regarded his anthologies of poems as 'flower gathering' (Introduction, *New Oxford Book of English Verse*, OUP, 1984, pvi) and George Moore described Yeats' lyrical gift 'withering, like cut flowers in a vase'. (*G.S.Fraser*, W.B.Yeats, Longmans, 1965.p5

[2] Walter de la Mare *Lewis Carroll*. London, Faber & Faber, 1932. p7

[3] There were 3: 1874, 75 & 76.

[4] Emma Barker, *The Changing Status of the Artist*. Open University Press. 1999. p207

continues to influence and inspire generations of writers, poets and artists.

The wild flowers grew unbidden and unplanned in the minds of men whose principal creative foci lay elsewhere. Neither Edward Lear, Lewis Carroll or William Gilbert saw themselves primarily as Nonsense writers: Gilbert and Carroll in particular resisted the fame it brought them and resented the attention it drew away from their more serious and intellectual concerns. Lear hoped to join the Pre-Raphaelite Brothers and make his reputation as a landscape painter, Lewis Carroll wanted to achieve fame for his mathematical treatise and Gilbert's seventy-five serious plays[5] attest to his desire to become a dramatist in the vein of Richard Brinsley Sheridan. But not only did the seeds take root in unsuspecting soil; they sprang forth with a spontaneous and uncultivated vitality which endures to this day. Although the wild nature of Nonsense made it a natural ally of the Romantics, Nonsense is not containable in any one particular movement. There is an unconscious, almost involuntary element in Nonsense which resists classification. Even attempting to define Nonsense precisely is fraught with difficulty as critics have discovered. Scholars have borrowed Nonsense to define surrealism, Dadaism and proto-modernism but it usually escapes.

Victorian Nonsense adheres to existing structures, obeys literary rules and follows a national tradition. It is almost always syntactically correct. It is almost never semantically coherent and the resulting tension is one of its charms. Nonsense comes from the conflict between logic and paradox: what you get is not what you might think, neither is what you get, what you see. An expectation of events is almost always confounded, even if the initial premise is realistic – which it mostly is not. For example, owls and cats are unlikely to go to sea together in the first place, just as fairies do not customarily give birth to arcadian shepherds who become Members of Parliament. Nonsense rejoices in incongruity and avoids simile and metaphor like the plague. Nothing is ever like anything else.

Nonsense poetry employs conventional metre and established rhyming patterns which allow an even wilder contrast between style and content. The sense of security induced by familiar spondees and dactyls is rudely shaken by the occupants of the Quangle Wangle's Hat,[6] just as it is horribly jarred by Gilbert's Ballads, with their nostalgic chorus, carolling folksy ditties about cannibals and dismemberment. Edward Lear made the limerick his particular servant but an immersion in the Romantic poetry of Byron and Tennyson coloured the music of his longer Nonsense poems: to nonsensically invert the Duchess' comment to Alice – take care of the sounds and the sense will come

---

[5] These were collected and published in five series of *Original Plays* by Chatto & Windus in 1876, 1881, 1881, 1195, & 1911. *Broken Hearts* and *Uncle Baby* are occasionally revived as curiosities but of the majority, no theatrical trace remains.

[6] Edward Lear, *Complete Nonsense*, London, Penguin. 2002. p391

of itself[7]. Much sound and little sense, for example, comes from the nonsense of Shakespeare's clown in *Twelfth Night*.

> 'When that I was and a little tine boy,
> With a hey ho, the winde and the raine,
> A foolish thing was but a toy,
> For the raine it raineth every day.'[8]

Germany has a rich tradition of Nonsense but perhaps only Christian Morgenstern is a familiar name today.[9] France, logically incapable of the illogical, compensated by producing Nonsense scholars Jean Jacques Lecercle, Maurice Merleau-Ponty and Gilles Deleuze. The peculiarly English relish for the absurd inspired writers from Chaucer to Eliot, yet neither before the mid-nineteenth century, nor after, has Nonsense appeared with such prolific and joyous abandon. Was it a reaction to the joyless rigidity of an aspirational bourgeoisie: an irresistible alternative to the sermonising morality of nineteenth century children's literature? How significant for the creation of Nonsense was the context of mid-Victorian peace and prosperity for an increasingly educated middle and upper-middle class? Where did Victorian Nonsense come <u>from</u>?

This study of Nonsense began over fifty years ago. My family communicated largely by exchanging lines from Belloc's *Cautionary Tales* or Eliot's *Practical Cats*. We children spent the long drives to Cornwall learning Lear's limericks off by heart and any suitor for my hand who could complete 'The Cormorant, or Common Shag/lays eggs inside a paper bag'[10] was in with

---

[7] Lewis Carroll *Alice's Adventures in Wonderland*, Penguin Classic Edition, 1998, p 79 Editor Hugh Haughton describes this motto as a play on 'take care of the pence and the pounds will come of themselves.'

[8] William Shakespeare, *Twelfth Night: or, What You Will*. Finale, V.i. 341-417. First Folio Edition, New York, Hamlyn, 1968. p293

[9] Nonsense is almost untranslatable although R.F.C.Hull, notable for his translation of Jung, has achieved the impossible with Morgenstern.

[10] 'The reason, you will have no doubt/is to keep the weather out. But what these unobservant Birds/have never realised is that herds Of wandering Bears may come with Buns/ and steal the bag to keep the crumbs.' Anon.

a fighting chance, as far as my father was concerned. My thesis, 'One Wild Flower', a more academic, disciplined and considered approach, continues a lifelong interest in the subject with a focus on selected Nonsense poetry from three Victorian Nonsense giants: Edward Lear, Lewis Carroll and William Schwenck Gilbert.

Although Nonsense itself has attracted a certain amount of earlier criticism, most studies have been concerned to analyse Nonsense philosophically, psychologically or linguistically. Nonsense has been debated in Chomskyan terms, in the language of literary theory and in relation to modern aesthetics, but it appears that no one has attempted to consider Nonsense <u>archaeologically</u>. The metaphor, borrowed from Michel Foucault, [11] illustrates a methodology of investigation through the 'sedimentary strata' or the existing social mores, and requiring the consequential shifting and sifting of friable and transitory matter. The origins of Nonsense lie in a combination of personal character, contemporary experience and unconscious volition: this thesis is an exploration of all three as they have lain behind the inspiration of Lear, Carroll and Gilbert.

My three heroes have been studied individually and each has their champion in a particular biographer whose lifework ~~their life work~~ has been: Edward Lear is represented by Vivien Noakes[12], Lewis Carroll by Morton Cohen[13] and W.S.G. by Jane Stedman.[14] (I should here acknowledge the particular contributions to Gilbertiana of James Ellis[15] and Ian Bradley.[16]) Although other books by other authors exist, most of which I hope I have read and consulted, the work of these remains magnificently pre-eminent. This study includes a resumé of Lear, Carroll and Gilbert biographies and it has attempted a review of the earlier critics and scholars who have written on my particular selected Nonsense verses. But I believe that no attempt has yet been made to link these three major Victorians,[17] nor to site their Nonsense so specifically among the political, social, artistic, theological or even musical concerns of the mid-nineteenth century. Only context can illuminate Nonsense: scholarship, convention and conformity may define it and analyse it almost to extinction but no amount of intellect will substitute for a recreative and

---

[11] Michel Foucault ,*The Archaeology of Knowledge*, London, Routledge, 1969.

[12] Vivien Noakes, *Edward Lear, The Life of a Wanderer*, London, Collins & Co, 1968, 1979.

[13] Morton Cohen, *Lewis Carroll*, London, Macmillan, 1995.

[14] Jane Stedman, *WS Gilbert – A Classic Victorian and His Theatre*, OUP, 1996.

[15] James Ellis, Editor, *W.S. Gilbert The Bab Ballads*, Massachusetts, The Belknap Press. 1970, 1980.

[16] Ian Bradley, Editor; *The Complete Annotated Gilbert & Sullivan*, OUP, 2001.

[17] Jackie Wullschläger, *Inventing Wonderland,* London, Methuen, 1995, analyses aspects of Lear, Carroll, Kingsley, Grahame, Milne and Barrie, but from the perspective of creating fantasy worlds as opposed to the reflections and context of Nonsense itself. Interestingly, her clever and imaginative study has been translated into French - *Enfances Revees*, 1997.

contextual interpretation through which we may glimpse the original creative spark. King Lear tells Cordelia: 'Nothing will come of nothing.'[18] Everything comes from something; something which this study aims to find.

Despite the familiarity of Lear's limericks and longer Nonsense poems, only a very few writers have concerned themselves with their analysis, exploration or context. It is as if the very absurdity of owls and cats rowing about in small boats together somehow inhibited any further rationale, a state of affairs which never prevented scholarly expositions for arguing chessmen or talkative eggs. A bearded and bespectacled topographical painter simply did not present such an interesting psychological study as the combination of an allegedly paedophiliac photographer and bachelor Oxford mathematics lecturer. The Alice books have been an academic playground since they were written and still attract psychoanalysts, literary theorists and postgraduate students in bewildering numbers: it seems that modern readers are equally bewitched by the Tenniel-striped figure of Alice Liddell. *The Hunting of the Snark,* far less analysed and written about, is far more nonsensical in its systematic arbitrariness and supernatural imagery. But there are no feistily appealing small Victorian girls in the wholly masculine adventure of *The Hunting of the Snark* and no competitions in popular fiction to recreate the hero/heroine.[19]

The *Bab Ballads* of W.S. Gilbert are continually thrown out of the nest by the libretti of the Savoy Operas, noisy, successful cuckoos who all but eclipse their original parents. Not all the Ballads inspired Gilbert and Sullivan's operettas but a great many lie behind their creation and they are the true Nonsense, flowering wildly against the deadlines of comic journals during the 1860s and 1870s. The carefully rehearsed and produced operas depend upon

---

[18] William Shakespeare *King Lear*. I. i 54-101

[19] Noel Streatfield's *Ballet Shoes*, 1936, featured a competition in which rival young actresses vie to be chosen for the role of 'Alice'.

illogical plots stemming from an absurd logic. Gilbert's perfectionism in the theatre militated against real Nonsense which requires an element of spontaneity. Nonsense cannot be thought out or deliberately created.

Nonsense exists in other forms than verse and in other ages than Victorian, but it is the peculiarly potent combination that has inspired this book. Between the years 1840 and 1875, it was as if the children's nursery rhyme had climbed upstairs to join the adults after dinner: here, it would metamorphose into poetry characterised by a uniquely English talent for the absurd. It would be cloaked in Romantic, sub-Tennysonian, metre, concealed in anthropomorphic allegories or drift unconsciously into a dream world where anything is possible. Just as the medieval jester could say what he liked, protected by his cap and bells from the very notion of being serious, so the Victorian Nonsense poet could explore themes of immense significance with a childish innocence and an enabling lack of fear. Occasionally, this would be unconscious, a fact responsible for the adoption of *Alice in Wonderland* as a surrealist text – following the first London exhibition of surrealist Painting in 1936, British Surrealists were dubbed 'The Children of Alice'. [20]

The formal structure of Nonsense verse in contrast to the free-flowing nature of Nonsense prose lends both significance and memorability. Apart from the signature opening of 'Once Upon a Time', almost no story, Nonsense or otherwise, carries a repeated motif that can be easily recalled. I could mischievously suggest that 'Nonsense Poetry' is oxymoronic, a contradiction in terms, as how can no-sense possibly be presented in a sensible, orderly fashion? But in fact, it is the power and rhythm of a verse which combine to convince the reader that its Nonsense needs to be taken seriously. As Nowottny says, 'A rhyme can take us back, not only to the one word with

---

[20] *International Surrealist Exhibition Catalogue,* New Burlington Galleries, London. 11 June - 4 July, 1936.

which it rhymes, but to the whole line'.[21] Moreover, the logic dictated by a rhyming pattern, justifies the oddest of ideas and serves to link undreamt of connections. At another level, Nonsense poetry may claim to be the purest poetry of all, depending for its effects upon sound, rhythm and repetition patterns. Nonsense words act as the instruments in an orchestra, combining and alternating in duets, trios, quartets and ensemble, but often meaning nothing whatever in themselves, an idea developed to startling effect in Edith Sitwell's *Façade,* set to music by William Walton.[22] In one episode, the reciter, together with six instruments, intones *Scotch Rhapsody;* (first line is 'Do not take a bath in the Jordan, Gordon'.)

'Til the flaxen leaves where the prunes are ripe
Heard the tartan wind a-droning in the pipe
And they heard McPherson say,
'Where do the waves go – what hotels
With their bustles and their gay ombrelles?'

It is poetry at the farthest possible distance from prose. Sitwell herself described it as the musical equivalent of Lizst's Transcendental studies – abstract modernism, a category which Nonsense verse occasionally slips into – a notion reinforced by Sitwell's declared inspiration from Stravinsky[23].

'I engage with the Snark every night
In a dreamy delirious fight
I serve it with greens in those shadowy scene
And I use it for striking a light'.

Chorus, *The Hunting of the Snark.*[24]

I hope this thesis will benefit from my amateur knowledge and love of the music which informs the rhythm and metre of so much Nonsense verse: not only in the speech patterns required by the lines, but occasionally in an actual song setting, such as Lear's own music for *The Pelican Chorus* or *The Ballad of the Yonghy Bonghy Bo.* Research has uncovered the music of Adrian Welles Beecham, son of Sir Thomas, for selected *Bab Ballads.*[25] The ultimate lollipop? Nonsense cannot be said to exist in music. The claim to describe that Richard Strauss' *Till Eulenspiegel* (1894) is the *Alice in Wonderland* of sound

---

[21] Winifred Nowottny, *The Language Poets Use.* London, Athlone Press. (Reprint) 1966. p15

[22] Edith Sitwell, *Façade Poems,* first published in the literary magazine *Wheels,* 1918. Walton's score dates from 1922, but was revised in 1949.

[23] John Press, *The Fire and the Fountain,* Oxford, OUP, 1955, p98

[24] Lewis Carroll, *The Hunting of the Snark,* London, Penguin Classic, 1995. p66

[25] 1931 & 1933: Welles Beecham never recovered from being the son of Sir Thomas and remains a footnote in most musical histories – a small oeuvre includes some Shakespeare song settings and a musical version of *Ruth.*

[26]and that Beethoven's yellow-hammer motif in the second movement, and oompah village band in the third movement of the *Pastoral Symphony* (1808) are nonsensical, falters against the underlying logic of the music. 'Scherzo' or 'joke' music offers light relief between weightier moments, but scherzi are not nonsense. Music, even of the most unstructured, contemporary or popular variety, requires rules to work, in contrast to Nonsense which makes up its own. There is unlikely to be a Nonsensical equivalent of formal counterpoint, banned consecutive fifths or those strictures which require a theme in the tonic to be followed by one in the dominant.

Nonsense Poetry is related to the nursery rhyme and to the folk song. The first connection lends it an inbuilt nostalgia for all our childhoods. Not because distance lends enchantment to a paradise lost of endless summers of cloudless skies and fly-less picnics, nor on account of the carefree irresponsibility of the very young with no homework, but because we associate childhood with true spontaneity and simplicity. This essentially Wordsworthian construction was widely available to Victorian readers and writers and proved highly influential. We know now that art needs to remain childlike: we need to remember Mann's Adrian Leverkühn in his version of Dr. Faustus and that sophistication and the intellect are death to creation.[27] Only Gilbert, of my three subjects, preserved a cautionary approach to his younger years, believing that happiness increased with independence and ability and that children needed rescuing from childhood. Neither Lear, Carroll nor Gilbert had children of their own, and only Gilbert married. Edward Lear and Lewis Carroll collected children like some adults collected stamps, and Mr and Mrs Gilbert entertained children to particular parties at their home in The Boltons to which no conventional adults were ever invited.

Nursery rhymes feature rhythm, repetition and a chorus for children to chant, skip or sing. Sometimes they seem to be Nonsense: sometimes they make perfect sense. We shall see just how Edward Lear built on those elements in his limericks and how they exist in *The Hunting of the Snark* and Gilbert's *Bab Ballads*. The nursery rhyme,

> 'Diddle, diddle dumpling, my son John
> Went to bed with his trousers on
> One shoe off and one shoe on
> Diddle diddle dumpling, my son John,'

is not so far from Lear's *Jumblies,*

> 'In a sieve they went to sea
> In spite of all their friends could say
> On a winter's morn, on a stormy day
> In a sieve they went to sea'.   CN, p253.

---

[26] George Edinger and E.J.C. Neep, *Pons Asinorum*, London. Kegan Paul, 1929. p18

[27] Leverkühn, supposedly based on Schoenberg and supported by the musical theories of Adorno, finally falters with his intellectual approach to musical creation.

Both stories have the added attraction of a certain defiance of both common sense and adult realist rules – and Lear's rhyme seems to imply a daft version of a romantic quest for the hopeless.

The 'ballad' character of the folk tradition is taken up by Gilbert in particular. 'Ballad' has a greater significance than its alliteration with 'Bab'; the word conjures up a romantic image of storytelling through song, of tales preserved by being passed down orally through generations and somehow acquiring sense through custom. For Gilbert, 'ballad' is shorthand for echoes of Nonsensical minstrelsy, wimpled damosels, knight-errants and rusty armour, rhymes and themes which were to inspire the Nonsense of both A.A. Milne[28] and *1066 And All That*.[29] The word echoes medieval England, a period taken seriously by Tennyson, the Pre-Raphaelites, Auguste Pugin and William Morris but parodied by almost everybody else.

'A troubadour, young brave and tall
One morning might be seen
A singing under Colter's Hall
Upon the village Green

He went through all the usual forms
And rolled his eyes of blue
As dying ducks in thunderstorms
Are often said to do.' (etc.)

W.S. Gilbert *Bab Ballad* . JE, p183.

(Note how 'the usual forms' gives the game away, self-consciously appealing to an adult awareness of literary pastiche). Carroll's long nonsense verse epic *The Hunting of the Snark* has 'ballad' qualities of a repeated chorus, sequential quatrains and simple vocabulary.

The connection of Nonsense poetry to the folk song, helps link Nonsense to the Romantic Movement of the early-nineteenth century. Romanticism is an important concept in this study of Nonsense and will rear its head throughout the book: like so many movements, (artistic, political, theological) it was a reaction to that which went before. In particular, the *Lyrical Ballads*, 1798, of Wordsworth and Coleridge were written with the vitality of vernacular speech as a deliberate contrast to the sculptural stylishness of the eighteenth century. The aim was to relate formal poetry to the reality of every day life: to make poetry as accessible and attractive as nursery rhymes, ballads and folk songs. The *Lyrical Ballads* may be said to have begun the Romantic movement, yet romanticism, unlike many partially reactive 'isms' – classicism, surrealism, symbolism, realism, pantheism – exists both intrinsically and inherently. It may exist on its own terms without relation to external events. It is not an ideology, but a loosely connected body of ideas in which expression, emotion and individual sensibilities were allowed freer rein than before. It is associated

---

[28] A.A. Milne, *Now We Are Six*, London, Methuen, 1927, in particular *The Knight Whose Armour Didn't Squeak*, p22

[29] W.C. Sellar and R.J. Yeatman, *1066 And All That,* London, Methuen & Co, 1930.

primarily with the new social order of post-Revolutionary France and post-Napoleonic Europe. Jacques Barzun has described romanticism as a question, not a solution, 'the one thing that unifies men in a given age is not their individual philosophy, but the dominant problem that these philosophies were designed to solve'.[30] The problem was to create a new world on the ruins of the old and over the tumbled stones of Classicism climbed Beethoven, Heine, Byron, Caspar David Friedrich and Tennyson. None of my three subjects – Lear, Carroll or Gilbert – could escape the long shadow of Tennyson and none of them tried: all acknowledged his influence by parody, imitation or metamorphosis.

Edward Lear knew Tennyson personally, adored Tennyson's wife Emily Sellwood, and set over twenty poems to music. (In addition, he conceived a project to illustrate over two hundred of them: it was never completed and only a few survive.) Carroll had been stalking Tennyson and his family with a rosewood box camera and was finally permitted to photograph Alfred's sons, Lionel and Hallam, in the Lake District. Gilbert based *Princess Ida* on Tennyson's *The Princess* and excitement was generated during one performance when 'Tennyson' was believed to be in the audience. The imposter was H.J. Lincoln, music critic of the *Daily News* whose unkempt appearances helped an occasional impersonation of the Laureate.[31] Gilbert and Tennyson briefly shared the services of a disreputable publisher, John Camden Hotten,[32] in the 1860's and may have met in his office – but no record appears to exist.

Carroll dared to poke fun. In *The Three Voices*[33] he impertinently parodied Tennyson's *Two Voices*[34] with a tale of a young man who encounters a battle-axe on a beach. The older woman nails his hat with her umbrella, shrieks feminist imprecations and disappears. Note that whilst the verse form is pastiche, almost parody, there is a crucial shift from the subjective 'I' in Tennyson to an objective and mocking 'He' in Carroll.

'A still, small voice spake unto me
Thou are so full of misery
Were it better not to be?
Then to the still, small voice I said
Let me not cast in endless shade
What is so wonderfully made?

To which the voice did urge reply
Today I saw the dragon fly

'The world is but a thought, said he
the vast unfathomable sea
Is but a notion – unto me'
And darkly fell her answer dread
upon his unresisting head
Like half a hundred weight of lead

The good and great must ever shun
that reckless and abandoned one

---

[30] Jacques Barzun *Classic, Romantic and Modern*. London, Secker and Warburg. 1961. p14

[31] Stedman, p203

[32] Known to posterity for a prodigious number of books on 'chastisement'. Matthew Sweet, *Inventing The Victorians*, London, Faber & Faber, 2001. p203

[33] Lewis Carroll, 'Three Voices' 1865. From *Collected Works*. Nonsuch Publishing, 1939.

[34] Alfred, Lord Tennyson. 'Two Voices' 1833. First published in *Poems, 1842.*

Come from the wells where he did lie' Who stoops to perpetrate a pun.
(Tennyson...etc)   (Carroll...etc)

A sense of humour is not always concomitant with Nonsense and not often associated with Lewis Carroll, but here and there, it pops up.

The Romantics were variously succeeded by the realists, the Symbolists and the Surrealists who became absorbed into modernism (occasionally dubbed the uncompleted project of the Enlightenment) which swept all before it. If Nonsense is an illegitimate child of the Romantics, it is godfather to surrealism. The movement proper was born in Paris during the 1920s when André Breton, doctor and psychiatrist who worked to heal the shell-shocked survivors of WW1 studied the writings of Sigmund Freud. A belief in the power of the unconscious, the significance of dream analysis and the value of free association as defined by Freud, provided the first surrealism manifesto, a movement which aimed to liberate the imagination and free human experience from restrictive custom and destructive rationality. Realism was seen as propping up ancient edifices in new forms of chaos and new contradictions. Surrealism functioned as an absurd extension to reality, thus operating in similar fashion to Nonsense. This thesis will examine the primary relationship of Nonsense poetry to surrealism, notable particularly in the work of Lewis Carroll, less so in Edward Lear and only occasionally in the *Bab Ballads*. Carroll was himself a reaction against the real; logic and mathematics brought him no joy and his only pleasure lay in a fantasy life largely prompted by dreams and he unconscious.

The freedom inherent in the personal eccentricity of Lear, Carroll and Gilbert bestowed freedom of the imagination on their Nonsense writing. Children's literature in the early nineteenth century may have escaped formal censorship, but many authors laboured under a presumption of evangelical Christianity and pedagogical earnestness. Only a minority of writers began to appeal to the particular imagination and character of children in the early nineteenth century: this study will compare the available books for children in the 1840s and 1850s and demonstrate the extraordinary impact of Nonsense upon a market reared on morality tales and religious virtue. Nonsense offered children the rare pleasure of a constant supply of small acts of anarchy against the norm. The extreme solemnity which characterised so much mid-Victorian endeavour at all stages of life, was declared by Humbert Wolfe to be the reason which made 'Lear and Carroll explode into Nonsense to avoid lunacy'.[35] Wolfe believes that 'Tennyson, Matthew Arnold, Arthur Hugh Clough and Charles Kingsley shared nothing but a fanatical seriousness'.[36] Was Nonsense a youthful rebellion: an undeclared conspiracy by Lear, Carroll and Gilbert to give logic a school holiday? How much did Nonsense unconsciously reflect the concerns of Victorian society whilst pretending a mild form of lunacy? Dr Paul Ryan [37] makes a convincing case for the explosion of science fiction films in England and America during the 1950s and 1960s as unconscious allegories for the struggle against communism and the cold war.

Michel Foucault argues that censorship is not just the ordering of society, but the society in which censorship takes place: that context is all. This underlines the value of studying the areas around a central field – of relativity, if you like – as well as the knowledge that nothing exists in isolation. The latent ambition of art must always be to achieve acceptance in an impossible combination of challenge and conformity. Approved art forms are represented and extolled by powerful academies and newcomers fight for inclusion if they are to survive. Unlike Groucho Marx, artists **want** to join the club that initially refuses them membership. But the effect of a canonical hierarchy, however contextually and philosophically interpreted by Foucault, has been to repress and stifle individual imagination: could the sheer survival of Victorian Nonsense qualify it for canonical inclusion?

Changing times, tastes and testaments of the twenty-first century allow liberties undreamt of in Victorian England – we no longer need to wrap our barbs in limericks, ballads or Nonsense songs. We let Cole Porter explain that

'in older days, a glimpse of stocking
was looked upon as something really rather shocking,
now, heaven knows – anything goes'.[38]

Nonsense requires a structure to operate both against and within, and we are obliged to acknowledge the force of Foucault's arguments: that the rare, wild flower of Victorian Nonsense may be considered as a valid form of Victorian literature precisely because it offered a contrast to the norm.

This introduction to Nonsense explains the background to my interest in

---

[35] Humbert Wolfe, *English Verse Satire*, London, Hogarth Press, 1929. p141. (And he forgot Kingsley's *Water Babies* who are not serious at all. LS.)

[36] Ibid. p141

[37] Lecturer in Film Studies and Modern Media at Brighton University. 2007.

[38] Cole Porter 'Anything Goes' written for Ethel Merman in the Broadway musical of the same name, 1934.

the subject and my rationale for the Nonsense poems and authors selected. A definition is attempted, but although boundaries must be drawn somehow and limits for the inquiry set, this thesis is far more concerned to establish where and how Nonsense came from, as opposed to what Nonsense is. Nonsense prose and poetry are compared and I relate Nonsense verse to Romantic poetry and the Romantic era as well as to various literary movements which followed. The introduction will conclude with a resumé of certain earlier writings on Nonsense and the variety of definitions so far extant, whilst allowing for the ultimate caveat that Nonsense is like an elephant: it is very difficult to describe until it is encountered. In legal terms, Nonsense ought to be patent upon examination.

THAT WHICH WENT BEFORE: NONSENSE.

One of the very first definitions of Nonsense came from the writer Edward Strachey, Lytton's Uncle, in a Preface to the Ninth Edition of Lear's *Nonsense Songs and Stories*: 'In contradiction to the relations and harmonies of life, Nonsense sets itself to discover and bring forward the incongruities of all things within and without us...Nonsense has shown itself a true work of the imagination, a child of genius and its writing one of the Fine Arts'.[39] Another early and staunch advocate of Nonsense was Chesterton[40] who regarded nonsense in its broadest meaning as a timeless phenomenon, distinguishing between satirical and symbolic nonsense and the new version of the cosmos as offered by Edward Lear, Lewis Carroll and W.S. Gilbert.[41]

Belgian poet and professor Emile Cammaerts began a tradition of literary distinction in Nonsense critics. His short, stylish book was one of the first to consider Nonsense seriously as a form of poetry: 'Nonsense seems particularly conducive to rhythm and to rhyme, even more than the solemn themes of life and death. Prose walks too slowly for it, it needs the wings of rhyme and the dance of rhythm. Like the jester in the old court, it moves to the tinkling sound of bells'.[42] As a biographer of G.K. Chesterton (1937) the author knew whereof he wrote, and as a foreigner, he could sensibly comment on Nonsense as an almost exclusively English phenomenon. Cammaerts notes the powerful link between the Romantic poets (Coleridge and Wordsworth in particular) and Nonsense poems, believing that if Nonsense is poetry run wild, such wilderness is more likely to be found in a country where poetry is highly developed.

Elizabeth Sewell, another poet-professor,[43] produced *The Field of Nonsense* in 1952 which remained the cornerstone of Nonsense studies until the philosophies of Jean Jacques Lecercle and Michel Foucault in the 1980s. Essentially, Sewell argued that Nonsense is not merely a denial of sense, a

---

[39] Edward Lear, *Nonsense Songs and Stories* with Introduction by Sir Edward Strachey, Bt. London, Warne & Co. 1888.

[40] G.K. Chesterton, *In Defence of Nonsense*. London, Brimley Johnson. 1901.

[41] W.S. G's influence on Chesterton alone ought to convince all waverers that Gilbert was a Nonsense writer; in *The Man Who Was Thursday*, Chesterton's anarchical policeman explains that 'burglars and bigamists are moral men who accept the essential ideal of man but merely seek it wrongly...that thieves respect property...they merely wish the property to become their property that they may more perfectly respect it'. *The Essential Chesterton*, OUP, 1987, p150

[42] Emile Cammaerts, *The Poetry of Nonsense*, London, Routledge. 1925. p39

[43] Author of *The Structure of Poetry*, London, Routledge, 1951 and *The Orphic Voice*, London, Routledge, 1961.

random reversal of ordinary experience and an escape from the limitations of life into a haphazard infinity, but on the contrary a carefully limited world, controlled and directed by reason, a construction driven by its own laws'.[44] Both Cammaerts and Sewell concentrate their analysis on the work of Edward Lear and Lewis Carroll, barely mentioning William Gilbert, much less any minor Victorian Nonsense poets. The poet Walter de la Mare (1873 – 1956, contemporary of Cammaerts and Sewell) characterised Nonsense as 'an indefinable cross between humour, fantasy and sweet unreasonableness' but does not answer his own query of how Nonsense differs 'from the merry, the comical, the frivolous, the absurd, the grotesque and the mere balderdash'.[45]

Wim Tigges builds on the work of Sewell with *An Anatomy of Literary Nonsense* [46] which began life as a Dutch doctoral thesis and in which he has taken scholarly pains to consult every known writer and critic on every possible aspect of Nonsense in any European language. Tigges distinguishes the genre of Nonsense from the related modes of light verse, fantasy, the grotesque and the surreal and traces the traditions of Nonsense that stem from Lear and Carroll. He defines Nonsense by a setting up of constant interaction between texts and theory, eventually producing a key to the literary-aesthetic interpretation of generically related texts, aiming to 'make possible a better understanding of the nature and workings of Nonsense devices'.[47] He argues that the true essence of literary nonsense 'is the maintenance of a perfect tension between meaning and non-meaning' and the creation of a reality through language.

Curiously, contemporary French scholars, Jean Jacques Lecercle in particular,[48] have concerned themselves in varying degrees with Victorian Nonsense. Lecercle argues that Nonsense is metasense – Nonsense texts are not explicitly parodic, or at least, they turn parody into a theory of serious literature: 'Lewis Carroll's metalinguistic comments of points of grammar can be fully understood only in the light of Chomskyan linguistics: Edward Lear's omnipresent reference to an aggressive 'they' in his limericks is crying out for an existentilist or Heideggerian account'.[49] His scholarly and complex study tackles the philosophy of Nonsense from a largely linguistic point of view: 'The deep seated need for meaning, which Nonsense texts deliberately frustrate in order to whet it, will be accounted for in the non-transparency of language, of the incapacity of natural languages to fulfil their allotted task of expression and communication'[50]. As Sewell wrote in simpler terms three decades earlier, in Nonsense, as in poetry generally, 'language has no direct

---

[44] Elizabeth Sewell, *The Field of Nonsense*. London, Chatto & Windus. 1925. p5

[45] Walter de la Mare, *Lewis Carroll*. London, Faber & Faber. 1932. p8 & p14-15

[46] Wim Tigges, *An Anatomy of Literary Nonsense*, Amsterdam, Rodopi. 1988.

[47] Ibid. p3

[48] This tradition seems to have begun with Henri Bergson's *Le Rire*, 1900, and must now include Gilles Deleuze, Maurice Merleau- Ponty and Michel Foucault.

[49] Jean Jacques Lecercle *The Philosophy of Nonsense*. London, Routledge, 1994. p2

[50] Ibid.p3

connection with reality'.[51]

A more historical study is Noel Malcolm's *The Origins of English Nonsense*,[52] an enjoyable, scholarly romp which traces the origins of Nonsense from mediaeval Europe to Victorian England, with a particular focus on the seventeenth century. He takes issue with Cammaerts and Chesterton in particular for maintaining the belief that Nonsense poetry was the exclusive product of nineteenth century England, and with all Nonsense writers who believe that Nonsense exists as a timeless, universal category that possesses only instances rather than origins. Malcolm argues than Nonsense is a literary genre, distinct from folk tales, nursery rhymes, drinking songs and ballads, linked to the high literary conventions of the day and developed in specific instances by individual poets of distinction. He makes a valiant attempt to revive the life and work of sixteenth century poets, John Hoskyns and John Taylor for example, and quotes some of their marvellously entertaining Nonsense rhymes – but the proof of the pudding must lie in its eating, and for all Malcolm's erudition, neither have been revived as household names.

The most recent consideration of Victorian Nonsense appears to be Jackie Wullschläger's *Inventing Wonderland*.[53] This throws paint over the broad canvas of Edward Lear, Lewis Carroll, Kenneth Grahame, J.M. Barrie and A.A. Milne, linking them together as five men who could not grow up; five men who told tales casually to entertain individual children and who never thought or expected their work to be published, even less to achieve their later reputation as Nonsense writers. Wullschläger's attractive study focuses on the fantasy world of Victorian and Edwardian children's literature which 'lasted until the First World War when to die ceased to be the awfully big adventure that Peter expected.'[54] She is particularly effective on Victorian images of childhood and 'the repressed sexuality that privileges innocence'[55] although never quite penetrating into the rougher aspects of Lewis Carroll, nor the questing melancholy of Edward Lear.

My own work treads a careful path between these studies, owing a certain allegiance to the shade under their branches and the depth of their stems but, eventually, my path leads me in a different direction. I do not attempt to explain Nonsense by itself. My approach is not concerned with Nonsense as philosophy, linguistics, mathematics or even insanity; my aim is to discover where Nonsense came from. What may we learn about Victorian concerns and priorities by uncovering its roots? How did it function in its original context? My study aims to illuminate Walter de la Mare's one, wild, flower by detailed reference to Victorian social mores, Victorian art, Victorian theological controversies, Victorian music poetry and drama, and Victorian science. This offers a lateral view of social history from a surprising standpoint: we do well to remember that much of life is far too serious to be taken seriously. Although

---

[51] Elizabeth Sewell *The Structure of Poetry*. London, Routledge & Kegan Paul. 1951. p4

[52] Noel Malcolm *The Origins of Nonsense*. London, HarperCollins. 1998

[53] Jackie Wullschläger, *Inventing Wonderland*. London, Methuen, 1996

[54] Ibid, p8

[55] Ibid, p9

I accept that analysis by biography may restrict a wider view,[56] I include brief biographical sketches of Lear, Carroll and Gilbert: my argument is that some personal history is unavoidable and indeed essential as no man, least of all a Nonsense writer, acts out of character or period.

---

[56] A reference to Roland Barthes' *Death of the Author*, 1967, an influential discourse on the perils of distilling meaning from the cultural, social, political or historical aspects of author identity, and now almost dogma.

INTRODUCING EDWARD LEAR

Edward Lear, born just twelve years into the nineteenth century, is the first subject in this book. He could fairly be acclaimed as the originator of the Limerick although verses in almost the same metrical form are found in earlier writers. He has become celebrated as the first of the Victorian Nonsense writers and the first name associated with our 'rare wild flower'. Despite the enduring popularity of the limericks, Lear's longer Nonsense songs and poems have a greater claim to fame: 'The Jumblies', 'The Owl and the Pussy Cat' and 'The Dong with the Luminous Nose' share emotion, poetry and Nonsense in almost equal measure with a 'romantic prelude of rich hues and haunting rhythms'.[57]

The first seeds of English Nonsense may be seen in Chaucer. Tiny shoots appear in Shakespeare, and contemporaries of the Bard, John Hoskyns and John Taylor, were once well known for Nonsense verses. Hoskyns' *Cabalastic Verses*, c.1611, in faultless iambic pentameter, deserves a mention.

'Even as the waves of brainless, buttered fish
With bugle horne writ in the Hebrew tongue
Fuming up flounders like a chafing dish
That looks asquint upon a three man's song'.[58]

Lear's first *Book of Nonsense* appeared in 1846. It was published by Thomas MacLean in London and contained seventy limericks in two volumes: each cost 3s 6d and the author was one Derry Down Derry[59] (who liked to see little folks merry). The books were an immediate success, although the anonymity of the author led to absurd rumours, the most persistent of which was that the Earl of Derby,[60] Lear's friend, patron and host, was somehow responsible himself for the dozens of delightful drawings and limericks.

In 1861, Edward Lear published an enlarged *Book of Nonsense* under his real name which went into thirty editions in his lifetime. A second *Book of Nonsense, Songs, Stories, Botany and Alphabets* appeared in 1871 which contained the more ambitious and original Nonsense poetry. The final *Laughable Lyrics* appeared in 1877 in which 'The Dong with the Luminous Nose' and 'The Courtship of the Yonghy, Bonghy Bo' are Nonsense poetry tinged with personal melancholy: watery sunshine after rain. John Lehmann

---

[57] G.K.Chesterton, *In Defence of Nonsense*. First published by R. Brimley Johnson, London, 1902. www.nonsenselit.org accessed 9/1/008

[58] Noel Malcolm, *The Origins of English Nonsense*, London, Harper Collins, 1997, p127

[59] Later, ominously, employed as a pseudonym by Lord Alfred Douglas.

[60] Earl is an anagram of Lear.

describes these as 'transposed Romantic poetry, written with remarkable skill, with a sense of rhythmic architecture and word music that recalls the masters, especially Lear's beloved Tennyson'.[61]

The *Books of Nonsense* have never been out of print. An early review in *The Spectator* described Lear as 'the parent of modern Nonsense writers...he is distinguished from all his followers and imitators by the superior consistency with which he has adhered to his aim – that of amusing his readers by fantastic absurdities, as void of vulgarity or cynicism as they are incapable of being made to harbour any symbolic meaning'.[62] Sir Edmund Strachey, writing about Lear's Nonsense in *The Quarterly Review,* 1888, called it 'a child of genius, one of the Fine Arts'.[63] George Orwell valued Lear's 'humour of pure fantasy which assaults man's notion of himself as not only a dignified, but a rational human being' and described *The Courtship of the Yonghy Bonghy Bo* as 'building up a fantastic universe which is just similar enough to the real universe to rob it of its dignity'.[64]Orwell enjoyed Lear's violent contrasts and compared him to C.S. Calverley:

'They call me cruel. Do I know if mouse or songbird feels?
I only know they make me light and salutary meals.
And, as tis my nature to, ere I devour, I tease 'em
Why should a low bred gardener's boy pursue me with a besom?
For me, they fill the milk bowl up and cull the choice sardine
But ah, I never shall be more the cat I once have been.
The memories of that fatal night, they haunt me now
In dreams I see that rampant he, and tremble at that Miaow'.[65]

(Calverley, 1834 – 1881, is a lesser Victorian Nonsense poet who deserves to be better known, if only for the immortal lines 'we are not as tabbies are' in his noble apology for tobacco). Holbrook Jackson, journalist, socialist, publisher and writer, edited a *Complete Nonsense* [66]in 1947, the eighteenth edition of which appeared in 1989 and whose familiar typographical cover was to be seen in almost every bookcase in Britain. Jackson wrote that 'Lear's nonsense is no mere tissue of quips and jokes. It is a thing in itself in a world of its own with its own physiography and natural history; a world in which the nature of things has been changed whilst retaining its own logical and consistent idiom'.[67]

Lear's Nonsense books became nursery staples and would have been

---

[61] John Lehmann, *Edward Lear and His World.* London, Thames & Hudson, 1977.
[62] *The Spectator.* Vol. 60, September 17, 1887. p1251
[63] Elizabeth Sewell, *The Field of Nonsense*, London, Chatto & Windus,1952. p5
[64] George Orwell, 'Funny But Not Vulgar'. *Collected Essays and Journalism*, 1944-45. London, Secker & Warburg, 1968. Book Club Associates, 1981. p673
[65] C.S. Calverley, from *Fly Leaves*, first published by Deighton Bell & Co, London. 1884.
[66] Edward Lear, *Complete Nonsense.* Editor, Holbrook Jackson, London, Faber & Faber. 1947.
[67] Ibid, pxxiii

familiar to Lewis Carroll and William Gilbert, among thousands of others. Despite their undoubted influence on all subsequent children's books and pictures (the contemporary Maurice Sendak and Dr Seuss in particular) their creator has attracted significantly less literary criticism and analysis than Lewis Carroll, though Vivien Noakes has redressed the balance to a certain extent. Elizabeth Sewell describes the 'unfailing mental delight afforded by Lear'[68] and considers that some of the Nonsense songs have equal moments to Yeats, Verlaine and Spenser. Scholars have discovered similarities to Lear's work in the writings of James Joyce, Gertrude Stein and Wallace Stevens[69] – others have derived a kind of existential philosophy from his Nonsense, finding in his work the freedom to make up one's own rules.[70]

Edward Lear was an artist. He was influenced by the paintings of J.W.M. Turner whom he might actually have glimpsed down the long corridors of Petworth House in the 1830s. Lear's early career as a botanical illustrator was frustrated through poor eyesight and uncertain health: warmer climates were thought necessary and so, in 1837, he travelled to join a community of artists in Rome, the starting point for what became a lifetime of travel and topographical painting. His larger oil pictures never found critical support but the beauty and skill of his smaller watercolour sketches have established his reputation during the past fifty years. Apart from regular visits to England, he lived abroad, first in Corfu, then various resorts around the Mediterranean before finally at home in San Remo on the Italian Riviera. In 1846, his *Illustrated Excursions in Italy* caught the eye of Queen Victoria and he was summoned to Osborne House to give a series of twelve drawing lessons to the young queen. In his turn, Lear studied life drawing with Holman Hunt in the 1860s. He wanted to improve his figure drawing and join the Pre-Raphaelite Brethren - the apprenticeship to 'Daddy' Hunt formed yet another life-long and intimate male friendship if it never quite enabled the serious artistic status and recognition that Lear craved.

The Nonsense was born, as Nonsense so often is, through a combination of chance and circumstance: the first limericks and illustrations amused Lord Derby's children at Knowsley, the later poems were light relief from the intense labour of painting huge and detailed landscapes. Almost all his Nonsenses were designed for a particular child, or children – *The Owl and the Pussy Cat* was a get-well present for John Addington Symonds' young daughter Janet in Italy[71]. He wrote constantly, in ceaseless correspondence with dozens of friends and acquaintances worldwide, as well as restlessly recording foreign travel and adventures. Nonsensical animals, the Piggiwiggia Pyramidalis and Nasticreechia Kroluppia among them, owe a certain credibility to Lear's botanical training, just as the stories and rhymes benefit

---

[68] Sewell, p5

[69] Alison Reik, *The Senses of Nonsense*, University of Iowa Press, 1992.

[70] A recent example of the continuing inspiration of Edward Lear was the Bubble Theatre, Elephant Lane, London SE16,4 JD production of *The Dong With The Luminous Nose* in July/August, 2007.

[71] Noakes, p227

from the practise of a pen whose ink never ran dry.

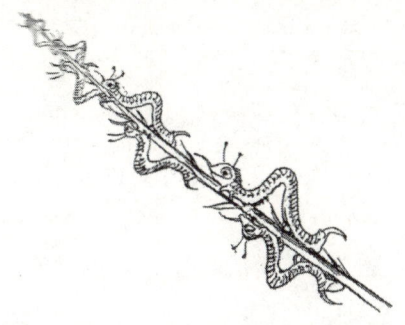

Nasticreechia Kroluppia

Edward Lear created pictures with words as well as words with pictures. He created a new way of arranging words so that their meaning became dislocated from familiarity. Sometimes, he invented a new vocabulary entirely with words that have become part of the English language: 'runcible', 'scroobious', 'uffish', 'mumbian' and 'slobacious'. Sometimes, his eccentric spelling – 'eggstrax, eggsibission, pollygize' – shakes an inattentive reader into focus. His illustrations perfectly captured the nonsense. Adult readers were startled, charmed and engaged. John Ruskin wrote that 'I really don't know any author to whom I am half so grateful for my idle self as Edward Lear. I shall put him first of my hundred authors'.[72] The disciplined child of 1846 thrilled to the non-moral grotesques of Lear's imagination, peppered with a dash of risible violence: the horrible ends of Nonsense characters were somehow perfectly acceptable in the Victorian nursery with its evangelical sense of sin and taboo. Lear's Nonsense world, where mice play the piano and spoons grow from plants, demonstrated that anything was possible.

---

[72] *Pall Mall Gazette,* February 15, 1886.

Like his mice, Edward Lear played the piano. He was a capable amateur musician, who composed settings for several of his longer Nonsenses as well as settings for Tennyson poems. He sang with a pleasing tenor voice, accompanying himself at the piano and inspiring the unrequited affection of at least one young woman. This book will examine the little-known music he wrote – it belongs to the rich and significant history of the Victorian Parlour song.

In a Gilbertian phrase, Edward Lear was a very plump and pleasing person. Despite his acute myopia, solitary wanderings, unreliable health and occasional irascibility, he was immensely popular with adults and beloved by children.

> 'He has many friends, laymen and clerical
> Old Foss is the name of his cat.
> His body is perfectly spherical
> He weareth a runcible hat.'   CN, p 428

His gift for friendship was in part due to his ability, almost that of a child, both to demand and to receive: in part due to his constant, cheerful correspondence and in part due to a hunger for emotional bonds, substitutes for the ideal marriage which could never take place.

EDWARD LEAR, BIOGRAPHICAL

Edward Lear was born in 1812, the twentieth of the twenty-one children born into the prosperous middle-class household of Jeremiah and Ann Lear. The family occupied Bowman's Lodge, Holloway, a village set high amidst woods and fields, made fashionable by the coach every half hour to the city of London. His childhood seems to have been sad and unhappy: early health problems[73] were compounded by the financial crises of his neglectful parents, and the only redemption came from the loving care of his older sisters, Ann and Sarah. Vivien Noakes believes that Lear never recovered from the disruption of his home and the scattering of the family caused by the debts of Jeremiah. The Yonghy Bonghy Bo possessed;

'Two old chairs and half a candle
One old jug without a handle'   CN,p324.

and the Discobbolos family shared a mistrust of possessions, wanting;

'No knives, no forks, no chairs,
No tables, nor carpets, nor household cares
From the worry of life we've fled
There is no more trouble ahead.'   CN, p321.

The year of Lear's birth was a memorable one. Robert Browning was born, the first two cantos of *Childe Harolde* and Turner's *A Frosty Morning* were composed and the cornerstones laid for the Brighton Pavilion. The first Blenkinsop/Murray locomotive was employed at the Middleton Colliery, Daguerre was perfecting his camera oscura and Aloys Senefelder accidentally discovered the principles of lithography. Passion vied with progress: the romantic flowered along with the railway lines.

Less tangible and much less congenial influence came from the dawning Evangelical Low Church movement whose most celebrated converts were William Wilberforce and Hannah More. The frightening doctrine of original sin, chillingly advocated by More in 1799, stated that, 'it is a fundamental error to consider children as innocent beings whose little weaknesses may perhaps want some correction, rather than as beings who bring into the world a corrupt nature and evil disposition which it should be the great end of

---

[73] Lear suffered from asthma, bronchitis and temporal lobe epilepsy. These terrible afflictions coloured his life and his work: they will be dealt with in later chapters.

education to rectify.'[74]

Two of Lear's sisters, Harriet and Mary, suffered the peculiar Evangelical narrowness which made repressing children a religious obligation. They, among many others, shared Charles Wesley's beliefs that 'all children were by nature evil...pious and prudent parents must check their naughty passions in any way they had in their power'.[75] When will it please God to knock religion on the head and substitute love, charity and common sense, Lear enquired later in life and told a dear child 'I'm sure we shall be allowed to laugh in Heaven'.[76]

The child, as a separate being, is a mid-nineteenth century concept, which, like Christmas, owes much to the German *Gemütlichkeit* of Prince Albert and Queen Victoria. The domesticity inherent in *Kinder, Kirche, Küche* arrived too late for Edward Lear, but proved effective in the upbringing of Lewis Carroll and William Gilbert, although the greater construction of 'childhood' meant that 'children' became a group more efficiently controlled. Kirsten Drotner suggests that the nineteenth century 'ghetto-ization of childhood was something completely different from adult reality and power'[77] and that 'the focus of anxiety spread from the upper classes to the lower, and from boys to girls'. In contrast, eighteenth century children were treated as little adults and when life was rough and hard for all classes, little attempt was made to soften it – yet eighteenth century children's life had a measure of freedom lost by the mid-nineteen hundreds.

Until he was eleven, Lear was taught lessons by Ann and Sarah, with kindness and humour. Home schooling was not unusual in the early nineteenth century: J.S. Mill's private tuition from his father included Greek at three, Latin at eight, science at ten and logic with political economy at the age of fourteen. Lear's early education was only particular in its feminine bias as the influence of Jeremiah Lear seems to have made little intellectual impression on his next-to-youngest child.

In effect, Ann and Sarah taught Lear the accomplishments deemed necessary for a young lady of the early 1800s – reading, writing, painting, sketching and music. They could not have realised that they were providing the foundations of an artist, writer and musician. Ann's story tales from classical mythology found a more fertile soil than her Bible readings as Christianity had become soured in a personal fashion by the extreme and suspect piety of her sisters. Homer's *Odyssey,* based on travellers' tales of one-eyed Cyclops and giant squids bore fruit in *The Jumblies* who embark in their sieve on a perilous Nekyia, or night journey, attempting to find the Utopian Hills of the Chankley

---

[74] Joan Perkin *Victorian Women*. London, John Murray. 1993. p11

[75] Cited in Ivy Pinchbeck & Margaret Hewitt *Children in English Society*. London, Routledge. 1973. Vol.2. p351

[76] Vivien Noakes *Edward Lear, The Life of a Wanderer*. London, Fontana Collins. 1968. p64

[77] Cited in Kirsten Drotner *English Children and their magazines. 1751- 1954*. London and New Haven, Yale University Press, 1988. Px-272.

Bore and a limitless supply of Stilton cheese.

Greek legends and Lear's longer Nonsenses share the unfathomable depths of the sea.

'Down the slippery slopes of Myrtle
Where the early pumpkins grow
To the calm and silent sea
Fled the Yonghy, Bonghy Bo'

'The Courtship of the Yonghy, Bonghy Bo'
CN, p 324.

Greece became important to Lear for more than antique legends. Firstly, it was the spiritual home of his childhood hero Lord Byron, secondly, it housed a landscape of picturesque, paintable scenery, ruins and populace, thirdly, it offered a sunny refuge from the English 'foggopolis'.

We know that Lear read Daniel Defoe's *Robinson Crusoe*:[78] as he was able to describe Thomas Stothard's illustrations,[79] as 'those exquisite creations of landscape which first made me, as a child, long to see similar realities'.[80] He could have read Tobias Smollett, Henry Fielding, Oliver Goldsmith and Samuel Richardson: he might have been more interested in the oriental tales of *Scheherazade: A Thousand and One Nights* which were translated and published in 1708 for children to delight in the exotic and unfamiliar adventures of Ali Baba, Sinbad and Aladdin. More foreign fare came from the Brothers Grimm whose *Kinder und Hausmärchen* appeared in 1823 with appropriate pictures by George Cruikshank. It is almost inevitable that Lear was subjected to the morality inherent in Maria Edgeworth's *Early Lessons*, (1809), where every tale was a thinly disguised lecture on good manners and correct social conduct, Mrs Sherward's *Rewards* which demonstrate God's blessing on Christian conduct and Bunyan's The *Pilgrim's Progress* (1678).

Children's stories in the early 1800s still tended towards the importance of moral rather than religious education, a situation exacerbated by religious publishers SPCK[81] and RTS[82] who were quick to harness fiction to the 'improving' aspects of Christianity in children's books. A typically painful example was *Mrs. Norton's Story Book* 1830, which spelled out a moral such as 'work hard - indolence is a sin and must be punished'[83] and *The History of The Fairchild Family*[84] where children are shown a gibbet to remind them of death and God's judgement. Exceptional were the stories of noisy, normal mischievous children such as those in Catherine Sinclair's *Holiday House*, (1838) featuring a giant so tall that he must climb a ladder to comb his own

---

[78] Daniel Defoe, 1719.

[79] Published by T. Cadell & W. Davies, London, 1820.

[80] John Lehmann, *Edward Lear and His World*. London, Thames & Hudson, 1977. p20

[81] Society for the Promotion of Christian Knowledge

[82] Religious Tract Society

[83] *Mrs. Norton's Story Book*. London, John Harris, 1830.

[84] Mrs. Sherwood, *The History of the Fairchild Family,* London, J.Hatchard. 1818.

hair.[85] Lear's first *Book of Nonsense* in 1846 was in direct conflict with contemporary moral attitudes in children's fiction: his Nonsense centred on the experiences and conflicts of childhood with reproving adults as a distant and vaguely ominous 'they'.[86]

> The first his parrient was – who taught
> The cove to read and write
> Latin and Grammarithmetic
> And lots of things besides.   CN, p 425.

The youthful cove learned Latin and Greek and the consequent obligation to practise writing it in verse – understanding the morse code of dactyls and spondees was normal education in 1820. Lear discovered the Romantic poets before his formal schooling: we know that the boy Lear loved the work of Byron in particular as well as Wordsworth and Coleridge, before his adult passion for Alfred Tennyson.[87]

It was Wordsworth's idea of nature endowed with life and powers beyond the human scale, together with Coleridge's theory that 'poetry has the power of exciting the sympathy of the reader by a faithful adherence to the truth of Nature'[88] which struck a chord in the young Lear. He was always unusually aware of his surroundings and travels to the Arundel home of an elder sister Sarah revealed the wide open beauty of the Sussex Downs. England was still, in 1815, a rural economy with most of the working population engaged upon the land or in trades connected with agriculture and Sussex, with no canals,[89] coal mines or cotton imports remained resolutely rural throughout the nineteenth century. Coach travelling was uncomfortable, tedious and occasionally dangerous; highwaymen had vanished by 1815 but robbers were still a hazard on lonely roads and in winter, outside passengers all but froze to death. Lear's adult journeys across seas, countries and continents were truly hazardous, but always undertaken with relish and excitement: the original purpose of finding a congenial climate to offer relief from asthma attacks augmented by an artist's need for fresh horizons. Travelling was a Romantic pastime, one which summoned up the spirit of the Grand Tour, visible in 1820s England through spectacular panoramas in fashionable, purpose-built theatres and assisted by Lord Elgin's looted antiquities in the new British Museum.

---

[85] Justin Schiller, *Edward Lear within the tradition of Children's Literature.* Programme Note, 16th July 2000, Redgrave Theatre, Bristol. p10 'How Pleasant to know Mr. Lear'.

[86] The 'nosy parkers' pressure groups and bureaucrats who constitute 'they' are frequently discussed in Lear biography: see John Vernon Lord *The Nonsense Verse of Edward Lear*, London, Methuen, 1986, pXV

[87] Noakes, p22/23

[88] Coleridge, *Biographica Literaria*, 1817. Quoted in Wordsworth's *Guide to the Lakes*, Devizes, Webb & Bower, 1984. p7

[89] Only the Wey-Arun Canal, 17 miles long, from Shalford, nr. Guildford to Wisborough Green. Built in 1816 with the backing of the Earl of Egremont and linking the Wey to the Arun at Dunsfold. Peak years were 1839-40 when 23,000 tons a year were carried: compare with 300,000 tons p.a. on the Kennet/Avon.

On a childhood visit to Arundel, Lear was introduced to Lord Egremont of Petworth House, a notable art collector and philanthropist with a magnificent baroque palace at his disposal.[90] The 3rd Earl famously patronised J.M.W. Turner, allowing him to stay in rooms at Petworth and paint in the Old Library, still sometimes called 'Turner's Studio'.[91] Throughout his professional painting career, Lear was to demonstrate the somewhat conflicting influences of Turner's swirling lightscapes with the detailed topography of Constable – both Petworth artists, friends of Egremont and inspiration to the young painter.

Edward Lear's childhood love of art matured into the desire to become a painter but there was no money for an art school training and so, instead of studying with Turner at the Royal Academy, Lear was obliged to teach himself by drawing nature from life. Aged just fifteen, he haunted the new Regent's Park (1811), where Stamford Raffles[92] and Humphrey Davy [93]had established a Zoological Garden, and helped Ann eke out a livelihood of sorts by hawking his animal sketches round the inns and taverns of north London. In 1830, he was invited to record the menagerie at Knowsley for Lord Stanley, heir to the 12th Earl Derby. This significant invitation led to a network of aristocratic connections who became life-long friends, patrons and collectors of his art. It introduced him to another menagerie – that of the Stanley children, grandchildren, nephews, nieces and miscellaneous smallfry for whom he wrote the first *Book of Nonsense* in 1846.

Lear's childhood tendency to bronchitis and asthma worsened in the English climate and, by 1837, his health had deteriorated to such an extent that only a warm, dry climate could help. Lord Stanley enabled his protégé to travel to Rome to paint and recuperate: from that day onwards, Edward Lear became a wanderer, never living long in one place and always anticipating the next. His gift for friendship which began so opportunely with the Derby family, was to console, inspire and motivate the next chapters of his life to a greater extent than ever before: he met Chichester Fortescue in 1845 and Franklin Lushington, a young barrister, in Malta during 1849 and their companionship and affection meant the world to him, as did the later bonds with Evelyn Baring, a lively and sensitive soldier, later the first Earl Cromer. Lear's capacity for romantic love manifested itself in intense male friendships, the exact nature of which properly remains a mystery, but most writers do not believe he was an 'active homosexual'. He identified with particular children, but never wished for his own, recording that an annual infant would drive him

---

[90] The Petworth Collection has been re-arranged since Lear's day and the original Turner watercolour sketches of the interior now hang in the National Gallery. An intriguing painting in the collection that Lear may have seen is an interpretation of Swift's *Gulliver's Travels* by Leslie entitled *Gulliver's Presentation to the Queen of Brobdingnag.*

[91] Since 1991, Turner's sketches of Petworth interiors have informed the redecorations and picture hangs and seeing the house through Turner's eyes is becoming increasingly possible. *Petworth House,* The National Trust, 1977, p87

[92] More widely known as the founder of Singapore as a British Colony in 1819: first President of the Royal Zoological Society.

[93] Chemist and inventor of the Miners' Safety Lamp.

wild: 'the row from 40 ill conducted little beasts is frightful'[94] he wrote from a Swiss hotel – he needed to escape into travel and Nonsense.

It was Lushington who introduced Lear to Alfred Tennyson for the poet's sister married Franklin's brother Edmund. There was some mutual admiration when Tennyson wrote 'To E.L. on his Travels in Greece' upon the publication of the *Journals of Landscape Painter in Greece and Albania.*

'Tomohrit, Athens, all things fair
With such a pencil, such a pen
You shadow forth to distant men
I read, and felt that I was there.'[95]

But it was an unequal business. Lear revered Tennyson utterly and longed to illustrate 300 of his poems, a project that he never forgot and never completed. Lear's more intimate friendship was with Tennyson's wife Emily who empathised with his hopeless passion for her brother-in law Franklin and who remained a loving correspondent all their lives. Tennyson was worshipped for his luxurious descriptions, his espousal of forgotten chivalry and the conscious artistry of his musical phrasing and he bestrode the nineteenth century like a colossus: he was to inspire Lear, Carroll and Gilbert.

Lear must have been heartened by the poet's praise, as his own confidence was flagging. As the century moved forwards, his larger oil paintings failed to attract critical attention, or indeed to sell at all. Fashion was moving against austerely classical landscapes and into the crowded panoramas of Francis Frith whose *Derby Day*, (1856), and *Ramsgate Sands*, (1851), made him the Dickens of the art world with their sprawling, busy canvases of public entertainment and familiar landmarks. Lear was obliged to paint small watercolours as potboilers which he constantly devalued, so that buyers never felt they were investing in art, but patronising a rather desperate friend.

Between the years 1865 – 1875, Lear's Nonsense was expressed with the deepest personal feeling, in sad and melancholic poetry which carries the romantic legacy of Keats, Wordsworth and Schubert.

'When awful darkness and silence reign
Over the great Grombolian plain
Through the long, long wintry nights
When the angry breakers roar
As they beat on the rocky shore
When the storm clouds brood on the towering heights
Of the hills of the Chankley bore.'

The Dong with the Luminous Nose'
CN, p422.

In 1869, tired of wandering, Lear finally decided to settle down under his own roof and chose the Italian resort of San Remo. Despite its nickname as the

---

[94] Holbrook Jackson, pxxi

[95] Noakes, p103

'town of flowers' San Remo's Ligurian shyness saves it from any form of attention and even twentieth century tourism has not spoilt the little town's artistic heritage. It lies between Capo Nero and Capo Verde, characterised by perched houses, steep streets and little squares. 'Villa Emily' (Tennyson) was his sanctuary for eight years until a neighbouring development ruined the view and he was obliged to move. In the transition between villas, Lear finalised the text and drawings of a hundred new limericks and Nonsense songs and stories, becoming yet another Dopty Duncle in his temporary hotel life and explaining the confusion of hotel cutlery with botanical specimens such as 'Manyforkia Spoonfolia'.

Lear turned sixty in 1872. He missed the company of his friends – but he seemed not to miss England, neither did he appear to be touched by England's adventures on wider shores: he made no obvious response to the Crimean War in 1854, or the Indian Mutiny in 1857, both of which avoidable conflicts had strong roots in religious dissension. Lear possessed faith, but no belief in organised Christianity. Edward Strachey recalls how Lear 'taught his manservant to say the Lord's Prayer with him every evening and that Lear felt it his duty to prevent the young man growing up without religion, expressing his horror at a Godless world'.[96]

In the last few years before his death in 1888, Lear suffered increasing ill-health, exacerbated by depressive melancholia and financial anxieties. His faithful servant Giorgio had a troubled family life, his friends mostly, unavoidably elsewhere, and only a faithful, tailless cat Foss (Adelphos) remained on his bed. He wrote what became understood as his own obituary, 'Some Incidents from the Life of My Uncle Arly' in 1884.

'So for three and forty winters
Til his shoes were worn to splinters

---

[96] Edward Strachey, *Introduction to the Nonsense Songs and Stories*. London, Frederick Warne & Co, 1894.

All those hills he wandered o'er;-
Sometimes silent, sometimes yelling;-
Til he came to Borley Melling,
And he'd wandered thence no more.

On a little heap of barley
Died my aged Uncle Arly,
And they buried him one night;-
Close besides the leafy thicket;-
There – his hat and railway ticket;-
There - his ever faithful cricket:-
(But his shoes were far too tight)'.

'Some Incidents in the Life of my Uncle Arly'.
CN, p456.

Vivien Noakes suggests that aspects of the poem represent the constraints that Lear felt might have crippled his life: the ill-health, the latent homosexuality, 'the deep, inexpressible realisation of the sadness of life that had grown from the depths of his own unhappiness. Yet perhaps even he knew that from this very perception of sadness had grown a compassion, an understanding and a pity for man's suffering and it was this compassion that made him the loved and loving man he was.'

THAT WHICH WENT BEFORE: EDWARD LEAR

Many early writers on Lear knew him personally and their work may be summarised as appreciative and anecdotally informative, but seldom and only incidentally analytical.

Carolyn Wells[97] described Lear and Carroll as 'Englishmen of genius, deep thinkers and hard workers' for 'their most meritous and interesting kind of Nonsense which embodies an absurd or ridiculous idea and treats it with elaborate seriousness'. This begins the distinguished American tradition of scholarship and commentary on Victorian England which is partially responsible for making subsequent generations of critics on both sides of the Atlantic take nineteenth century Nonsense seriously as a literary form. The American Michele Sala is a contemporary successor to Wells, debating in academic terms how the limericks of Edward Lear 'introduce a number of possibilities, including dangerous and violent ones, and at the same time, disconnect those possibilities from the real world'. In *Lear's Nonsense Beyond Children's Literature* she concludes that 'on a purely narratological level, Nonsense is this: a free play of words and strange events on the surface structure, caused by lack of meaningful opposition in the deep structure'.[98]

An art school training and maverick approach to literature made the turn-of-the century views of G.K. Chesterton[99] unsurprisingly controversial: he preferred the 'fresh, abrupt and inventive rhymes of Mr. Lear' to the 'portentous sciences and philosophies of the nineteenth century' and argued that the 'Dong with the Luminous Nose' was as original as the first ship or the first plough. For Chesterton, the absence of personal information on Lear, in contrast to the voluminous material already accumulating around Carroll, was helpful in creating the 'completeness of Lear as a citizen in the world of the unreason' and a 'purely fabulous figure on his own account'.

In *How Pleasant to Know Mr. Lear*, Bertha Coolidge[100] took the opposite position, arguing that Carroll was an intellectual and a genius and that Lear was neither. 'Carroll's work went deep below the surface...his serious work

---

[97] Carolyn Wells *Preface to a Nonsense Anthology*. Charles Scribner's Sons, New York. 1903.

[98] Michele Sala *Lear's Nonsense Beyond Children's Literature*, 2000. From Internet Site marco@nonsenselit.org accessed 9/1/2008

[99] G.K. Chesterton *In Defence of Nonsense*. From *The Defendant*, originally published by R. Brimley Johnson, London. 1902.

[100] From Internet Nonsense site but originally published in *The Colophon,* a Book Collector's Quarterly, Part 9, New York. 1902.

was touched with a humour utterly beyond the simplicity of Lear'. Despite her partisan approach, Coolidge supported the Nonsense literature of both authors and upbraided posterity in 1902 for ignoring Lear.

Lear scholars seem to share a particular literary and intellectual pedigree. Angus Davidson, a minor Bloomsbury scion, wrote the first full length biography in 1938.[101] *Animal Farm* was written in 1945, the same year that Orwell wrote about Lear in 'Funny but Not Vulgar'[102] and Orwell debated Lear's 'amiable lunacy and perversion of logic' as well as his 'poltergeist interference with common sense'.[103] There is an occasional resemblance in Lear's animals (pigs in particular) to the livestock on Mr. Jones' farm in Orwell's classic satire but this may be as much connected with an undoubted porcine intelligence and character as any influence from Edward Lear on George Orwell. But Lear's animals are equally assertive, determined to fight an unknown 'they' who represent a crushing and dispiriting authority: anthropomorphism is more equal than anything. Aldous Huxley praised Lear's fantasies as a declaration of freedom in 1933. [104]

Orwell's Etonian King's Scholar contemporary, John Lehmann, contributed to the Lear bibliography with a largely pictorial study in 1977.[105] It is of particular interest from a biographer of Lewis Carroll, Rupert Brooke, Virginia Woolf and a consequent legatee of the Hogarth Press. In 1965, the

---

[101] Angus Davidson, *Edward Lear: Landscape Painter and Nonsense Poet.* London John Murray. 1938.

[102] 'The Leader', 28th July, 1945.

[103] George Orwell, Preface to *The Book of Nonsense*, London, Megroz Penguin Edition. 1938.

[104] Aldous Huxley *On the Margin.* Chatto & Windus, London. 1933. pp 162-172

[105] John Lehmann, *Edward Lear and His World.* Thames & Hudson, 1977. John Lehmann (1907-1987) brother of the novelist Rosamund Lehmann and the actress Beatrice Lehmann.

British Council and the British Book League commissioned Joanna Richardson to write about Edward Lear for their series of supplements to *British Book News*. Richardson, biographer[106] and Englishwoman of letters, is most notable for winning the Prix Goncourt. Her short study is admirable and precise, even if offering no new insight or critical theory.

Susan Chitty produced *That Singular Person Called Lear* in 1988, a title, similar to many in the genre, borrowed from the writer himself. Poet (and ex-Jesuit) Peter Levi brought out the most recent biography in 1995:[107] It was inspired by his research on Alfred Tennyson, in similar vein to the study by Joanna Richardson. Levi's choice of biographical heroes from Greek mythologists to Shakespeare, Yevtushenko and Pasternak elevates Lear to a higher literary canon than usual. But the bestselling biographies of Vivien Noakes have done more to bring Lear to contemporary notice and attention than any other scholar. Her three books[108] have become the cornerstones for literary critics, academic research and general readers alike. In 2002, she edited *Edward Lear The Complete Nonsense and Other Verse*[109] which contained previously unpublished Nonsense and she remained a frequent lecturer and broadcaster on the life and work of Edward Lear, before her death in 2011.

The modern American writer Clifton Snider[110] proposes a Jungian interpretation for the Nonsense of Lear, following in the footsteps of Erich Neumann and his Jungian analysis of *Alice in Wonderland*. According to Jung, 'the polaristic structure of the psyche is, like any other energetic system, dependent upon the tension of opposites' which might explain what cats and owls are doing rowing about in a boat together. And then again, it might not. After positing the rationale for Lear as jester to serious minded Victorian thinkers, Snider suggests we may best understand Lear as 'Trickster' a social archetype defined by Paul Radin (and of particular interest to the contemporary Irish poet Paul Muldoon):

'Trickster is both creator and destroyer. He wills nothing consciously. At all times he is constrained to behave as he does from impulses over which he has no control. He knows neither good nor evil, yet he is responsible for both. He possesses no values, moral or social, is at the mercy of his passions and appetites, yet through his actions, all values come into being'.[111]

---

[106] Presumably, the British Council selected her on account of her *Tennyson - the Pre-Eminent Victorian*, published by Jonathan Cape, London. 1962.

[107] Peter Levi, *Edward Lear, a Biography*. London. Macmillan .1995.

[108] Vivien Noakes, *Edward Lear Life of a Wanderer*. London, Collins, 1968.Vivien Noakes, *Edward Lear Selected Letters*. Oxford, Clarendon Press. 1988.Vivien Noakes, *Edward Lear*. New York, Harry N. Adams, 1986.

[109] Penguin Books, London. 2002.

[110] *Psychological Perspectives*, The Jung Institute of Los Angeles, No. 24, Spring-Summer, 1991.

[111] Paul Radin, *The Trickster: A Study in American-Indian Mythology*. Schocken, New York. 1956.

Radin saw Trickster in medieval jesters, Punch and Judy, circus clowns and certain animals such as the raven, the hare and the spider. Snider trawls through sociology to uncover yet another role model for Lear – the American/Indian *berdache,* a morphological man who does not fit modern society's standard male role and who has a non-masculine character. Snider is one of the many writers on Edward Lear who believe that his emphasis on long noses is a phallic assertion, demonstrating latent, if not actual, homosexual inclinations. Early European settlers tried to extinguish the *berdache* whom they considered 'abhorrent sodomites' even allowing for their characteristic creativity, hard work, love for children and sense of humour. As Snider fairly points out, Lear lived in an age which needed to laugh. Evangelical religion and pedagogical earnestness spread like smog, inspiring Noakes to describe Lear as believing that joy was synonymous with levity and merriment was a step along the broad road to destruction.

No versions of either Lear's life or his work have been translated into film, as far as I can be aware. In this, he differs strikingly from Carroll and Gilbert who have attracted film makers from Walt Disney to Mike Reed and any number of loosely connected three-dimensional tributes. But the contemporary actor Charles Lewsen has produced a one man show entitled *How Pleasant to Know Mr Lear* which tours to great acclaim. A recent programme[112] for a show at the Redgrave Theatre, Bristol, included essays by Vivien Noakes, Rowena Fowler, Ruth Pitman, Justin Schiller and Dr John Swales as well as poetic contributions from Roger McGough – and Alfred Tennyson.

---

[112] 16th July 2000, Redgrave Theatre, Bristol.

EDWARD LEAR AND THE HERITAGE OF ROMANTIC POETRY

Lear's birth in 1812 fell in the centre of that unique period between the outbreak of the French Revolution in 1789 and the first Reform Bill in 1832: when the largest movements of history impinged with the greatest force upon the private experience of individuals. The art and culture which sprang from those storms of revolution created the intellectual atmosphere of Lear's childhood – the poems of Wordsworth, Byron and Coleridge, the drawings of Blake and the paintings of Turner.[113] When Lear was a boy, poetry used to be part of daily life; 'Poetry was not an esoteric mystery, not something hidden in the privacy of the library, not cabinet literature, but a social instrument, an open celebration, a common possession'.[114]

> 'For what, we ask, is Life
> Without a touch of poetry in it?
> Hail, Poetry, thou heaven born Maid
> Thou gildest e'en the Pirate's trade.
> Hail, flowing font of sentiment
> All Hail, Divine Emollient!'

W.S. Gilbert: Pirate Chorus,
The Pirates of Penzance, 1880.

By the time Gilbert's 'divine Emollient' had been lauded by the cultivated Pirates (who liked a glass of sherry before raids, rapes and pillage), the great romantic poets of the early nineteenth century assumed a mythic status. Tennyson alone remained as a living colossus but Shelley, Keats, Wordsworth, Byron and Coleridge were long dead. Nonsense poetry recalls them with echoes of romantic imagery, onomatopoeic sounds and rhythmic metre. Contemporary readers of Victorian Nonsense verse would be familiar with the affectionate parody of the Romantic giants and both benefited from mutual acquaintance. 'Some poems that Tennyson, Browning, Hardy and Kipling clearly intended to be taken seriously, use the tactics and achieve something

---

[113] Vivien Noakes does not mention that Lear listened to music as a child, but it seems almost impossible to imagine that Bowman's Lodge did not have a fortepiano in 1812, nor that some of his elder sisters wouldn't have played Mozart duets or sung Schubert songs.

[114] Herbert Read, *Phases of English Poetry*, London, The Hogarth Press. 1928. p33

like the effects of comic poetry'.[115] And surely it is no coincidence that England, a country famed for the greatest and most eternal poets, produced the greatest and most eternal Nonsense. In another sense than the parodic, Nonsense poetry may be described as the purest of all poetry as the rhythm of the metre and the sound of the words create an effect all on their own.

'On the Coast of Coromandel
Where the early pumpkins blow
In the middle of the wood
Lived the Yonghy Bonghy Bo' .

'The Courtship of the Yonghy
Bonghy Bo'. CN, p324.

'The great achievement of English Romanticism was its grasp of the principle of creative autonomy, its declaration of artistic independence'.[116] The Romantic style came to mean imaginative, individual and subjective: the romantic content came to be understood as emotional, religious and natural, but there were as many exceptions as standards, as many interpretations as variations, and as many adherents as opponents.

Byron remains the ultimate 'romantic' literary personality and became a byword for aggressive self-assertion, love of liberty and cult of love but his poetry owes more to the classical satire of Pope and Dryden. Blake is often linked with Coleridge and Wordsworth[117] in the first wave of English Romantic poets who actually experienced the initial euphoria in France and, in some sense, reacted against it, but Blake cannot be so easily categorised. C.S.

---

[115] Donald Gray, 'Victorian Comic Verse, or Snakes in Greenland'. VP 26, No.3(1988)211-223

[116] Northrope Frye,' 'Blake After Two Centuries'. *English Romantic Poets; Essays in Criticism*. OUP 1960. p65

[117] Great personal friends and jointly known as 'The Lake Poets' for their sojourns in Windermere.

Lewis believed that Shelley (together with Milton) is the logical successor to Dante and that the concentration of his fantastical, almost supernatural imagery is unique in nineteenth century poetry: this has been linked to the influence of 'Gothic' novels which were among Shelley's favourite reading as a boy.

So 'romantic' although a useful and evocative word, is insufficient and some other distinctions must be found in order to consider the inheritance of poetry in Lear's Nonsense verse. Herbert Read[118] has suggested that all poetry belongs to either a popular tradition or an artistic one. Popular poetry makes simple statements with straightforward definition. The metre is usually a regular and progressive beat devoid of artifice or elaboration. These 'ballad' poems derive from traditional songs and operate as a communal activity, linking people together in easily-remembered music, sung, spoken or chanted. Repeated chorus and strophic verses are another characteristic of popular poetry as is the lack of either author or central narrative voice. Traditional poems are both of the community and for it: individuality has no place here. Themes of popular poetry are equally common to all: love, family, animals, hunting, God and the weather.

'Oh, Western wind, when wilt thou blow
That the small rain down can rain?
Christ, that my love were in my arms
And I in my bed again!'

Anon, 16th.[119]

Into the popular tradition may come 'O Mistress Mine' from Shakespeare's *Twelfth Night* and certainly 'There Was a Lover and His Lass' from *As You Like It*. Shakespeare, like Chaucer and Byron, knew how to write both popular and artistic poems.

Artistic poetry differs from the popular tradition in that it expects what Herbert Read calls a 'paper eternity' as opposed to being said or sung out loud. Artistic poetry depends upon representing sound by symbols which may, or may not, indicate a literal sense. (Nonsense poetry may occasionally be found in this category.) Verses may be constructed with complex rhyming patterns and a variety of metres ranging from the simple to the elaborate. Crucially, the sentiments expressed will be subjective and emotional, away from straightforward expression and experience. Yet 'poetry draws mankind together, breaks down barriers, relieves loneliness, shows us ourselves in others and others in ourselves. It is the friendly art. It ignores time and space. National, racial and secular differences fall at its touch, which is the touch of kinship and when we feel this, we laugh shamefacedly at our pretensions, timidities and reserves'.[120] In the fine writing that is artistic poetry, ideas and words are one: there is less the sense that a poet expresses ideas that already exist but more the feeling that the poet creates ideas as he writes.

---

[118] Herbert Read, *Phases of English Poetry*. London, Hogarth Press. 1928.

[119] *Oxford Book of English Verse,* Oxford, Clarendon Press. 1931. p53

[120] George McLean Harper 'Coleridge's Conversational Poems'. *English Romantic Poets, Essays in Modern* Criticism. OUP 1960. p146

Thomas Gray provides a classic example:

'Full many a gem of purest ray serene
The dark, unfathomed caves of ocean bear;
Full many a flower is born to blush unseen,
And waste its sweetness on the desert air.'[121]

The musical sounds and romantic concepts of this celebrated extract illustrate another function of artistic poetry: to 'clothe' thoughts in beautiful dress. Here is no philosophical truth nor revelatory idea, but a romantic notion of drowned jewels and faraway blooms expressed in perfect rhyme; two metaphors for modesty. The hidden treasures represent the purest of human qualities by marvellous comparison to real and crystal flowers – something is like something else, unlike Nonsense poetry, where nothing is ever like anything else. Gray illustrates prevailing themes of both artistic poetry and popular verse: an exploration of the self and of the soul together with awe and admiration of Nature.

Edward Lear felt a particular empathy with Lord Byron and when the news came of his death at Missolonghi, the eleven-year old boy burst into inconsolable tears. Byron brought a vivifying effect to his artistic poetry, much of which is as attractive and accessible as colloquial prose. There is a sense of harnessed energy in Byron, a champagne bottle waiting for the cork to fly off and liberate the contents, splashing wildly over the waiting glass. Vivien Noakes points out that Byron was a mature hero for a young man and it is unlikely that Lear realised that Byron, too, suffered from epilepsy. Only a few years later after Byron's death, Lear wrote a poem about the domestic upheaval suffered by the family after his father's financial collapse.

'In dreary silence down the bustling road
The Lears, with all their goods and chattels rode
Ten carts of moveables went on before
And in the rear, came half a dozen more:
A hackney coach, the Lears themselves enshrouds
To guard them from the gaze of vulgar crowds
The vehicle has reached the turnpike gate
Where wondering toll men – throngs of people wait:
The loaded carts, their dusty way pursue,
Shrill squeak the wheels – dark London was in view'.

CN, p3.

Lear's natural rhyming sense first appeared in these early poems where the influence of Byron is particularly clear.

'Farewell, Mother, tears are streaming   And the midnight moon is weaving

---

[121] Thomas Gray *Elegy Written in a Country Churchyard*. Oxford Book of Collected Verse, Oxford, Clarendon Press, 1931. p518

Down thy tender pallid cheek
I, in gems and roses gleaming
One eternal sunshine dreaming
Scarce this sad farewell may speak
Farewell, Mother, now I leave thee.
And thy love unspeakable
One to cherish, who may grieve me
One to trust, who may deceive me

E.L. CN p20

Her bright chain o-er the deep
Whose breast is gently heaving
As an infant is asleep
So the spirit bows before thee
To listen and adore thee
With a full but soft emotion
Like the swell of summer's ocean.
Farewell, Mother, fare thee well.

Lord Byron 'To Music'[122]

Both are popular poetry with an easy metre, simple vocabulary and direct expression. But as Lear developed his Nonsense rhymes during the 1860s and 1870s, a much greater artistic element is involved.

'And the golden grouse came there
And the pobble who has no toes
And the small Olympian bear
And the Dong with the luminous nose.
And the blue baboon who played the flute
And the Orient calf from the land of Tute
And the Attery Squash and the Biscuit Bat
All came and lived on the lovely hat
Of the Quangle Wangle

'The Quangle Wangle's Hat'
Quee".CN, p391

This is pure poetry, because it is rhythm and metre and sound allied to no very obvious points of reference. It is unlike the comic verses of, for example, Thomas Hood or C.S. Calverley whose popular ballads actually meant something, however peculiar: Hilaire Belloc's 'Charles Augustus Fortescue' is a direct descendent.

'The Nicest Child I ever knew
Was Charles Augustus Fortescue
He never lost his cap, or tore
His stockings, or his pinafore
In eating bread, he made no crumbs,
He was extremely fond of sums.[123]

This funny, ballad verse is neither Nonsense nor poetry. (Most children would consider it nonsense...)

Tennyson combines elements of both artistic and popular poetry and he remains the single most clearly observed influence on the Nonsense verse of Edward Lear. They met in 1849 and their lives touched at regular intervals

[122] *Oxford Book of English Verse*, Clarendon Press, Oxford, 1931. p690
[123] Hilaire Belloc *Cautionary Tales* London, Duckworth & Co, p75

until Lear's death in his Villa Tennyson in 1888; they admired one another's work but were never friends. Tennyson wrote a stanza in recognition of a painting by Lear and Lear planned to illustrate 300 Tennyson poems, by paint, and by music. 'The way to enjoy Tennyson is to look to him for what he is – a superb landscape painter, a consummate musician' wrote F.L. Lucas,[124] and it was the music in Edward Lear which enabled a particular appreciation of musical dreamscapes such as Tennyson's 'Lotos Eaters'.

> 'There is sweet music here that softer falls
> Than petals from blown roses on the grass
> Or night dews on still waters between walls
> Of shadowy granite, in a gleaming pass:
> Music that brings sweet sleep down from the blissful skies
> Than tired eyelids upon tired eyes.'[125]

Compare the *Lotos Eaters* with the following verse by Edward Lear. (And note the echoes from *In Memoriam*.)

> 'Cold are the crabs that crawl on yonder hill
> Colder the cucumbers that grow beneath.
> And colder still the brazen chops that wreath
> The tedious gloom of philosophic pills!
> For when the tardy film of nectar fills
> The ample bowls of demons and of men
> There lurks the feeble mouse, the homely hen
> And there the porcupine, with all her quills.'

CN, p386.

This is artistic poetry from the great romantic tradition. It is inspired by Tennyson and yet it is also Nonsense. Artistic poetry suffered in contrast to the increasing dominance of prose during the mid-nineteenth century and novelists became the new literary lions. (D.H. Lawrence and Thomas Hardy were rare exponents of both.) Popular poetry evolved into hymns, parlour song, the music hall ballad or even Savoy Opera libretti. Today, even popular poetry struggles to find a significant audience despite isolated champions (usually Irish) and Wendy Cope.[126]

Nonsense poetry divides neatly into both popular and artistic categories. Limericks, with their straightforward metre, familiar words and compact story, are popular verse. Their oft-repeated last line is the chorus, easy to remember and satisfying to chant. Lear's limericks, unlike many of their successors

---

[124] F.L. Lucas, 'Tennyson' in *Ten Victorian Poets*, Cambridge University Press, 1940. p13

[125] Alfred Tennyson 'Song of the Lotos-Eaters'. *Oxford Book of English Verse*, p828

[126] Newly notable for refusing the Laureateship in 2009, declaring that poetry cannot be written to order. Popular poets who have found an audience are Philip Larkin and John Betjeman.

which were written by and for an intellectual élite, were designed to amuse children.

> 'There was an Old Person of Bar
> Who passed all her life in a jar
> Which she painted pea green, to appear more serene
> That placid Old Person of Bar.'

CN, p358.

'The Owl and the Pussy Cat' is popular verse of the highest order.

> 'The Owl and the Pussy Cat went to sea
> In a beautiful pea green boat
> They took some honey and plenty of money
> Wrapped up in a five pound note
> The owl looked up to the stars above
> And sang to a small guitar.
> 'O lovely Pussy!, O Pussy my love
> What a beautiful Pussy you are,
> You are.
> You are!
> What a beautiful Pussy you are!'

CN, p238.

This Nonsense lyric contains almost every possible theme in popular verse and indeed some more usually found in serious and artistic poems. Love, nature and music are represented, so is the difficult quest to a faraway land. Money and food are physical symbols of sustenance and the ring denotes the eternal. Ostensibly, it is Nonsense, except that it has become so familiar that we accept it as truth. It has become mythic, just as Jason's Argonauts or Aesop's fables. Unlike the epics of Tennyson or the lyrics of Browning, Lear's Nonsense verse is not rooted in reality.

'The Pobble who has no toes,
Had once as many as we.
When they said, some day, you may lose them all,
He replied, 'phum phiddle de dee.'
And his Aunt Jobiska made him drink,
Lavender water, tinged with pink,
For she said, 'the whole world knows
There's nothing so good for a Pobble's toes'.

CN, p395.

Ina Rae Hark believes that Lear's toe-less Pobbles represent Darwinian survival and that 'although solicitude for the Pobble's toes has been the overwhelming concern of his aunt, once they are gone, they are gone'.[127]

Readers of Lear's Nonsense verses today are probably less familiar with the Romantic inheritance of poetry and reactions to them are uncoloured by an easy association with Byron, Tennyson and Shelley. Sometimes, an ignorance of English poets might even be helpful: 'Carroll and Lear moved beyond travesty itself to make poems in which reference to the language of other poems is almost entirely obscured'.[128] And although it is certainly true that a knowledge of both deepens an appreciation of the other, comparisions can be odious.

[127] Ina Rae Hark 'Edward Lear: Eccentricity and Victorian Angst'. *Victorian Poetry*, 26, 3(1988)112
[128] Donald Gray, 'Snakes in Greenland'. VP, 26,3 (1988) 210-223.

EDWARD LEAR AND ART

Edward Lear <u>became</u> an artist with words although his initial ambition had been to be an artist with paint. He first learnt drawing and sketching at home with his sisters Ann and Sarah in the domestic tradition of the nineteenth century: although his father, Jeremiah, possessed some good paintings at Bowman's Lodge, it seems that the young Edward never desired to emulate the Old Masters but became inspired by nature, wildlife and the artistic romanticism of contemporary painters.

Edward's first real brush with art came on boyhood visits to a married sister in Arundel, West Sussex, and family visits to Petworth House. The huge baroque palace, built along the lines of Versailles, is a treasure trove of sculpture, furniture, interior design – and painting. The collection was initially established by the 2nd Earl at Egremont House, Piccadilly[129] but it was his son, the 3rd Earl, who ushered in what became known as Petworth's Golden Age, twice extending the North Gallery in 1824 and 1827 to house an ever-growing collection of Dutch, Italian and French Old Masters, new paintings by Joshua Reynolds, John Constable, William Blake and Joseph Mallord William Turner.

It is possible that Lear met Turner at Petworth; he certainly saw many of Turner's landscapes and developed a lasting admiration for Turner's flexible style of capturing light and atmospheric effects with his swirling strokes, impressionist brushwork and dramatic representation of nature. Yet another early and influential supporter of Turner proved to be John Ruskin whose *Modern Painters, I,* (1843), was entirely inspired by his crusade to support Turner against *The Literary Gazette, Blackwood's Magazine* and *The Athenaeum*, all of whose reactionary critics attacked Turner and compared him unfavourably to Claude Lorrain and Salvator Rosa. Ruskin championed Turner's impressionistic accuracy with typical brio: in *Modern Painters, II,* he softened his approach somewhat, but never failed in his support for the modern romantic school of English landscape painters. As we shall see, Ruskin read and enjoyed the work of Edward Lear, choosing him as a Nonsense writer and poet first among his favourite books.[130]

Turner began his career in the eighteenth century tradition of topographical pencil sketches which determined the subsequent placing of a colour wash, but his technique developed into freer, bolder and braver expression: a 'fantastic world bathed in light and resplendent with beauty, a world not of calm but of movement, not of simple harmonies but dazzling

---

[129] 94, Piccadilly, and known colloquially as the In and Out Club. The building still exists as one of the last remaining great London houses and is becoming a luxury hotel.

[130] Peter Levi *Edward Lear* London, Macmillan, 1995. p330

pageantries.'[131] Like Turner, Lear drew directly from Nature and, like Turner, Lear was particularly attracted by the sharp clear light and bright colours of the Mediterranean. In marked, direct and contemporary contrast were the straightforward and truthful representations of John Constable, 1776–1837. Lear's later landscape sketches and drawings show the Constable/Turner dichotomy of reality softened by impressionism, of truth released by freedom, and the literal translated into the romantic.

Another Petworth artist whose life and work was to prove a significant influence on Edward Lear was William Blake, (1757–1827). Poet, visionary, illustrator and painter, Blake's range of achievement still resists easy categorising, but 'illustrator' must be what relates most strongly to Edward Lear. Blake's series of 102 water colour pictures for Dante's *Divine Comedy* may have sown the seeds for Lear's project to illustrate 120 Tennyson poems, as might Blake's illustrations for 'The Book of Job' or smaller-scale illustrations for the poetry of Thomas Gray, notably 'Elegy in a Country Churchyard' and 'Hymn to a Favourite Cat Drowned in a Bowl of Gold Fish'.

When Jeremiah Lear retired in 1827, fifteen year old Edward went to live with Ann and to begin earning his own living by sketching from nature and selling the drawings. There was no money for a real art training, preferably at the Royal Academy where Turner taught, the absence of which Lear was always keenly aware. Ann's new home near the zoo gave opportunities for watching and studying wild animals and birds in as nearly a natural habitat as possible. It was the age of the naturalist: John James Audubon, 1785–1851, had created a sensation in 1826 with his *Birds of America*, a series of highly dramatic bird portraits drawn to record species threatened by invading colonists, and Thomas Bewick, (1753–1828), made such an impression with his *British Birds*, (1804) that a species of wild swan was named after him.

Young Edward Lear had an introduction to Prideaux Selby and Sir William Jardine who were preparing *Illustrations of British Ornithology* in 1825 and it appears likely that he acted as an assistant. 'It was a fortunate apprenticeship for it taught Lear to be bold and lively and imaginative in his work, encouraging characteristics that were probably always there'.[132] Lear began work on his own book *The Family Psittacidae* in 1828. The precision, skill and beauty of Lear's parrot drawings immediately established his reputation as an ornithological draughtsman and led to the Knowsley commission, as well as collaborative ventures with a number of publishers in pioneering natural history studies. We shall never know what might have happened to Lear if poor eyesight and troubled health had not made him want to leave England for Italy in 1837 and spend a lifetime wandering on the continent.

Between 1840 and 1870, Lear wrote and illustrated seven books of his

---

[131] E.H. Gombrich 'The Break With Tradition'. *The Story of Art*, London, Phaidon, 4th Ed. 1974. p390

[132] Noakes, p30

travels[133]. Whilst working on the hundreds of topographical watercolour sketches and dozens of oil paintings required for the travel books, he squeezed in quantities of Nonsense drawings, pictures and illustrations. The first collection was actually published in 1846 although the limericks and drawings had been produced ten years earlier for the Stanley children at Knowsley. Nothing like *The Book of Nonsense* had been seen before. Children's books of the time were not child-centred: if they managed to escape an evangelical moralising, they might be accompanied by very adult, if very beautiful, drawings like those by Thomas Stothard, (1755–1834),[134] (Lear knew and admired Stothard's work, especially Stothard's illustrations for *Robinson Crusoe*). A typical illustrated children's story of the day comes from *The Children's Magazine*, January 1st, 1829 showing dialogue in the manner of a *Punch* cartoon. Father is propped up on the mantelpiece in conversation with two stodgily overdressed children. Drawing and text are equal in mind-numbing banality.

Father. 'Here's a parcel from the Post Office, Robert and it has something in it for you, I'm sure'.

Robert. 'For me, Father? Oh! What can it be? Has the little magazine come at last?'

Father. 'It has indeed'.

Robert. 'I'm so glad! Sister Jane! Our magazine has come'. Etc, etc.

Contemporary artist-illustrators such as George Cruikshank, John Leech[135] or Richard 'Dicky' Doyle produced elaborately cross-hatched social comments and satire. Only perhaps the black and white line drawings of Wilhelm Busch (1832–1908), which illustrated his own doggerel verses *Max Und Moritz* can be considered in the same terms as Edward Lear. Yet his slapstick character *Schadenfreude* lacks the charm of Lear's invention and the drawings lack bite. Busch's fellow countryman Dr Heinrich Hoffmann wrote and illustrated the *Cautionary Tales of Strewwelpeter* which appeared in England during 1848 – these are darker and more disturbing children's stories which do not have the antidote of Lear's contradictory illustrations: Lear's young person of Janina has her head fanned off by her old uncle, but she is smiling sweetly. Edward Lear was known to dislike Ger-man, Ger-women and Ger-children but there seems little doubt that he was influenced not only by Hoffmann and possibly by Busch but by the earlier Grimm Brothers *Kinder Und Hausmärchen,* marvellously illustrated by Cruikshank, What became known as 'The Golden Age' of illustrated children's books with the work of John Ruskin, Charles Kingsley, Lewis Carroll and George MacDonald lay two decades ahead, together with the mass of new illustrated journalism of the 1860s.

---

[133] These illustrated travelogues were familiar to early nineteenth century. readers: James Fenimore Cooper published several similar records of journeys through Europe in the 1830s.

[134] Stothard, a follower of Rubens, painted frescoes including 'War' and 'Intemperance' as social commentary at Burghley House during 1799–1803.

[135] Leech illustrated Barham's *Ingoldsby Legends.*

Edward Lear's Nonsense drawings were unique in their day and perhaps remain so in ours. They were revolutionary when they first appeared and just as revolutionary when their creator died, although they had not developed at all. They are indivisible from their accompanying limericks, songs and stories and indeed indebted to the words of the verse: perfectly matched text and writing which is not necessarily the inevitable result of an author illustrating his own words. W.S. Gilbert did perfectly conjoin both in *The Bab Ballads* and Lewis Carroll attempted to illustrate Alice: Carroll's primitive sketches remain valued for a certain otherworldly innocence and amateur fantasy, qualities lost in the slick cross-hatching of Sir John.

Thomas Byrom[136] emphasises the occasional contrast between words and text: an example is the small dog owned by an Old Man of Ancona who is illustrated as being a very large dog indeed, or the Old Man on a hill who strides over a flat surface. Byrom believes that in nearly every pictured poem there is a discrepancy, but this is not usually the case and perhaps the American Byrom has taken Nonsense a shade too literally. In the manner of their subjects, who are often half human and half animal, the illustrations are caught between the act of writing and the act of drawing. Ann Colley believes that 'the reader's eyes follow the segments spread out across the flat surface of the page while his ear attends to the syllables in the articulated rhythms of the stanza'.[137] This writer admires the extra dimension afforded by Lear's limerical pictures and believes in their utmost synergy. To me, pictures and poems have become indivisible: literal interpretations of the absurd supplying unforgettable, often anthropomorphic images such as The Old Man Who Said Hush (CN, p173) or The Old Man In a Tree. (CN, p 161).

---

[136] Thomas Bryom, *Nonsense and Wonder: the poems and cartoons of Edward Lear.* New York, Penguin Books, 1977.
[137] Ann Colley 'Edward Lear's Limericks and the Reversals of Nonsense'. VP 26,3(1988)285-299

Despite the Nonsensical adventures in the limericks, the drawn characters inhabit a real world. Old Men, Old Women and Young Persons are subjected to familiar problems and situations to which they respond with the usual human mixture of courage and cowardice. As John Vernon Lord has noticed 'hardly any of them are Righteous'.[138] Very few typical early Victorian idealised heroes and heroines can be seen in the drawings of Lear's Nonsense, and almost no typical moral issues. No limerick, for example, deals with Feckless Mothers, Irish Protest or Demon Drink[139], as do some poems and ballads of the period - Lear never ventured the challenge to authority implicit in Tennyson's 'Charge of the Light Brigade' There is a pervading sense of the individual competing against the norm: of an outsider fighting against a nameless and slightly sinister 'they'. Yet although Lear was never an active rebel, he remained a permanent outsider, isolated from contemporary concerns by sojourns abroad, ill-health and insecurity of all description.

All Lear's topographical drawings, Tennyson pictures, large oil canvases and the Nonsense art can be best considered as illustration. This is obvious when applied to landscape, animals or poetry, but less expected in the Nonsense drawings which illustrate very much more than merely the verses they accompany. Limerical characters spontaneously demonstrate a variety of Lear's unconscious emotions and, in this sense, some of Lear's Nonsense art borders on the surreal. Surrealism's ideological origins are derived from Freud's belief in the exploration of the unconscious to release the mind from conscious control, allowing dormant images the freedom to float to the surface. The importance of surrealism is 'the belief in the superior reality of certain forms of association neglected heretofore, in the omnipotence of the dream and the disinterested play of thought'.[140] In addition, Surrealism demonstrates a hyper-realism in which the form and function of familiar objects are underlined by an unfamiliar yet obviously related context such as the steam train which emerges from the domestic fireplace in René Magritte's *Time Transfixed*, 1938.

Lear's Nonsense drawings have a terrific feeling of movement. Limerical characters are often on tip-toes with outstretched arms and flying clothes.

---

[138] John Vernon Lord, 'Illustrating Lear'. Essay for the Inauguration of the New Brighton University, 1991. p17

[139] 'Father's a Drunkard and Mother is Dead' is the classic, by Mrs Parkhurst, 1868.

[140] Hugh Honour and John Fleming, *A World History of Art*. London, Macmillan, 1982. p591

Bold, confident lines portray dynamic gestures and eloquent facial expression. There is a sense of instant and spontaneous execution, a quality significantly lacking in Lear's larger oil pictures. In the Nonsense drawings, everything and everyone is dancing, running, stepping or falling over. Nonsense animals are informed by Lear's natural history studies – lobsters, newts and horses are difficult subjects for amateur artists to draw convincingly, but Lear has no trouble with them at all.[141] In contrast, Lear knew that his figure drawing needed attention and enrolled as an adult student at the Royal Academy in 1849 where he practised copying antique busts and casts, although to little practical effect. Even individual teaching from Holman Hunt could not constrain him into becoming a Pre-Raphaelite – observing the precepts of the Brotherhood to paint from nature led him to absurd lengths, such as wiring a stuffed jackdaw to a tree for *The Quarries of Syracuse*, (1853).

Yet there was a link between Nonsense art and the Pre-Raphaelites as both understood illustration as an essential means of conveying and enhancing a narrative. 'Truth' – religious, social or moral – became a Brethren watchword, exalted over the quest for 'beauty' and dominating their search for expression. Just as romanticism was a reaction against the order, logic and system of the classical, Pre-Raphaelites reacted against the corruption of truth by what they believed to be false ideals of beauty. They aimed to return to an art unsullied by theatrical insincerity and formal posturing; they shared a Victorian dream of innocence and simplicity inspired by nature and vindicated by Ruskin's exuberant and fulsome support. 'Illustration' may never have the slightly snobbish cachet of fine art but the possibility of art as illustration is an old battleground upon which blood is still spilt. The partnership of artists such as Hablot Knight Browne (Phiz) with Dickens or George Cruikshank with the Grimm Brothers established an iconic imagery in fiction, just as their

---

[141] See Noakes, p263

successors Arthur Rackham[142] (Rip Van Winkle) and Pauline Baynes[143] (Narnia). We may not know the tales that lie behind the fantasies of Hieronymous Bosch, nor all the characters in Rubens' Flemish allegories but they undoubtedly existed and the fact that so much earlier art portrayed scenes whose stories we do know from religion, mythology or history should not blind us to ignoring tales behind the rest. [144] Nonsense art does tell the story, just as plainly as the morality tales of Hogarth or the satirical observations of Cruikshank. The adage that every picture tells a story remains true: what might not be true is the story itself.

Lear drew 'Nonsenses' throughout his life, and not always to illustrate limericks. Frequent sketches decorate his letters, diaries and table mats. They became an essential alternative to the serious business of painting for a living and, increasingly, Lear became proud of them. But for many years, his Nonsense drawings were obliged to occupy space not reserved for normal work patterns, late at night and in odd scraps of spare time and sunlight. Lear found the larger scale oil paintings a terrible drain, partly due to the wearisome attention to detail and partly because they were a reworking of subjects that had long since ceased to command his attention. 'I certainly do hate the act of painting', Lear wrote in a letter to Lord Carlingford 'and although day after day I go steadily on, it is like grinding my nose off'.[145]

The drawings themselves have always attracted critical attention. In 1887, an anonymous reviewer praised Lear's 'fantastical absurdities' which are 'as void of vulgarity or cynicism as they are incapable of being made to harbour any symbolical meaning', adding how much pleasure was given by Lear's 'happy gift of pictorial expression enabling him to double, nay quadruple the laughable effect of his text by inexhaustible profusion of the quaintest designs'.[146] Emile Cammaerts suggested that all Nonsense writers must necessarily illustrate their own work as interpretations of unreality offered dauntingly limitless horizons: 'when we observe the care taken by Kipling over the *Just So Stories* and by G.K. Chesterton to illustrate *Biography for Beginners* and *Greybeards at Play*, more or less subjected to the spirit of Nonsense, we are led to think that there is more than a coincidence in the fact that Nonsense writers are also Nonsense draughtsmen'.[147] Yet Kipling's illustrations never achieved an abstraction from the mores of contemporary design and his folkloric fables are drawn in the art-nouveau style of the 1890s. The contemporary scholar Ann Colley believes that the limericks and

---

[142] Arthur Rackham, 1867–1939 British artist celebrated for his children's book illustrations who worked in a striking vein of Nordic fantasy.

[143] Pauline Baynes, created the iconic images for the first C.S. Lewis children's book *The Lion, The Witch and The Wardrobe* in 1949.

[144] For example, Edouard Manet does not tell the viewer that *The Balcony'* 1868, is a double portrait of celebrated violinist Fanny Claus and the artist Berthe Morisot whose 'fan' and 'umbrella' represent a paintbrush and a violin bow, respectively.

[145] Cited by Brian Reade in 'Introduction to Edward Lear Exhibition.' Arts Council of Great Britain, 1958.

[146] *Spectator,* September 17th, 1887. p1251

[147] Emile Cammaerts *The Poetry of Nonsense,* London, Routledge. 1925. p60

illustrations emerge as 'reverse images' of the oil paintings, supporting the value of linear abstraction. She theorises that the literalism of Lear's caricatures allows a humanity to emerge that would be lost in the shadows of paint and that the sparse, one line construction of the sketches with no background detail inhibits any contextual association and contemporary reference. This allows an abstraction which survives, instead of dating period references which might not. 'In addition to explicating the implicit, the limericks reverse the paintings and literalise experience by pushing aside associations, eradicating shadows and images and expelling superfluous dimensions'.[148] Colley's theories are ingenious and force a closer comparison between Lear's Nonsense drawings and his professional topography but she fails to make any distinction between Lear's large scale oil paintings and his watercolour sketches.

Brian Reade[149] comments that 'Lear's subjects descended from preconceptions fashionable in the period of Turner, but his technique as a watercolourist went even further back to the "stained drawings" of eighteenth century masters, although his style, unlike theirs, was impulsive'. The antique nature of Lear's watercolours is connected with his classical subjects – the ruins and landscapes of ancient Greece and Italy, countries in which, like childhood, he felt infinitely comfortable. It is worth noting that many of Lear's Nonsense characters, even if drawn in the 1870s, wear Regency clothes. Their Empire line dresses, poke bonnets, drain pipe trousers and large checks are fashions familiar from Prinny and the 1820s.

Despite the union of Lear's Nonsense verses and his Nonsense art, brave artists have, from time to time, attempted new interpretations, contending with the reader's knowledge of the original drawings which, for most of us, are signally resistant to change. William Foster re-drew *The Owl and the Pussy*

---

[148] Ann Colley, 'Edward Lear's Limericks and the Reversals of Nonsense'. VP.26,3(1988) 285-299

[149] Brian Reade, Introduction to Edward Lear Exhibition, Arts Council of Great Britain, 1958.

Cat for Frederick Warne in 1889, followed by Leslie Brooks in 1890. Helen Oxenbury recreated *The Quangle Wangle's Hat* in 1969 which won the Kate Greenaway medal for the best illustrated children's book that year, followed by yet another version from Kevin Madison in 1981. Owen Wood produced an Owl and Pussy Cat in 1978 which, like Juan Wijngaard's limerick illustrations in 1982, perhaps stray too far from Lear's original ideas.

As a Sussex student, I have a natural bias for the work of contemporary Sussex artist John Vernon Lord[150] who has not only recreated the Nonsense of Edward Lear, but Lewis Carroll's *Hunting of the Snark* which constitutes another major part in this thesis. John Vernon Lord, who taught art at Brighton College of Art (now subsumed into Brighton University) for many years, took his role as a modern interpreter of Lear's Nonsense extremely seriously: he 'wished to express in my illustrations the paradoxical association of joy and wistfulness which haunts so much of Lear's writing'. Lord believes 'that Nonsense provided Lear with a protective cloak that insulated him from the frustrations that lay deeply within him'. His 330 new Nonsense illustrations are roughly divided into thematic groups 'the drinkers, the screamers, the musicians, the conspicuous noses and insect pests' to name but a few. The drawings are fresh and exciting, carefully re-imagining the unimaginable, but their attractive confusion and thoughtfully imposed background and context diminishes some of the original sparse abstraction, and sites Nonsense in an oxymoronic familiarity.

---

[150] John Vernon Lord, *Illustrating Lear*. Brighton Polytechnic Press, 1991.

A book on Nonsense cannot concern itself over much with Edward Lear as a serious oil painter, nor as an esteemed wildlife artist and topographical illustrator. Yet, as conclusion to this chapter on art, there is a valid and instructive comparison to be considered between Lear's battle to be taken seriously for his large scale landscapes and his contemporary Robert Schumann's struggle to be recognised as a symphonist.[151] Both artists were driven to produce what the prevailing fashion seemed to dictate, by admiration of the giant figures of Holman Hunt and Beethoven and by the need to sell their work. Mid-Victorian society was obsessed by sensations implicit in the colossal, the mammoth and the immense: the Midland Hotel of St. Pancras, the Great Exhibition, Francis Frith and 'loose baggy monster' three volume novels are just some of the most obvious examples. Schumann's natural creative form was the miniature and his unique genius flowered most obviously in the piano collections of 'Carnaval' 'Papillons', 'Davidsbundlertanze', the romances, songs and chamber music. His themes are not particularly orchestral and did not lend themselves readily to large-scale expansion. Yet he strove for recognition and success in a field to which he was not always suited, just as Lear tried so hard to become master of an alien medium. Today, we follow Schumacher and know that Small can be Beautiful. Lear can enjoy a belated fame as master of watercolour sketches and Nonsense drawings. Schumann can be revered for the miniature piano pieces.

---

[151] The all-too-controlling figure of Clara Wieck enters the picture here. Schumann was greatly influenced by his wife's ambition.

EDWARD LEAR AND MUSIC

Oscar Schmidt's comment that England was 'das Land ohne Musik' has always been taken far too literally. He actually wrote 'die Englander sind das einzige Kulturvolk ohne eigne Musik',[152] or the English do not possess their <u>own</u> music, which may be truer and perhaps tolerable from a German, but we should be very careful before we accept the notion that England had no musik. London around Lear's birth in 1812 was a very cosmopolitan town and home to French and Italian refugees – musicians in particular. The German born, naturalised Englishman Handel, wrote Italian operas for his new national audience, and in even greater spirit of international rapport, composed *Judas Maccabeus*, a Hebrew legend adapted to celebrate the English victory in the Scottish battle at Culloden in 1746. Handel, who made his home in Burlington House, Piccadilly, established the oratorio from a heady mix of Italian operas, German passions and the English choral tradition – a Handel Festival in Westminster Abbey during 1791 drew record crowds to hear popular arias and chorales from *The Messiah* (1741). During Lear's lifetime, oratorio became considered as the highest form of musical art and was to inspire Sullivan's oratorios *Prodigal Son*, (1869), *Light of the World,* (1873), and *Martyr of Antioch,* (1880), as well as numerous productions by lesser musicians bravely competing with Handel, Mendelssohn and Spohr.

We know how much music meant to many Victorian artists including John Ruskin,[153] Alfred Tennyson, George Eliot and Thomas Hardy: we shall see how important music became to the life and work of Edward Lear. The wider musical scene of his childhood was flourishing and never more dynamic in this country than between the years 1800 and 1843, when Lear left England to live and travel overseas. New developments such as the mass sight singing movement, musical education in State-supported schools, cheap octavo editions of choral works, colleges of music and diploma-granting professional organisations supported new musical practice and awareness outside the home.[154] The Academy of Ancient Music, established 1710, gave regular, well-attended concerts in London and Samuel Arnold founded the Glee Club in 1787 for social, male voice music. Haydn wrote his 96th Symphony for an

---

[152] Oscar Schmidt *Essays on English Social Life and Politics*. London, Jarrolds, 1926, translated by H. Herzl, but actually written in the 1850s. Schmidt was a curious combination of naturalist, scientist, composer of dozens of piano miniatures and an essay entitled 'Was Goethe a Darwinian?'
[153] Ruskin edited four volumes of Tuscan songs in the 1880s and wrote a small portfolio of his own.
[154] Nicholas Temperley *The Lost Chord,* Bloomington, Indiana University Press, 1989.

English audience in 1792 and led it himself from the harpsichord.[155] The Philharmonic Society gave their first performance of Beethoven's 5th Symphony in 1816 which so thrilled the musicians with its strange 'bold beauty'[156] that they commissioned further works and invited Beethoven to London.[157] Numerous instrumental and choral societies promoted performances around the country with the aid of the impresario Salomon, the composer Dussek or the irrepressible pianist/salesman Clementi. [158] The Royal Academy of Music, patron, His Grace the Duke of Wellington, was founded in 1822.

Music during Lear's childhood in England was becoming not only accessible, but available for a significant new market. The most frequently performed composers at Her Majesty's Theatre, London during 1810–1840, Mozart, Donizetti, Bellini and Rossini, wrote operas which provided a chain of favourite and familiar airs: the charm of Rossini in particular did much to make opera going a less formidable pastime. Inside the home, music remained the ultimate accomplishment. The ability to play the piano demonstrated technical prowess, social respectability and the chance to channel dreams – domestically.

Ann and Sarah taught Lear music and the piano at home in Bowman's Lodge. He remained a more enthusiastic than distinguished pianist, but acquired sufficient ability to accompany singers with his own favourite broken chords, to play by ear and to compose a little. He possessed what he described to Edward Strachey as a 'good voice'[159] perhaps singing some of the tens of thousands of strophic parlour songs of the 1830s and 1840 and certainly hearing them. Composers of these ballads such as John Blockley, Fred Weatherley, and J. Carpenter are forgotten and only perhaps Sir Henry Bishop, dubbed by Carlyle as the 'English Mozart', remains familiar with 'Home Sweet Home'.[160] (And the 'Dashing White Sergeant'.) If the names of the composers have faded from consciousness, their songs have not and the Victorian Parlour Song can still be heard. Longfellow's 'Excelsior' by the Irish composer Michael Balfe, 1808–1870, and his 'I Dreamt I Dwelt in Marble Halls,' [161] are sung today, even if not always entirely seriously. Balfe, a figure of immense importance in the early Victorian musical theatre, anticipated Lear with his Tennyson settings. 'Come Into the Garden, Maud', was written for

---

[155] Dr Burney, inevitably, was in the audience and thought it 'superior to any music yet in England'.

[156] *Beethoven* George Marek. London, William Kimber, 1969.

[157] Deafness and money worries stopped this epochal event happening – but the Philharmonic sent 100 guineas for Beethoven in 1827, hoping for a 10th Symphony. He died before he could fulfil his part of the bargain.

[158] Clementi owed much to the patronage of the English country house, in his case, Peter Beckford at Fonthill.

[159] Sir Edward Strachey Bt. *Introduction to Edward Lear Nonsense Songs and Stories.* London, Frederick Warne & Co, 1894.

[160] From Balfe's opera *Cari, or The Maid of Milan.* 1843.

[161] From *The Bohemian Girl.* 1843.

Sims Reeves in 1855.

Jeremiah Lear typified the 'Veneering' *nouveau riche* with his interest in music and painting as patronised by the aristocracy – visible proof of distinction for the upwardly mobile. A hallmark of a new gentleman such as Jeremiah was that his wife should not work. Mrs Lear might occupy herself with charitable good works or genuine sympathy, but paid employment was out of the question, even if it existed, or twenty one children allowed it. Lower class menials cooked, cleaned and helped with the children: a lady must find other means of passing her time. Middle class parents dispatched their daughters to school to acquire those elegant accomplishments of the aristocracy necessary for filling leisure hours: a little French, some dancing, needlework, but above all, an ability to play the piano. No doubt there were genuine music lovers in early nineteenth century England for whom pianos provided comfort and solace – alongside were an incalculable number for whom the purchase of a piano constituted the first step towards respectable gentility.

By the time Lear was attending school, the piano had all but replaced the harp and the harpsichord both in general popularity and the music composed for it. Mozart and Haydn carefully wrote for both, not wishing to lose adherents of either, but technical innovation made the purchase of an upright piano a possibility for most educated families and by 1820, J. Broadwood & Co were producing c. 1,000 uprights and 400 grand pianos a year. Despite their popularity, even the smallest 'cottage' upright was not cheap, at between 40–70 guineas c.1840. Hire purchase was invented specifically to enable the average family on an income of c.100 guineas a year to buy an upright piano.[162]

Lear's lack of formal musical training did not deter him from playing the piano and singing. It gave him pleasure and represented one more accomplishment he could pride himself on. Even more important, he knew it gave pleasure to others and thus warmed his aching heart. The idea of setting Tennyson to music seems to have paralleled his idea of illustrating Tennyson's poems with paint, and both concepts took root before he actually met the Laureate in 1849. In 1852, he submitted a list of 124 poems from the *1842 Poems* and described his ambition in a letter to Emily. 'My desire has been to show that his words have the power of calling up images as distinct and correct as if they were written from those images, instead of giving rise to them'.[163] Lear read Tennyson constantly and his head was so full of the poems that lines were continually bubbling to the surface. His journals abound with Tennysonian quotations – some of the Nonsense songs are written in 'Tennysonian'.

'On bare islands of yellow sand
And when the sun sinks slowly down
And the great rock walls grow dark and brown

[162] Cyril Ehrlich, *The Piano, a History*. Oxford, Clarendon Press, 1999.
[163] Anne Henry Ehrenpreis, 'Edward Lear sings Tennyson songs' Harvard Library Bulletin, 27 (1979) 65-85.

When the purple river rolls fast and dim
And the Ivory Ibis starlike skim
Wing to wing, we dance around
Stamping our feet with a flumpy sound
And this is the song we nightly snort...'

Edward Lear, 'The Pelican Chorus'.
CN, p412.

The landscape project was never completed, neither were the musical settings But Lear did find time to write at least twenty-one accompaniments which he frequently performed to admiring audiences: testimonies agree that his great feeling and expression more than compensated for his musical limitations and Lady Strachey recognised the source of Lear's effectiveness with music; 'A man who sings like that must understand other people's feelings'.[164] One unusually enthusiastic listener was a Miss Cotton in 1855 whose raptures over Lear's singing gave her a sleepless night although her motives seem not to have been entirely of musical origin.[165] She might have been startled at Lear's occasional substitute singing of 'The Cat and the Fiddle' to some particularly solemn air: Lear's Nonsense was always at hand to distract from emotion grown too painful by intensity. Lear's admiration for Tennyson did not inhibit a parody.

'Delirious bulldog, echoing calls
Splendour falls from castle walls,
My daughter, green as summer grass,
and snowy summits old in story,
the long supine plebian ass
the long light shakes across the lake
the nasty crockery, boring falls
and the wild cataract leaps in glory.

Tom Moore'y pathos, all things bare,
Blow bugle blow, set the wild echoes flying
With such a turkey, such a hen
blow bugle blow, answer echoes
And scrambling forms of distant men,
dying, dying'.[166]

'Oi! Aren't you glad that you weren't there?'[167]

Julia Margaret Cameron lived near Farringford and occasionally sent her grand piano, carried by an eight man team, across the shingly garden, to enhance Lear and Tennyson's pastime of singing songs together. (Tennyson's piano was always out of tune). Lear heartily disliked Cameron, despite her

---

[164] Cited in Ehrenpreis, p73.

[165] Vivien Noakes, *Edward Lear*. London, Fontana, 1979. p128

[166] Tennyson *The Princess*. Stanza iii. 1847.

[167] *Later Letters of Edward Lear:* 28th February, 1872, to Chichester Fortescue. London, Ayer Publishing, 1911. p140

generosity, always complaining about her habit of unannounced visits and hoping that his incivility would keep her gruff voice at a distance.[168]

Strictly speaking, Edward Lear's Tennyson settings, transcribed with the assistance of musical scholar Edward Francis Rimbault, are not within the bounds of any inquiry into Nonsense. Yet they help illustrate the range of Lear's musical talent and so perhaps I may be allowed to say here that they demonstrate a partiality for the key of E major, a restricted tessitura and kinship to Mendelssohn's *Songs Without Words.*[169] Taken as a whole, they seem to me to lack the tiny original spark heard in Lear's music to his own Nonsense verses. 'Home They Brought The Warrior Dead','Come Not When I am Dead' and 'O Let The Solid Ground' are mournful hymn tunes, rich in both Victorian sentiment and arpeggiated chords, grimly appropriate for the favourite Victorian theme of death. Only the lyric ballad 'Edward Gray' shares the charm and harmonic invention of 'The Ballad of the Yonghy Bonghy Bo'.

Yet one of Lear's Tennyson songs achieved immortality in the unlikely setting of Swinburne's *maison de convenance*, Woodbine Villa, 7, Alpha Place, St. John's Wood in 1853. The over-furnished room provides the backdrop for Holman Hunt's portrait of sexual angst, 'The Awakening Conscience', where a young girl's face eloquently expresses the remorse aroused by her lover playing 'Oft in the Stilly Night' by Tom Moore on the piano[170]. Lear's setting of Tennyson's 'Tears, Idle Tears'[171] lies plainly on the floor. As Ruskin remarked 'there is not a single object in that room, common, modern, vulgar, that does not become tragic if rightly read'.[172]

A parallel may be drawn between the overblown emotion of Lear's Tennyson settings[173] and the overworked detail of Lear's formal oil landscapes. The essence of Lear's genius lies in the spontaneous creation of his sketches: landscapes, Nonsense or music. If one aspect of romanticism is its immediacy of expression, then Lear's watercolour sketches, Nonsense verses and illustrations and his Nonsense music are Romantic.

---

[168] Amanda Hopkinson, *Julia Margaret Cameron*, London, Virago. 1986. p122

[169] Grove lists 3 books of Mendelssohn's *Songs Without Words*, published by Simrock in 1830, 1833 & 1836. The six piano solos in each book were immediately successful and echoed round Victorian drawing rooms; Novello published the English editions and they remain small masterpieces of 'salon' music.

[170] The lover is no pianist. Not on THAT chair.

[171] 'Tears, idle tears, I know not what they mean/Tears from the depths of some divine despair/Rise to the heart and gather to the eyes/In looking on the happy autumn fields/And thinking of the days that are no more'. *New Oxford Book of English Verse*, 1984, p647

[172] Lionel Lamborne, *Victorian Painting*. London, Phaidon. 1999. p383

[173] A selection of Lear's Tennyson settings has been recorded by Robert Tear, accompanied by Garth Morell. Cabaletta Recording, CDN 5004. The CD is entitled *Tears, Idle Tears*. Oh tear…

EDWARD LEAR'S NONSENSE SONG SETTINGS

Lear composed his own music for 'The Courtship of the Yonghy Bonghy Bo' and for 'The Pelican Chorus'. He was known to have sketched out a setting for 'The Owl and The Pussy Cat' and often sang it, but no printed version exists. (Igor Stravinsky wrote one c.1930 for his wife Vera who told Robert Craft it was the first English verse she ever learned.)[174] His Nonsense songs are characterised by a gentle melancholy, very much in sympathy with the tear-laden tunes of the Victorian Parlour Song. Lear 'never borrowed the prevailing ethos of the bourgoisie that their songs would persuade the working class of the righteousness of bourgeois morality'.[175] His 'otherworldliness' stems from an isolated life on the continent as well as an apparent disregard for the lot of the man on the Clapham Omnibus. Nothing in Lear's Nonsense and especially nothing in the music and the song settings appears to relate to social protest or political awareness. The rebel movements which inspired Negro Spirituals, many Irish ballads and some Nonconformist hymns failed to touch any chord in Edward Lear. The only overt political reference that I can find is contained in a limerick and refers to William Ewart Gladstone.

> 'There was an Old Man at a Station
> Who made a promiscuous oration
> But they said, take some snuff – you have talked quite enough
> You afflicting Old Man at a Station'.

CN, p338

And even if we didn't know that Gladstone liked public speaking from railway stations, the following verse makes Lear's antipathy clear.

> 'When Grand Old men persist in folly[176]
> In slaughtering men and chopping trees

---

[174] John Vernon Lord. *Illustrating Lear* Brighton Polytechnic, 1991. Section 20/21. I wonder what poor Mrs Stravinsky thought about English poetry if that was her introduction...

[175] Derek Scott, *The Singing Bourgeois*. OU Press, 1989. p190

[176] This echoes Oliver Goldsmith's 'when lovely woman stoops to folly/and finds too late that men betray/what charm can soothe her melancholy/what can wash her guilt away/a pattern subsequently also adopted by T.S. Eliot in *The Waste Land*: 'when lovely woman stoops to folly and/paces about her room alone/she smoothes her hair with automatic hand/and puts a record on the gramophone'.

What art can soothe the melancholy
Of those whom futile statesmen tease?'

CN, p452.

'The Courtship of the Yonghy Bonghy Bo' is a gentle and lyrical ballad of unrequited love which shares the romantic appeal of a Celtic folk song.[177] The song may reflect Lear's failed courtship of Gussie Bethel or indeed may reflect Lear's wider anxiety about replacing the lost love of his mother: there is no interpretation beyond a tragic one. His drawings show the Bo with huge head and tiny body, representing an overabundance of cerebral activity at the expense of physical endowment. In contrast, Lady Jingly Jones is a shapely young woman with demure aspect and Regency clothes, conversational with her Dorking hens.

The strophic song for voice and piano accompaniment has eight verses of eleven lines each, the last repeated as in a chorus. The key is E major (a Lear favourite), 2/4 time signature and syncopated rhythm. The first 4 bar question phrase on the tonic is answered by a second 4 bar reply. The second set of question/answer phrases on the 3rd, ascends slightly and is given a dramatic turn by the two sharpened As of the E major diminished 7th. The penultimate 4 bars on the dominant return to the tonic for a matching final phrase and the perfect security of a 1cV1 cadence.

'The Pelican Chorus' shares the key of E major but is differentiated by the 6/8 dotted rhythm time signature. Essentially, the song comprises a repeated 8 bar phrase with a repeatable 8 bar chorus over 6 verses. The melody begins on the dominant which remains the focal note of a brief central melody based on an E major arpeggio. The limited harmonic vocabulary is no handicap to a good tune: consider Figaro's 'Non Piu Andrai' or 'Three Blind Mice'. The chorus is a bouncy rhythmic chant which emphasises the slightly silly words, 'Ploffskin, Pluffskin, Pelican Jee, we think no birds as happy as we'. Harmony throughout remains straightforward with only one accidental E sharp in the 5th bar of the chorus.

---

[177] Given Lear's reference to Tom Moore in his Tennyson parody, we know he was familiar with Moore's Irish Melodies which appeared in 10 volumes between 1808–1834.

CANTO.

On the coast of Co - ro - man-del, Where the ear - ly pumpkins grow, In the

PIANO.

There is a sea-change in the atmosphere of the 'Pelican Chorus' in contrast to the Yonghy Bonghy Bo; here all is cheerful, uplifting music with no hint of romantic melancholia. It would make a good marching song. No matter that the words express a nonsensical wedding between the King of the Cranes and a certain Miss Pelican,

'who won her heart
With a crocodile's egg and a large fish tart.'

CN, p412.

The music reassures the listener that everything is perfectly normal with entirely predictable phrases and the customary perfect cadence. Unlike Lear's limericks and line illustrations which have only a toe-hold on reality, Lear's music for his Nonsense songs remains in comfortable convention. Dr Ian Copley has described Lear's musical style as 'based mainly on stepwise movement varied by occasional leaps through the notes of a chord. Occasionally, the mediant is stressed and there is a decided fondness for a cadence figure where in the melodic line moves by leap upwards from the dominant to the mediant and then by step down to the tonic'[178]

---

[178] Ian Copley, 'The Music of Edward Lear'. *Musical Opinion*, October, 1980. p9. Quoted from John Vernon Ward, 'Illustrating Lear'. Inaugural Lecture at Brighton Polytechnic. 27th May, 1987, Brighton, 1991. p50

EDWARD LEAR AND MUSIC IN HIS LIMERICKS

Twelve limericks tell a musical story. Most instruments featured are monosyllabic flutes, bells, harps and lyres for obvious rhyming reasons. Music is always shown to have a beneficent effect.

'There was an Old Man of the Isles
Whose face was pervaded by smiles
Sang hum diddle diddle and played on the fiddle
That amiable man of the Isles'.

CN, p 82.

Another Old Man's delight was to play the trumpet all night, whilst a Young Lady of Tyre who swept the chords of a lyre, enraptured the deep. The Old Man on the Border who lived in the utmost disorder was redeemed, not by the tea which he made in his hat, but by dancing serenely with his cat. Clearly, the Old Man with a flute frightened off the snake who ran into his boot, whilst another, more sympathetic musician, played the jig for several white pigs.

Dancing is popular. Like poetry and music it shares a reliance on rhythm. The Old Person of Filey, of whom all persons spoke highly, danced perfectly well to the sound of bell and the Old Person of Skye (whom we have met before) entranced the folk in that most North-Westerly region of Scotland by the choice of his dancing partner. One old person of Slough dances most injudiciously on the end of a bough. The Old White Man of Whitehaven danced quadrilles with a raven, in colour contrast to the very black Old Person of Ischia whose conduct grew friskier and friskier. Many Learic characters seem poised on tiptoes to dance through their stories, although very curiously, none of them sing.

MUSIC IN OTHER NONSENSE BY EDWARD LEAR

The Dong, in 'The Dong with the Luminous Nose' plays 'a pipe with silvery squeaks' as he dolefully searches for his Jumbly Girl over the great, Grombolian plain. Throughout the poem, the 'plaintive pipe' echoes the mournful nature of the hopeless quest. The musical nature of this Nonsense song has attracted some contemporary musicians, including a new composition by Dr Alastair Borthwick of university of Hull whose short, 15 minute composition 'The Dong With the Luminous Nose' was premiered in 2005. Already mentioned is the Bubble Theatre's version of the same poem which toured in 2007.

The Melodious Meritorious Mouse played a Merry Minuet in the Piano Forte in one of Lear's Nonsense Alphabets and Mr Floppy Fly in 'The Daddy Long Legs and The Fly' asks Mr Daddy Long Legs to 'sing a mumbian melody' as the 'silvery sound would please the shrimps and cockles round'. Daddy Long Legs refuses because his legs have grown too long.

'My six long legs, all here and there
Oppress my bosom with despair
And if I stand or lie or sit
I cannot sing one little bit'.

CN, p246.

More doleful Nonsense is sung by Mrs Broom and Miss Shovel.

'What nonsense you're singing today,
Said the Shovel, 'I'll certainly hit you a bang',
Said the Broom 'and I'll sweep you away!'

CN, p241.

It seems that the only cheerful songs in Lear's Nonsense are those of the courtship of the Pussy Cat by the Owl, and the vivifying numbers of Mr and Mrs Spikky Sparrow.

'The owl looked up to the stars above
And sang, to a small guitar.
'O lovely Pussy! O, Pussy my Love
What a beautiful Pussy you are, you are
What a beautiful Pussy you are'."

CN, p238.

Are there elements of Don Giovanni's mandolin serenade here? Or a comical reference to the long tradition of rhapsodising Latin lovers which lies behind it? Could Lear be remotely parodying the nonsensical seduction of every girl in sight by a disguised Leporello and his master? Stranger things have happened. And might not Mozart lovers be reminded of Papagena and Papageno by the sartorial togetherness of Mr and Mrs Spikky Sparrow? We shall never know…

Postscript

Proof of the enduring musical appeal of Edward Lear's Nonsense lies in the continual attempt to set the songs and limericks to music. No doubt there are many settings which this thesis can neither know or find, but mention should be made of Charles Villiers Stanford who, under the pseudonym Karel Drofnatsk[179] composed a score for selected Lear Nonsense Rhymes in the 1890s and Matyas Seiber, the Hungarian composer who wrote an effective SATB with orchestral accompaniment = Soprano/Alto/ Tenor/Bass: familiar musical chord abbreviation with orchestral accompaniment for 'The Owl and the Pussy Cat' in 1957. The distinguished and versatile American composer and critic Virgil Thomson (1896–1989) whose highly original body of work was rooted in American speech rhythms and hymn book harmonies, set a number of Lear verses to music. Most notable among these is the *Cantata on Poems of Edward Lear,* (1973), which featured a solo soprano, chorus and orchestra.

EDWARD LEAR AND HIS TRAVELS

It is tempting to read Lear's limericks as a personal travelogue and relate the Old Men, Old persons and Young persons of an international list of towns, places and countries to actual places visited or known by Edward Lear. But despite his daunting schedule of journeys, not even Lear ever travelled to Siberia, Moldavia, Russia, Sweden or Peru. He might not have known locations much closer to home on which some limericks are based: history does not record visits to Ealing, Putney or Rye, nor still less likely trips to Woking,[180] Chertsey, Basing or Slough. There are connections to be found with his place names, but these are not inevitable, neither does every place name actually exist. It may surprise the modern reader to discover that Minety, Brill, Ibreem, Brulak and Brigg are real places but I can find no mention of El Hums in any atlas, nor the towns of Teog, Fagoo, Jodd and Narkunder. Geography in the Nonsense of Edward Lear tells us two important facts — firstly, that he was immensely well educated with a breadth of knowledge and reference that would be remarkable in an internet age, and secondly, that he visited a breathtaking number of towns, countries and landscapes on horseback, on foot and even on elephant in the days before the railways.

Edward Lear became a traveller because constant movement soothed his epilepsy and warmer climates were necessary for his debilitating asthma: he continued to travel because his career as a topographical artist required the stimulus of new landscapes and because he had no familial ties in England. The dictum of Horace 'they change their climate, not their souls who rush across the sea' [181] might apply to tourism, but it does not apply to the genuine traveller whose perception, knowledge and understanding is transformed by the genuine experience of travelling. Lear travelled with companions and he travelled alone — his journeys were often difficult and sometimes dangerous. Perhaps they exacerbated Lear's underlying melancholy and introspection for however far the journey, there was no escape from himself.

Lear made his first journey to Italy in 1837, travelling slowly overland to record his impressions of European landscapes and cities en route. But unlike the vaguely dilettante travellers of the Grand Tour, that eighteenth century 'gap year' for wealthy and privileged youth, Lear both wanted and needed to work. His inspiration in Rome was not the hedonistic James Boswell, but JMW Turner, some of whose Italian sketches were to illustrate *Childe Harolde*. The Byron paintings, exhibited in London in 1832, were captioned

---

[180] Every modern poet has had fun with Woking and John Betjeman wreaked havoc with Slough.

[181] Quoted in A.C.Grayling *The Meaning of Things*. Weidenfeld & Nicolson. 2001. p193

'And Now, Fair Italy, Thou Art the Garden of the World', an authentic hymn from Turner who had first visited Venice, Rome and Naples in 1819 and subsequently in 1828. Turner's watery vignettes captivated John Ruskin who made the first of his twenty trips to Italy in 1833 and based his Theory of Beauty in *Modern Painters 2,* (1845), on examples of Italian art. (Posterity had cause to celebrate Ruskin's love affair with Venice even if Effie Ruskin did not[182])

But it was not only the English painters who travelled south. The early nineteenth century revered Greek and Roman antiquity in all its forms and much intellectual effort was inspired by the Greco-Roman culture of language and philosophy. Even so unlikely a tourist as William Ewart Gladstone first visited Italy in 1832 to see the land of Dante, the writer, next to Homer, that he most venerated. In his *Pictures from Italy,* (1844), Charles Dickens made a determined effort not to consider paintings and sculpture but atmosphere, contemporary personalities and landscape. 'There is probably not a famous picture or statue in all Italy but could be easily burrowed under a mountain of printed paper devoted to dissertations on it',[183] and Dickens was more interested in the apothecaries shops in Genoa and the phenomenon of Vesuvius. The newly married Robert and Elizabeth Browning sailed to Florence on April 20th, 1847 where they were based for the next fifteen years. Italy past – and present – inspired and informed their poetry.[184] Lear met Elizabeth in Rome during 1859 but 'found her so smothered with bores and snobs' and asked Emily Tennyson 'what good does one get of anyone's society when it is like one beautiful small rose tree planted in the midst of 43 sunflowers, 183 marigolds, 96 dahlias and 756 china-asters?'[185]

Edward Lear joined the 'English ghetto' colony of artists in Rome, sketching and painting the ruins, palazzos and piazzas which rose from the still unpaved streets. The combination of Roman buildings such as the Colosseum and the Arch of Constantine, sunlit by cerulean skies and surviving in a society which blessed and encouraged artists, proved irresistible, as did the wilder landscapes around the Bay of Naples. Modern visitors to the Colosseum will only find smaller and more domesticated cats than heretofore as well as hundreds of feral dogs. Lear might not have minded cats but he thoroughly disliked dogs, Italian or otherwise.

'There was an Old Man of Leghorn
The smallest as ever was born
But quickly snapped up he, was once by a puppy
Who devoured that Old Man of Leghorn.'

CN, p73.

---

[182] Ruskin's original 450,000 word study *The Stones of Venice,* 1853, described that city's architecture in language as voluminous and picturesque as Venice itself.

[183] Charles Dickens *Pictures from Italy.* 1844. Published by Penguin Classics, London, 1988. Preface 'The Reader's Passport' p5

[184] Browning's great poems with specifically Italian settings include 'My Last Duchess', 'Fra Lippo Lippi', 'Andrea del Sarto' and 'Pippa Passes'.

[185] Cited in Noakes, p172

Lear found lodgings near the Spanish steps, in the shadows of Keats and Shelley where letters of introduction from his patron Lord Stanley ensured him a unique position between bohemian artists and the aristocracy.[186] He returned to England briefly in 1840 before returning to the Mediterranean in 1841 to visit Sicily and to make a journey across central Italy through the Abruzzi to the Adriatic coast.

'There was an Old Man of th' Abruzzi
So blind that he couldn't his foot see
When they said 'that's your toe' he replied 'is it so?'
That doubtful Old Man of th'Abruzzi.'

CN, p79.

Over the next six years, Lear travelled around Italy, with only occasional visits home. He was anxious to see as much of the countryside as possible before the storms of incipient revolution broke out. His limericks record inhabitants of Sestri, Ancona, Rimini, Lucca, Aosta, (an Old Man of which possessed a Large Cow, but he Lost Her) and Apulia.

'There was an Old Person of Pisa
Whose daughters did nothing to please her
She dressed them in grey and banged them all day
Round the walls of the city of Pisa.'

CN, p348.

Next on his itinerary were Corfu, Greece and Athens. He could tread in the footsteps of his hero Lord Byron and draw yet another clutch of picturesque ruined temples set amidst scraggy olive groves in brilliant Mediterranean sunshine. (It is likely that he knew Thackeray's *Notes of a Journey from Cornhill to Grand Cairo*, written in 1845 and widely read.) Yet he missed his sister Ann and he missed England, writing home to Lord Derby that he would always remain an Englishman and that 'a day in England is worth a week

---

[186] During the revolutionary storms of 1848, the British Ambassador to Naples became William Temple, brother of Lord Palmerston. He succeeded Lord Hamilton, more famous for the adventures of his wife…

elsewhere'.[187]

> 'There was an Old Man of Corfu
> Who never knew what he should do:
> So he rushed up and down 'til the sun made him brown
> That bewildered Old Man of Corfu.'

CN, p80.

This may have unconsciously reflected Lear's own anxieties. Travelling eased his illness and soothed a restless soul, but it brought attendant difficulties and not inconsiderable dangers. He journeyed through the wild and strange lands bordering the Eastern Mediterranean, including Janina in remote Greece: did he know Alexander Dumas' *Count of Monte Cristo* (1844) and read about Princess Haydee, daughter of the Ali Pasha of Janina and her love for Edmund Dantes? Despite capture and imprisonment, Dumas' princess kept her head.

> 'There was a Young Person of Janina
> Whose Uncle was a-fanning her
> When he fanned off her head, she smiled sweetly and said
> 'You propitious Old Person of Janina!'

CN, p350.

An unexpected legacy in 1849 enabled Lear to return to England and to embark upon a course of study at the Royal Academy Schools, but his stay was shortlived. Despite the company of old friends and an important new association with Holman Hunt and the Pre-Raphaelites, the wet darkness of English winters made him ill. In 1853, he sailed to Egypt to explore Cairo and the valley of the Nile: he particularly wanted to explore the island of Philae 'the beautiful little oasis of ancient temples and palm trees, the home of Isis, sister-bride of Osiris.'[188]

> 'There was an Old Person of Philae
> Whose conduct was scroobious and wily
> He rushed up a palm when the weather was calm,
> And observed all the ruins of Philae.'

CN, p167.

---

[187] Noakes, p58
[188] Noakes, p121

In Egypt, Lear met the pelicans of the Nile which inspired 'The Pelican Chorus' of 1867, but published ten years later. Pelicans, like Greeks, appealed to Lear's particular sense of humour and he enjoyed his time whenever he met them.[189]

Lear hoped to divide his time between London, where he could sell his paintings and a warmer climate in which to work, but it became clear that he would be established nowhere and that travelling, which had begun as an occasional adventure, was likely to become a way of life. He returned to Corfu in 1855 where he had started to make friends and to feel at home, even to be offered the post as Art Director of Corfu University, an honour he declined. Paradoxically, he needed the stimulus and company of friends, but he also needed independence, space and solitude in which to paint and work. He planned a journey to Palestine and the Holy Land, accompanied by his Suliot manservant Giorgio who was to be his mainstay for the next twenty seven years.

'There was an Old Person of Sidon
Who bought a small pony to ride on
But he found him too small to leap over a wall,
So he walked, that Old Person of Sidon.'

CN, p113.

After more than the usual frightening moments travelling through alien country – and some disagreeable revelations of Christian dissent – Lear returned to the comparative safety of Rome. He continued to visit London regularly to attract interest in his large oil paintings but they never sold sufficiently well, and he was obliged to rely on selling larger quantities of smaller watercolours; the quality of these has now been recognised but pleasure in their acquisition was dimmed by Lear's own conviction that they were of secondary importance. By the late 1860s, Greece and Corfu had settled down to quiet monarchical calm, and Lear returned to wander, paint and draw through the lands of the Eastern Mediterranean. In 1869, he finally decided to

Levi *Edward Lear*, Macmillan, London. 1995, p119

settle in the Ligurian town of San Remo and built the first of his two own homes, Villa Emily, followed by Villa Tennyson.

It was from Villa Emily that he set out for his last major expedition in 1872. Lord Northbrook, cousin of Lear's old friend Evelyn Baring, invited him to India and, after a false start, he finally reached Bombay in 1873, journeying for the next thirteen months from Lucknow to Calcutta, from Simla to Ceylon and in climates which varied from the biting Himalayan winds to the oppressive tropical heat. It says much for Lear's attraction as a friend that Northbrook, newly appointed Viceroy by Gladstone's Liberal government, found time from maintaining the Empire to organising travel arrangements for a visiting painter.[190] He saw pilgrims bathing in the Ganges at Benares, painted mountains of Kinchinjumga from Darjeeling and marvelled at Agra and the Taj Mahal. He met the Nizam, a local ruler: did he meet an Akhond?

'Who or why or which or what, Is the Akhond of Swat?
Is he tall or dark or fair?
Does he sit on a stool, or a sofa, or a chair?
Or Squat?
The Akhond of Swat
Is he wise, or foolish, young or old?
Does he drink his soup and his coffee cold
Or Hot?

The Akhond of Swat
Does he sing or whistle, jabber or talk
And when riding abroad, does he gallop or walk
Or Trot?'

> 'The Akhond of Swat'.
> CN, p399.

The Akhond was a real ruler of a native state on the north west frontier of Pakistan and, in Lear's time, the Akhond was a highly charismatic and ascetic Muslim Sufi who united the Swatis. Swat, a beautiful valley town in the kingdom of Gandhara, veered between secular and religious rulers but the entire tribal state was abolished in 1969. The Akhond of Swat, however comical a rank, is not without rivals on the subcontinent: the Nawab of Tonk is worth a mention.

India inspired a handful of limericks in the 1870s, most of which capitalise on wonderfully rhythmic Indian names.

'There was an Old Man of Mahasso
Who sang both as tenor and basso
His voice was that high, it went into the sky
And came down again, quite to Mahasso.'

> CN, p 403.

---

[190] When the Conservatives were returned to power in 1874, Northbrook struggled with Salisbury's policy towards the Indian States and he resigned as Viceroy in 1876.

The Cummerbund is a more serious bit of melodious and romantic Nonsense.

> 'And where the purple Nullahs throw
> Their branches far and wide
> The silvery Goreewallahs flew
> In silence, side by side –
> The little Bheesties twittering cry
> Rose on the flagrant air
> And oft the angry Jampan howled
> Deep in his hateful lair'.

CN, p405.

There are echoes of the Snark and the Jabberwocky here in the notion of a lurking and unknown terror. Lear possessed a copy of *Alice in Wonderland* and Noakes quotes a letter to Lear from his friend Fortescue which inquired 'have you read Alice in Wonderland? It is very pretty Nonsense'.[191]

Most of Lear's longer Nonsense songs and poems share the notion of journey but one without a known destination, or at least one which might be recognisable to posterity. The Pobble with No Toes does touch the shore of the Bristol Channel and the Pelicans live on the Nile delta, but Mr Daddy Long Legs and Mr Floppy Fly are typical in finding a little boat.

> 'Whose sails were pink and grey
> And off they sailed among the waves
> Far, far away'.

CN, p246.

Wandering is the destination itself, often across water. The Jumblies went to sea in a sieve, and the Owl and the Pussy Cat sailed away, for a year and a day. There is an almost Orphic sense of loss in Lear's wandering quest for happiness, health or security, none of which he possessed in sufficient quantity. Most plaintive of all is 'The Dong With the Luminous Nose' who seeks the Eurydice of his Jumbly Girl.

> 'Oh, somewhere in valley or plain
> Might I find my Jumbly girl again
> For ever I seek by lake or shore
> Till I find my Jumbly Girl once more.
>
> Playing a pipe with silvery squeaks
> Since then his Jumbly Girl he seeks
> And because, by night, he could not see
> He gathered the bark of the Twangum Tree
> On the flowery plain that grows

---

[191] Noakes, p242

And he wove him a wondrous Nose,
A nose as strange as a Nose could be! Etc

CN, p422.

The subtle shifts of rhythmic metre in this poem express shades of meaning and incipient melancholy that a regular pattern could never convey. Lear's longer Nonsense poems are characterised by their constantly varying rhyming patterns, one way in which mere doggerel is transformed into poetry and art.

Travelling concerns itself with the journey and not the destination and, in one sense, Lear never arrived. Even the last few more settled years under his own roof at San Remo were bittersweet with health and money worries. There could never be a refuge from the melancholy of epilepsy and impossible love: there could only be work and Nonsense and perhaps it is in the latter as much as in the landscape watercolours that the true spirit of Lear the traveller exists.

'And far away in the twilight sky
We heard them singing a lessening cry
Farther and farther till out of sight
And we stood alone in the silent night.
Often since, in the nights of June,
We sit on the sand and watch the moon.
She has gone to the great Gromboolian plain
And we shall probably never meet again.'

CN, p 412.

EDWARD LEAR IN SICKNESS AND IN HEALTH

About fifty of Edward Lear's 300-odd limericks feature food and drink. It was an important subject for Lear, as we know from his letters and drawings, and perhaps his particular relish for eating followed a childhood deprivation: the financial struggles of his father had led to a short term of imprisonment for debt which reduced the family to poverty and hunger in the 1820s. Edward's mother appeared to be more concerned to bring her husband nourishing food in prison than to worry about food for her twenty-one children at home, but fortunately for Edward, his motherly elder sister Ann took him under her wing and provided sustenance both practical and emotional.

It was not only the Lear family who suffered food shortages. A steep slump in trade during the early 1830s was followed by two bad harvests. Food for working people became painfully short in supply and fights broke out over rotten bones. Our New <u>Poor</u> <u>Laws</u> introduced by Earl Grey's Whig Government in 1834 attempted more efficient relief of the worst poverty, sponsoring Parish workhouses and adoption societies but some of the abuses recorded in the workhouse were as bad as anything outside it. A weekly workhouse food allowance for an adult in 1834 was 126 oz. of bread, 20 oz. of suet and 20 oz. of meat pudding: systematic famishing to save supplies actually attempted to reduce this in some of the hardest hit areas. The boy Charles Dickens suffered similar hardship to Lear when his father, aka Mr Micawber, went to the workhouse and young, starving children dared to ask for more. Lear fancifully reflects upon both his own twenty siblings and current food shortages in:

'There was an Old Man of Apulia
Whose conduct was very peculiar
He fed twenty sons upon nothing but buns
That whimsical Man of Apulia.'

CN, p95.

Peter Levi notes how much 'Lear's early experience of life coincided with that of Dickens who was born a few months earlier in the same year'[192] but whereas Dickens' miseries were engraved upon his memory, Lear completely obliterated his unhappy boyhood. The two men's paths crossed when a cousin of Edward's was articled to the same firm of lawyers, Ellis and Blackmore, who employed the young Dickens as a clerk in 1827.

Largely cocooned at Knowsley during the 1830s, Lear 'devoured some of the good things with great complacency'[193] but recorded both ennui and unease at the elaborate dinners of the Stanleys with their endless courses of boiled fowls, venison, mutton and small, bony, roasted birds. Here, he was safe from all practical aspects of food shortages, but he knew that his wider family in Highgate were suffering and no one in England could have been immune from what became known as 'the Hungry Forties', nor the consequent stirring of working class radicals.

> 'Twere the hungry forties when I were a lad
> An'fowks were clemmed an weak in t'airn and in t'brain
> We lived on demmicked taties and our bread gone sour
> An wakened up o'nights canoodled with t'pain'.[194]

When Lear travelled to his sister's Sussex home in the 1820s, he would have gone by horse-drawn coach through a rural landscape with villages whose occupants worked on the land, subsisted from their own small holdings and spun wool sheared from their own flocks in spinning wheels by their firesides. Ten years later, he probably journeyed by railway to Knowsley through the black, satanic mills of Yorkshire towns, newly swollen with workers for Arkwright's machines, hungrily adrift from their traditional ways of life and packed together in unwholesome slums. The new class system which emerged, stratifying workers, managers and the aristocracy, was acknowledged and accepted by Disraeli's 'two nations'[195] and Mrs Alexander's celebrated hymn of 1838.

---

[192] Peter Levi *Edward Lear*. London, Macmillan. 1995 p11-12
[193] Noakes, p31
[194] F.W. Moorman, Ed. *Songs of the Ridings*. From www.inkamara.ukgo.com. Accessed 18/3/2008
[195] The rich and the poor, from *Sybil*, Disraeli's 'condition of England' novel, 1845.

'The rich man in his castle
The poor man at his gate
God made them, high and lowly
And ordered their estate'.

On Lear's first journey to Italy in 1838, he found things rather different. 'Today, for instance, we had coffee and eggs at 5 – at 12, beautiful macaroni soup, boiled beef and mutton cutlets, strawberries, cherries and a bottle of wine each – at supper, macaroni and an omelette, wine and oranges...equivalent to 2/8d of our daily money!'[196]

Yet food in Lear's Nonsense is often handled with a violence not normally associated with comfort and a love of good living.

'There was an Old Man of Peru
Who watched his wife making a stew.
But once, by mistake,
In a stove she did bake
That Unfortunate Old Man of Peru'.

CN, p72.

There is a sadistic pleasure on the face of the large wife as she immolates her puny husband which contradicts the idea of a 'mistake'. Another Old Man, this time of the south, chokes on fish, just as,

'There was an Old Man of Calcutta
Who perpetually ate bread and butter
Til a great bit of muffin on which he was stuffin
Choked that horrid Old Man of Calcutta'.

CN, p74.

---

[196] Letter to Ann Lear. Noakes, p54

Even more violent is,

'The Old Person of Bangor
Whose face was distorted with anger
He tore off his boots and subsisted on roots
That borasible person of Bangor'.

CN, p174.

When an Old Person of Rheims[197] is troubled by horrible dreams and can't sleep, he is forcibly kept awake by having cake stuffed into his mouth. Food has become the enemy. Did an early struggle for subsistence beget feelings of anger and rage towards the need to eat? Or was the act of swallowing large morsels, so often depicted in Lear's limerical drawings, representing the hunger for an emotional need which could not be met, even by the largest piece of fish or meat?

In contrast, food saves the Old Person of Fife[198], who, though greatly disgusted with life, was cured by a ballad and a small bowl of salad, just as underdone veal relieves the man of Three Bridges. Limerical characters drink as well as eat. They consume brandy, beer, soup, tea, broth and perhaps necessarily senna, although generally in a palliative, as opposed to a peaceful sense. Food can become a weapon against loneliness, isolation and despair. 'Comfort eating' has become a modern mantra but if the phrase is new, the experience is as old as the hills.

Not altogether surprisingly, Edward Lear grew considerably fatter as he grew older. The slender young man of the 1840s with a neat haircut and small moustache became a whiskery and rotund figure by the 1870s. He became a professional diner-out, a habituee of grand houses and long meals: he did not possess his own kitchen until the Villa Emily in 1869 and the advice of Mrs Beeton[199] in 1859 'that there is no more fruitful source of discontent than a housewife's badly cooked dinners and untidy ways' was irrelevant, although he might have agreed that 'men are so well served out of doors at their Clubs, well ordered taverns and dining houses' that a wife is hard pressed to compete.

[197] CN, p84
[198] Ibid p340
[199] Mrs Beeton *Household Management*. Facsimile by Chancellor Press, London. 1984.

No one could have competed with Lear's Nonsensical chef Professor Bosh whose several recipes appeared in Lear's *Nonsense Gazette*, August, 1870. Gosky patties required a live pig and a broom handle, among other ingredients but the patties could never be cooked as the pig was generally let loose beforehand. An awareness of his changing shape is demonstrated by several limericks including the Old Person of Pinner[200] who was thin as a lath if not thinner – a contrast to the Old Person of Hurst[201] who didn't mind if he got fatter.

'There was an Old Man who when little
Fell casually into a kettle
But growing too stout, he could never get out
So he passed all his life in that kettle'.

CN, p329.

Other Nonsense songs, stories, botany and alphabets frequently feature food. 'The Seven Families from Lake Pipple Popple' lived together in the utmost fun and felicity despite a diet of boiled periwinkles, sponge biscuits, sago pudding and buttered toast and 'The Jumblies' provisions for their journey in a sieve included a pound of rice, a cranberry tart and no end of Stilton cheese. Lear began to refer to himself as a 'globular topographical artist' and described himself in the third person, as follows:

'He sits in a beautiful parlour,
With hundreds of books on the wall.
He drinks a great deal of Marsala,
But never gets tipsy at all.

He has many friends, laymen and clerical,
Old Foss is the name of his cat.
His body is perfectly spherical,
He weareth a runcible hat'.

'How Pleasant to know Mr. Lear'.
CN, p 428.

Edward Lear may be allowed an unusual interest in food: he needed comfort more than most. He suffered from asthma, bronchitis and a delicate stomach when he was a child, but his most serious and life-long malady was a form of epilepsy. This was present in his family as a sister Jane died in adolescence from convulsive epilepsy and whose fits Lear later recalled with horror. 'How I remember my sister Jane's attacks! How! Child as I was then, and quite unable to understand'.[202] The 'terrible demon' as Lear dubbed his affliction, affected all his life profoundly. 'The presence of the demon would

---

[200] Ibid p335

[201] Ibid p95

[202] John Swales, 'Edward Lear and Epilepsy.' Theatre programme essay, Redgrave Theatre, Bristol. 16th July, 2000.

have prevented happiness under any circumstances', he wrote in his diary, adding 'that it is a merciful blessing that I have kept up as I have, and not gone utterly to the bad, mad, sad'.[203] Lear referred frequently of his sorrow, so inborn and ingrained, expressing surprise that life with the demon was ever tolerable at all. It is unclear whether he knew his friend Tennyson suffered from epilepsy as did Swinburne, Paganini, William Pitt and Tchaikovsky: it seems possible that Lewis Carroll suffered a mild form of the disease.

'There was an Old Person whose tears
Fell fast for a number of years
He sat on a rug and wept into a jug
Which he very soon filled with tears'.

CN, p120.

One remarkable aspect of Lear's epilepsy was his concealment of it. He was completely successful in hiding up to twenty attacks each month and there seems no doubt that most of his friends were unaware of his troubles. It was helpful to have the epileptic 'aura' as an early warning system – an abnormal taste, smell, or inexplicable emotional response not apparent to others. Travel soothed the illness: alcohol exacerbated it. 'Biographers have tended to treat Lear's depression and despair as an understandable response to a distressing and stigmatising disease'[204] but in fact, they are symptomatic of it. The difference is one of volition.

The terror and shame of epileptic fits for a young child in the 1820s can scarcely be imagined. Further nightmares arose with the possibility that epilepsy, so little understood, would lead to dementia or insanity: it was believed to be a form of madness associated with demonic possession which could not be disassociated from personal blame and guilt. Almost worse was the widespread belief that childhood epileptic seizures were the result of

---

[203] Lear's diary for Monday, 31st July 1882. Cited in Noakes, p241
[204] Swales, as in Note 11.

masturbation which added lack of self control to Lear's perception of his failings.

'There was an Old Man whose despair
Induced him to purchase a hare
Whereon one fine day, he rode wholly away
Which partly assuaged his despair'.

CN, p329.

Epilepsy is a disorder of the central nervous system and has been known since ancient times, although now subject to semantic revision and described as a 'neurobiological disease'. It takes three forms – grand mal, petit mal or Jacksonian – all manifest by convulsive seizures of varying severity and regularity which first appear between the ages of ten and twenty. Eccentricity and perversity of behaviour are characteristic, as are heightened mood swings between ecstasy and depression.

The notion of links between creativity and madness are long established and the symbiosis between real and surreal, construct and destruct, sanity and insanity continues to engage scholars and critics. Foucault claims that 'we owe the invention of the arts to deranged imaginations – the caprice of painters, poets and musicians is only a name moderated in civility to express their madness'[205]. Foucault argues that madness is connected with the strange paths of knowledge and that 'if madness is the truth of knowledge, it is because knowledge is absurd, and instead of addressing itself to the great books of experience, loses its way in the dust of books and idle debate'. Daniel Nettle cites Dryden;

'Great wits are sure to madness near allied
And thin partitions do their bounds divide'.[206]

Nettle invents a new species of Homo Imaginans. They exist to provide

---

[205] Michel Foucault, *Madness and Civilisation*. London, Routledge 1995. p29
[206] Daniel Nettle, *Madness, Creativity and Human Nature*. London, Routledge 1995. p10

imaginative, impractical fictional representation to charm, entertain or impress, thus providing contrast to the reason of *Homo Sapiens* or the practical skills of Homo Faber. Edward Lear would be Homo Imaginans. Psychologist Andrew Steptoe[207] argues with Peter Medawar's belief that any connection between genius and insanity is a 'gothic illusion', claiming that although modern brain imaging and neuro-chemical investigations provide clues to organic dysfunction, <u>evidence</u> <u>for</u> <u>dimensions</u> <u>of</u> <u>unusual</u> <u>cognitive</u> <u>processes</u> <u>among</u> <u>the</u> <u>mentally</u> <u>disordered</u> is growing. There is no doubt that a true artist such as Lear possessed heightened sensibilities which made a sanguine temperament impossible. Like most creative personalities, he suffered from dizzy heights of ecstasy alternating with a melancholic depression.

Into this equation comes the question of Lear's sexuality. Most writers seem certain that he was homosexual, borrowing the many images of elongated noses in the limericks as proof of penile infatuation. It is likely that he was abused by a male cousin when he was ten, but childhood abuse does not necessarily form an adult homosexual. Edward Lear could not be a homosexual if the word meant a congenital abnormality over which he had no control and whose consequences were widely regarded as encouraging sinful and evil practices: but if the word becomes 'homoerotic' with connotations of bonded male friendships and love for particular companions, then indeed Lear could be so described.

It seems likely that morbids and demons, far more than any practising homosexuality, were the cause of Lear's resolute bachelor status, providing more serious checks than sexual perversity to his recurrent impulse to propose marriage to Gussie, daughter of his friend Lord Westbury.

The modern psychotherapist Virginia Graham Miftari maintains that emotional fragility produces alienation.[208] She believes that the abandonment of Lear's mother – and his position as almost-last child in the enormous family of twenty siblings – would fatally damage his sense of self. Not only would he always lack the confidence necessary for constructive interaction with his fellow man, but he would be frightened of intimacy with most women. Her reading of Lear's friendship with Gussie Bethel, a comfortable, homely woman in middle age, is that of an unthreatening relationship that offered companionship and security. She argues that he seems extremely unlikely to have been an active homosexual: certainly the mother-child relationship is crucial in learning emotional patterns, but most same-sex proclivities derive from an overly-intense parental involvement, rather than the reverse. His creativity enabled an empathy and an understanding of what people wanted from him: weapons in the constant battle to 'fix' emotional pain and hurtful feelings were his Nonsenses.

About twenty of the limericks feature unhappiness in a range of emotions

---

[207] Andrew Steptoe, Editor. *Genius and The Mind: Studies of Creativity and Temperament.* OUP, 1998. p9

[208] I am grateful to my daughter Mrs Graham Miftari, Senior Addiction Consultant at the American Therapeutic Hospital, Cottonwood, 17, Wimpole St, London, with whom I took the liberty of discussing Lear's case as if he were a modern patient.

from loneliness to rage, through anxiety, melancholia and uncertain identity. The Old Man of Cape Horn[209], wished he had never been born, and sat on a chair and died of despair, tears streaming down his great, round face. Sadness overwhelms the figure whose head, like that of the Yonghy, Bonghy Bo is hugely out of proportion, a caricature of the cerebral taking precedence over the physical.

The Old Person in Gray,[210] whose feelings were tinged with dismay, relieves her anxiety by feeding some carrots to several parrots, a more active remedy than that proposed by the Old Man of Hong Kong who, whilst he never did anything wrong, just lay on his back with his head in a sack.

One of the most oppressive images of all is the Young Lady in White who looks out at the depths of the night where the birds of the air, fill her heart with despair. Unusually for Lear, the young lady floating in the moonlit sky a la Chagall is drawn against a black background which increases à sense of ominous dread. Owls, accessories of witches, broomsticks and black magic from ancient folk tales to Harry Potter, circle round the sorrowful young lady who sports a Regency bonnet and trailing nightwear.

Anxiety becomes rage in several limericks, notably the Young Person of Smyrna[211] whose grandmother threatened to burn her (nastily, she suggested

---

209 CN, p97

210 CN, p368

211 CN, p159

that her Grandmother burn the cat instead) and the Old Person of Newry[212] whose manners were tinctured with fury. Like the Old Person of Pett[213] who was partially consumed by regret, some of the limericks are clearly driven by the rhymes of their names, but no choice is entirely accidental and it is the unconscious drive behind them which illuminates their creator. Identity is queried by the Old Person of Bow[214], whom nobody happened to know, or the very provoking Old Person of Woking[215] who sat on a rail with his head in a pail.

---

[212] CN, p357
[213] CN, p357
[214] CN, p368
[215] CN, p339

EDWARD LEAR AND ANIMALS

The history of animals in Nonsense is a long one, dating back to the sixth century BC and the fables of Aesop. These anthropomorphic tales are among the first to have been recorded in a vernacular European language and their simple messages remain true. We still understand how grudging others what we may not possess ourselves is the story of the dog in the manger, how we may be fooled by a wolf in sheep's clothing and how belling the cat is an easy idea but an impossible solution – for mice.

'Beast poetry' was popular in the fourteenth and fifteenth century German *Ludendichtung,* [216] which seems to have influenced medieval nonsense verse in both France and England. A handful of narrative animal nonsense poems survive from the Middle Ages, including this brief account of an animal battle:

'The cricket and the grasshopper went out to fight
Already dressed in helmet and coat of mail
The fly carried the banner as a doughty knight
The scarab beetle trumpeted with all his might'. [217]

The trickster figure of 'renart' or 'reynard the fox' as a peasant-hero character appeared in Europe around the fifteenth to sixteenth century together with a cast of characters such as Bruin the Bear, Baldwin the Ass, Chantecleer the Rooster and Hirsent, the She-Wolf in satires on the aristocracy and the clergy, forshadowing the fantasy tales of Swift and Orwell. Reynard makes a token appearance in Chaucer's *Nonnes Preestes Tale* and stars in Caxton's *The Historie of Reynard* (1485). Charles Perrault's (1628–1703) influential nursery rhymes and tales of *Mother Goose,* including *Puss in Boots* and *Little Red Riding Hood,* [218] appeared in the 1670s in Europe and an English version by Robert Samber entitled *Tales of Past Times told by Mother Goose* was published in 1729.

Despite the proliferation of animals in early Nonsense, it seems that the animals on record in this context are largely reflections of the human condition. They do not possess their own individual characteristics, other than those which display an equal human trait: early writers used what they imagine to be the cunning of the fox, the power of the bear, the folly of the ass or the speed of the hare as metaphors for man. Lear's unique combination of

---

[216] German 'tall story' nonsense poem narrated by an eye witness.

[217] Noel Malcolm, p 58

[218] Some of Perrault's stories were later adapted by the Brothers Grimm.

Nonsense writer and naturalist allowed animals their own voice – the chance for boat- rowing owls or the arsonist-inclined apes to be taken seriously for the same variety of nonsensical capers as bipeds. Anthropomorphism is kept to the minimum, but honourable exception must be made to the frogs who accompany Lear on a walk to rehouse their forty-nine tadpole offspring whilst discussing planned emigration to either Malvern or Mesopotamia. (CN p192)

Levi relates how the young Edward Lear drew pages of comical animals, one of which was entitled 'Portraites of the inditchenous (sic) beestes of New Olland'[219] which included 'Ye Peculiar or Prickly porkyoupine' as well as drawings of the little-known duck-billed platypus and a possum up a gum tree. All Lear's animals, whether funny, nonsensical or serious, have immense and irresistible charm.

But life for most animals in eighteenth century England could best be described as nasty, brutish and short.[220] 'Large mammals in captivity in the mid-1800s lived an average of two years and faced an immeasurable amount of disease, suffering and death'.[221] Exotic animals, exhibitionist souvenirs from scavenging voyages of the Grand Tour, reflected the exalted status of their owners far more than any love or understanding of their nature. A rhinocerous which arrived on an East Indian vessel during 1684 was exhibited at the Bell Sauvage on Ludgate Hill and was almost as celebrated a spectacle as the elephant Chunee who entertained large crowds in The Strand during 1826 until his fatal attack of musth made him dangerously unstable and he was, with some difficulty, put to death. Travelling menageries, forerunners of the circus, met the craze for sensation by exhibiting dangerous animals: Hannah Twynnoy was killed by one of George Wombwell's tigers at Malmesbury, Wiltshire and the American Isaac van Amburgh was the first man to entertain an audience by putting his head in a lion's mouth. Lord Byron did have a genuine affection for Bruin, his tame dancing bear kept in his rooms at Cambridge during 1806, but Bruin represented a serious protest: in boasting that Bruin would be sitting for a Fellowship, Byron was attacking the low standards of the university and the widespread corruption associated with elections which resisted all efforts at

---

[219] Levi, p62

[220] Quotation adapted from Thomas Hobbes' (1588–1679) description of the lot of medieval man.

[221] Ashton Nichols 'Romantic Rhinos and Victorian Vipers: the Zoo as 19th c. spectacle' www.libraryindex.com/pages 2189 16/1/2008.

reformation.[222]

Around the period of Lear's birth, a certain collective sentimentality concerning animals set about banning the rustic sports of bear-baiting, cock-fighting and bull running, practices which vigorous Non-Conformists allied with sexual liberties. The Evangelical movement was equally opposed to such animal entertainments – if not entertainments of most descriptions. Pioneering work by Astley Cooper and Charles Bell focussed public attention on the sufferings of wild animals in cramped cages, such as William Bullock's Museum of Natural and Artificial Curiosities which opened in Piccadilly in 1809 or the equal horrors which attended domesticated animals on the battlefield of Waterloo in 1815. The first stirrings of the animal rights movement and the RSPCA[223] were given momentum by the establishment of the Zoological Gardens in the north east corner of the new Regent's Park – an institution which now appears to represent capture and repression, but which offered the chance for sanctuary and botanical science in the 1830s.

Animals appeared at the London Zoological Gardens, Regent's Park, in 1828; there were bears, hyenas, llamas (2) an ostrich, tapir, leopards, jaguars and wildfowl. The first elephant appeared in 1831, rhinoceros in 1834 and the giraffe in 1835. Declared aims were to create opportunities for studying animals in a replicate habitat – not for vulgar admiration, nor the chance to gawp smugly at powerful species contained behind bars. Humphrey Davy wrote that 'it would become Britain to offer another and very different series of exhibitions to the population of her metropolis, namely animals brought from every part of the globe to be applied either for some useful purpose or as objects of scientific research'[224].

Around 1828, Lear's introduction to Prideaux Selby, working on *Illustrations of British Ornithology* with Sir William Jardine inspired him to produce his own *Illustrations of the Family of Psittacidae* or parrots. These 'superbly observed and confidently drawn' birds gave Lear an immediate reputation as an ornithogical draughtsman and he was nominated as an Associate of the Linnean Society.[225] During 1831, Edward and his sister Ann had moved to live in No. 61, Albany Street which runs down the eastern side of Regent's Park, just moments from the new zoo. He was a frequent visitor to watch and draw the animals and birds – he actually produced the draft of a *Guide to the Animals of London Zoo* with three plates which show the head of a sleeping lion, a polar bear and a harpy eagle but it was never published, probably due to a lack of subscription. He did publish lithograph illustrations to the *Transaction of the Zoological Society, Vol. 1, 1883,* and *The Zoology of the Voyage of HMS Beagle,* the boat on which Charles Darwin had been employed as a naturalist. The Royal Botanical Society also established quarters in Regent's Park even if specimens such as manypeopliaupsidedownia and nasticreechia krowluppia do not feature in early catalogues. But a glint of human mischief does feature in many of Lear's beautiful and serious animal

---

[222] Fiona MacCarthy *Byron Life and Legend*. London, John Murray. 2002. p68

[223] Founded in 1824 as the Society for the Prevention of Cruelty to Animals.

[224] Archive, Library of the RGS, Regent's Park.

[225] Noakes, p 31

studies: owls in particular seem to wink knowingly at their patron and the turtles waggle in a comical fashion. Lear's parrots – the family psittacidae – have some very human expression.

Attracted by Lear's growing reputation as an ornithological artist, Lord Edward Stanley, heir to the 12th Earl Derby, invited him to record his menagerie at Knowsley, Cheshire in 1836. Lear's flawless anatomical precision and true sense of design make his naturalist paintings to be the equal of Audubon, but unlike Audubon who worked from gradually decaying carcass, Lear drew from live birds, often held down with great difficulty by a keeper.

Lord Stanley, who succeeded as the 13th Earl in 1834, was a quiet and scholarly naturalist who had made detailed studies of birds and animals from his youth and had directed his attention towards scientific research and to collecting and breeding rare and exotic animals to be successfully naturalised in England. His small menagerie at Knowsley became the finest in the country, only rivalled by the zoological collection of Earl Fitzwilliam at Wentworth and of Sir Robert Heron in Lincolnshire. (Today, Knowsley Safari Park combines a tradition of animal breeding and research with popular support as a visitor centre on Merseyside).

Lear's first collection of Nonsense animals appeared in the limericks of his 1846 *Book of Nonsense,* drawn for the Stanley children at Knowsley, and the menagerie continued to grow until 1871 with the last collection of *Nonsense Songs, Stories, Alphabets and Botany.* In art, if not in zoos or the farmyard, animals in this period remained romantic symbols, celebrated for their natural qualities amidst the sublime elements in nature – for their innocence in contrast to a corrupted world.

A sentimental, as opposed to a romantic, approach to animals is familiar from paintings such as Landseer's *Monarch of the Glen* or John Fernley's anthropomorphic *Council of Horses,* (1840), inspired by the rational Houyhnhnms of *Gulliver's Travels* (1782–72). Every household would own at least one Landseer engraving: notable among many would be *The Old Shepherd's Chief Mourner,* (1837), depicting a sorrowing collie dog and

Laying Down the Law, (1842), which transfers human institutions to animals in a picture of a Poodle Judge and mixed-breed Jury. Edward Smith-Stanley, the 12th Earl Derby, epitomised an alternative inclination: he trained fighting cocks and race-horses, launching The *Oaks* (named after his Carshalton estate) in 1779 and subsequently The *Derby* as an Epsom classic the following year. Smith-Stanley belonged in that time-honoured English tradition of aristocratic sportsmen who reared pheasants to be slaughtered by the bucketful, bred dogs to kill dying birds and raced exhausted horses for money. (Wilde's dictum of the unspeakable in quest of the uneatable, lay in the future as did various measures to outlaw hunting wild animals with dogs.)

Lear's Nonsense animals are informed by this complex and inconsistent relationship between the English and animals which cannot be easily dealt with by the words 'sentimental' 'romantic' or 'scientific, 'pragmatic' or even 'sensational'. Nonsense was one avenue of exploration: it allowed a variety of animals to interact equally with bipeds in surreal adventures. Lear's limerical animals are neither innocent or subservient – they are sentient equals with a damaging propensity for mischief. They challenge a hierarchy which placed animals in some lesser status to that of their owners, before Darwin's theories forever altered the concept of animals as separate and unrelated forms of life. In the limericks of Lear, dogs do not fetch and carry for their owners – they eat them.

Or they lead them on a string as did,

'There was an Old Man of Kamschatka
Who possessed a remarkably fat cur
His gait and his waddle, were held as a model
to all the fat dogs in Kamschatka.' [226]

CN, p76.

Or they are quite the size of their owners, in true equality.

'There was an Old Man who said 'hush'
I perceive a young bird in this bush
When they said, 'is it small?' he replied, 'not at all
It is four times the size of this bush'.

CN, p173.

A hare, upon which an Old Man rides away to escape his despair, is the size of a small horse and assumes a wide-eyed and sympathetic dominance. (The hare carries a familial resemblance to the Rock Hyrax, *hyrax capensis*, Lear's beautiful and serious drawing of which was sold at Agnew's, London, in 1993 for £5,012.09p.[227] A spotted calf eats the shawl of a young woman who has shrunk to half her size in contrast. Pigs are fed figs by thoughtful, musical owners who sing to them and a crab the size of an elephant affrights a

---

[226] Kamschatka, a fishing peninsula in East Russia, was unknown to Lear , but 'the sound of the name delighted him'. Levi, p60.

[227] Courtesy of Agnew's, New Bond St. 0207 7290 9250. 17/1/2008.

honeymoon couple in Hyde Park.

Many limerical animals are inherently comical – fowls, geese, cows, frogs and rooks – who cannot lay claim to the dignity of stags, elephants, giraffes, eagles, or lions. Lear has a particular predilection for penguins. Their monosyllabic names make easy rhymes. Their identification with their human partner is always affectionate and benign, a state of affairs which occasionally belies the traditional role of the animal concerned. Sometimes, identification may be taken to the ultimate, as in the case of,

'There was an Old Person of Skye
Who waltzed with a Blue Bottle fly
They buzzed a sweet tune to the light of the moon
And entranced all the people of Skye'.

CN, p377.

There is a curious freedom implicit in this human adoption of animal mores. The human is released from normal codes of behaviour and may be allowed to buzz, bark, fly or twit-twoo as he pleases. Yet Edward Lear was not one of those adults who prefer the company of animals to his fellow man: animals were company and solace, his cat Foss ('Ye common nature Catte') [228] in particular, but he had a gift for human friendship and was beloved by men, women and children of all ages.

---

[228] Levi, p62

INTRODUCING WILLIAM SCHWENCK GILBERT

William Schwenck Gilbert is the second subject of this thesis. Playwright, critic, librettist, artist and journalist, he is neither invariably nor immediately associated with Nonsense. Yet it is the Nonsense of *The Bab Ballads* for which Gilbert achieved immortality: a collection of short illustrated verses whose lunatic inventions are the basis for the Savoy Operas. (Gilbert never liked to waste a good idea). The operas themselves are not Nonsense – they parody, burlesque and satirise events, institutions and individuals 'all rattled off to a popular tune',[229] but they are carefully rehearsed and orchestrated theatre, lacking the mayhem spontaneity of true Nonsense. Each piece was written out by Gilbert at least twelve times. As Emile Cammaerts observed, 'Nonsense ceases to be Nonsense when it takes itself too seriously: there must necessarily be a certain unfinished quality, it cannot be elaborate or well thought out'.[230] The Ballads were written in a hurry to meet the deadlines of *Fun*.[231] They were composed almost carelessly when Gilbert was a young journalist under pressure and they were rarely revised. Like Edward Lear's Nonsenses, squeezed in between painting large oil landscapes, Gilbert's *Ballads* were trifles between the serious business of writing plays. Walter de la Mare's 'one wild flower' of Nonsense in Victorian literature blooms wildly in the *Ballads* and they, not the operas, are the focus of this chapter. 'All of Gilbert is in the Bab Ballads' wrote *The Times* 'as all the flower is in the bud'.[232]

The Ballads are not nonsense in the same fashion that Lear's limericks are Nonsense – but they are nonsense in their absurd premises, their arbitrary interventions and their comical brutality. Like most Nonsense, they contain elements of parody and satire;[233] they, and only they, allowed Gilbert the full rein of his high-spirited, competitive, energetic creativity.

The introduction will be followed by a review of those existing

---

[229] *Patience,* Act 1.

[230] Emile Cammaerts, *The Poetry of Nonsense*. London, Routledge. 1925. p70

[231] *Fun*, 1861–1901. A lively illustrated periodical which carried comic stories as well as political news, sport and travel: a rival to *Punch,* but ever-so-slightly downmarket.

[232] *The London Times*, June 1911. Quoted by Reginald Allen in *First Night G & S*. London, Chappell & Co, 1958.pxii

[233] WSG parodied Lear's limerick 'There was an Old Man in a Tree/Who was terribly bored by a bee/When they said, does it buzz/They replied yes it does/It's a regular brute of a bee' with the following nonsense version: 'There was an Old Man of St. Bees/Who was stung in the arm by a wasp/When they said, does it hurt/He replied, no it doesn't/But I thought all the while 'twas a hornet!'

biographies and critical comments on Gilbert which focus on his boyhood, youth and early life before the partnership with Arthur Sullivan. Success doth make cowards of us all and the wild Nonsense which abounds in Bab became more restrained as the century advanced and the box office ruled. Studies of twinned 'Gilbert and Sullivan', which invariably concentrate on the Savoy Operas, never provide a sufficiently thorough examination of either, much less an understanding of the Ballads which lay behind them.

After the biographical resumé will come an examination of Gilbert's initial choice of careers and the London of the 1830's in which these were based. His curriculum vitae mirrors masculine endeavour in mid-Victorian England whose institutional rituals were a pantomimic gift; successive chapters chart the genesis of Bab through the army, the civil service and the bar. Bab's relationship to the Victorian church and to the theatre, musical scene and artistic climate occupies three further chapters, whilst the more introspective and intangible aspects of Gilbert and Bab are dealt with in chapters relating to gender, nationality, identity and transformation.

Unlike the limericks of Edward Lear or the stories of Lewis Carroll, Gilbert's one hundred and thirty seven *Bab Ballads* were not written for children, general or particular. They were written by one: by a Precocious Baby and this effort by Gilbert to distance himself from the childish nonsense with which we are concerned is in itself of particular interest. The *Bab Ballads* first appeared in collected form in 1869: *More Bab Ballads* were published in 1873, followed by *Fifty Bab Ballads* in 1877, selling through several editions by Routledge & Kegan Paul. In 1898, a sizeable new version of the ballads together with *Songs of a Savoyard* appeared with a introduction by WSG himself. The imprint was acquired by Macmillan in 1904 and several new printings included a Pocket Library edition in 1925, a standard size volume in 1951 and a reprint in 1979. James Ellis' definitive, annotated study for the Belknap Press of Harvard University first appeared in 1970, was reissued in 1980 and required a third printing in 2003.

This chapter will redress the notion, inherent in most accounts of Gilbert's early life, that his father was a shipboard surgeon with an unsavoury interest in mental asylums; another generally accepted canard appears to be Gilbert's own declaration that 'my father never had an exaggerated idea of my abilities: he thought that if I could write, anyone could, and forthwith he began to do so.[234] Closer examination of Gilbert Senior's *Memoirs of a Cynic* reveals a very different story.[235] This study does not purport to be primarily biographical but a correction of two serious misunderstandings is vitally important: firstly for the new light it throws upon the theatrical influences of Gilbert's boyhood and secondly for the questions it raises concerning Gilbert's economy with the truth. As a young boy, Gilbert Senior's greatest treat was a visit to the pit of the theatre where an 'unswerving belief in the reality of theatrical illusion' was to persist all his life.

---

[234] Edith Browne, *William Gilbert*, 1907. Quoted in Dark and Grey, London, Methuen. 1932. p2
[235] Dr. William Gilbert, *Memoirs of a Cynic*, 1880. London, Tinsley Bros.

A school friend who lived near the East India Docks inspired Gilbert Senior to a naval career and he served as a midshipman on board the vessels of the Honourable East India Company. Uncertain if his future lay with the navy, a ship's doctor advised him of the security of medicine: 'you'll always find a berth on a whaler for £5 a month with food and cabin', but Gilbert thought medicine was a "dead-end" and no comparison to the possibilities of the law,' through which you may rise to the highest offices in the State and become a Member of the House of Peers'.[236] Later, he confessed that his attraction to the Bar had largely derived from two daughters of a barrister who lived in Hastings. Gilbert Senior did study medicine, and became a Member of the Royal College of Surgeons in 1830 even though the autopsy room made him queasy. The significant turning point was a visit to France with his medical mentor who encouraged a 'gap year' of travel and experience through Europe in general – but theatres in particular.

We shall be examining the status of the English theatre in the 1830s and 1840s, but suffice it to say here that the position of theatres on the continent was very different. The status of the actor in early Victorian England ranked along with vagrants and vagabonds in a world of travelling theatrical troupes where the material was dire and the audiences rowdy. In France and Germany, theatres were 'a desirable social amenity as opposed to a disreputable luxury':[237] Schiller and Hugo accepted the theatre as a challenge they were happy to accept, in contrast to the English Romantic poets who mostly preferred to ignore it. (George Rowell suggests that neither Shelley or Byron would have submitted to the discipline of the theatre.[238]) In this new, colourful world of Italian opera and French drama, Gilbert Senior lived backstage. He learned French and Italian, attended early productions of Bellini (*I Capulletti*) , flirted with 'Juliette', and began to write reviews of the theatre. Yet his admiration was not wholly uncritical: he wrote that the repertoire of one touring company, 'contained such an immense variety of subjects as to totally preclude their perfection in any,' [239] and that 'of their moral character, as a whole, perhaps the less said, the better.'

Gilbert Senior eventually returned to England and lodged with a journalist uncle in Brompton. He continued to develop a career writing theatrical reports for newspapers and periodicals, becoming an editor through the alcohol-induced incapacity of elderly relations and finally inheriting their substantial estate. To stave off the ennui produced by a handsome legacy and no employment, Gilbert took his new wife and young family for prolonged travels around Europe.

His son shared his father's passion for the stage. But no respectable parent in 1845 would mark his son down for future success in the arts, although painting and literature were marginally more acceptable than the theatre. Even

---

[236] *Memoirs of a Cynic*. p34

[237] Michael Baker, *The Rise of the Victorian Actor*. Croom Helm, London. 1978. p19

[238] George Rowell, *The Victorian Theatre*, CUP, 1978 p32

[239] *Memoirs of a Cynic*, p208

Gilbert Senior's friendship with Charles Kean,[240] – that rare figure on the Victorian stage, an educated, meticulous and hardworking actor characterised by utter professionalism and unimpeachable private life[241] – did not enable Gilbert Junior to become an actor and his attempt to join Kean's company when still a schoolboy was rebuffed. Yet his father's familiarity with the theatre and his friendship with actors had a profound and lifelong impact on Gilbert Junior.Themes from Shakespeare appear constantly in the operas – *Measure for Measure* becomes the Mikado's punishment by death for flirting – and the Baronets of Ruddigore who step out of the picture on the stage represent a device borrowed from several nineteenth century plays, notably Planché's *The Court Beauties,*1835.[242] A closer examination of James Robinson Planché's 176 plays (which include 23 melodramas, 9 musical revues, 23 fairy tale extravaganzas and 9 burlesques of classical mythology) might undermine some of Gilbert's reputation as an original writer but creative plagiarism from Bach to Britten is nothing new. What remains to be regretted today is not Gilbert's theatrical borrowings but a general lack of respect and recognition for Planché.

Gilbert was obliged to aim for a theatre of war. He attempted to win a commission in a line regiment, offering himself for service in the Crimea, but when peace was unexpectedly declared, Gilbert sat one of the new competitive examinations for a clerkship in the Civil Service. This 'detestable thraldom' [243] lasted four years after which he was released by a legacy which enabled pupillage in a barrister's chambers and a call to the Bar in which he was hilariously unsuccessful. He joined the Volunteer Militia and was promoted to Captain of the Royal Gordon Fusiliers which allowed a picturesque Scottish uniform and the chance to dance Highland reels.

Despite his failure as a barrister, certain qualities in Gilbert remained those

---

[240] Charles Kean, 1811–1865. Director of Queen Victoria's Theatricals.

[241] Kean married Ellen Tree in 1842, a popular and gifted actress in her own right.

[242] Michael R.Booth, *Victorian Spectacular Theat*re, London, Routledge. 1981. p18

[243] Cited in Max Keith Sutton, *W.S.Gilbert*. Boston, USA, Twayne. 1975, p15

of a lawyer: a disconcertingly accurate memory, a pugnacious belief in justice and consequential concern for the underdog. Concomitant was the beginning of an alternative career as a writer of criticism, political comment, humorous prose and doggerel Nonsense for the growing legion of magazines and periodicals. Journalism was beginning to be familiar activity for briefless barristers – or even successful lawyers, as we shall see. Gilbert married in 1867 and determined upon a more solid career than writing Nonsense for *Fun*. He wrote extravaganzas, entertainments and theatricals and began to achieve a certain notoriety for his burlesques, if not for his straight plays. Tiring of setting new lyrics to old tunes, he collaborated with an ambitious young Irish composer and wrote *Thespis, or The Gods Grown Old*, the first Gilbert and Sullivan opera, produced by John Hollingshead at the Gaiety Theatre, London, in 1871.

The partnership of Gilbert and Sullivan became known as one of the glories of the Victorian age. It changed the status of the English musical theatre. It revived the fortunes of the stage. It made stars of the cast, the theatre and the impresario. 'Gilbertian' entered the language and the lyrics entered popular consciousness. *Gilbert and Sullivan* operettas remain popular, if slightly outmoded: a vehicle for amateur dramatics or controversial interpretations by Jonathan Miller. There has been a *Black Mikado*[244] and a

children's *Gondoliers*. In the main, Gilbert and Sullivan has been too popular to attract serious criticism, itself an interesting comment on intellectual and musical snobbery, but its continued survival demands attention and respect.

---

[244] 1975; set on a tropical island, Sullivan's music was adapted for calypso band with reggae and rock overtones and Patricia Ebigwei starred as the most heart breakingly beautiful Yum Yum.

THAT WHICH WENT BEFORE – WILLIAM SCHWENCK GILBERT

The first biography proper appeared in 1929 when Isaac Goldberg, an American journalist, author, critic, editor, publisher and translator (and biographer of H.L. Mencken, George Gershwin and Arthur Sullivan) produced *Sir William Gilbert, A Study in Modern Satire.* Goldberg's multifarious career enabled some fascinating detail concerning the possible Sullivan-Carroll collaboration and an insightful, quasi-psychological approach for Gilbert. In a subsequent study,[245] he understood that underneath everything Gilbert wrote 'there was something that cut beneath the etiquette to instincts that do not always follow the book'[246] and that his personality encompassed both the candles and crinolines of his childhood and the hectic, unresolved Freudianism of the 1920s.

Gilbert's friend, Henry Roland Brown, planned a biography in the 1920s but died before the project could be realised. His sister, Lilian Roland Grey, collaborated with Sidney Dark in 1923 to provide a valuable, first hand collection of memoir, anecdote and personal impressions.[247] The authors describe Gilbert's genius for changing both the perception and the reputation of theatrical libretti: mere vulgar doggerel was elevated by his creative imagination to become a fine art, even if this was not the achievement for which he wished to be remembered. According to them; 'No one with the smallest critical faculty can read the Gilbert comedies and find in them more than a suggestion of the genius that riots through the *Bab Ballads* and the libretti. The strangest and most ironic of Gilbertian paradox is that he never accepted that his serious plays were not equal to his magnificent excursions into the land of Topsy Turvydom, the country of the Happy Impossible'.[248] Gilbert wanted to be remembered for *Broken Hearts*[249] and not *The Mikado,* (much less for *Captain Reece*), just as Sullivan would have preferred fame as the author of *Ivanhoe,*[250] not *Iolanthe.* Jane Stedman supports the theory that Jack Point's 'they don't blame you as long as you're funny' in *The Yeoman of the Guard* is a bitter self-portrait of a man who would be taken seriously, but

---

[245]Isaac Goldberg, *The Story of Gilbert and Sullivan, or The Compleat Savoyard.* New York, Crown Publishers, 1929.

[246] Goldberg, p 505

[247] Sidney Dark and Roland Grey, *W.S.Gilbert, His Life and Letters.* London, Methuen. 1932.

[248] Dark and Grey, p.60

[249] 1875. A tearful play about four women who have withdrawn from the world of men.

[250] Libretto by Julian Sturgis, adapted from Scott: the purest romantic tosh and a dramatic flop.

never is.[251]

Comedy and cruelty can lie too close for comfort was the essence of Q's criticism in a Cambridge lecture on Gilbert in 1929.[252] Q rejoiced in the *Bab Ballads*, declaring them infinitely superior to the opera libretti, but believing Gilbert to be 'essentially cruel and delighting in cruelty'[253].Yet if one is 'repelled' by Gilbert's cruelty, one may as well be repelled by Falstaff's debauchery or Don Giovanni's lust. Later supporters rounded on Q, notably James Ellis and Jane Stedman – two distinguished and contemporary American Gilbertians. Ellis argues that Q's response 'unassailable, if unappreciative, is that of a reader unable or unwilling to make the purely intellectual transformation of a scene demanded by Gilbert'.[254] Certainly Gilbert poked fun at elderly ladies with no waists but as Stedman points out, Gilbert's dame figures satirised not the middle-aged follies which his contemporaries conventionally ridiculed, but the premium which Victorians placed on youthful beauty as the most desirable quality in marriage.

David Eden presented Gilbert as an insufferable monster of egomania and neurosis, claiming that Gilbert's personality was arrested at an early stage of development, even that he was some kind of infantile sado-masochist.[255] More of the same could be read in Eden's subsequent study based on the semi-autobiographical novels of Gilbert's father.[256] The picture drawn of WSG's father is of 'a hard, selfish man, probably alcoholic and mentally unstable after

---

[251] G&S, p891

[252] Sir Arthur Quiller-Couch. Cornish-born, Trinity-educated poet, writer and scholar: described as 'a courtly gentleman of the old style' by Selina Hastings (*Rosamund Lehmann*, London, Chatto, 2002, p45), a gallant, and a Liberal: urbane, sentimental and amusing and unlikely to appreciate WSG's tart wit.

[253] Arthur Quiller-Couch. *WSG*. 1929. Quoted in John Bush Jones *W.S. Gilbert; A Century of Scholarship*. New York, New York University Press, 1970. p168

[254] James Ellis, Preface to *The Bab Ballads*. HUP, Massachusetts, 1970. p16

[255] D.J. Eden, *Gilbert and Sullivan - The Creative Conflict*. Cranbury, N.J. Fairleigh Dickinson.U.P. 1986.

[256] D.J.Eden, *W.S. Gilbert - Appearance and Reality*. Saffron Walden, The Arthur Sullivan Society. 2003.

the death of his first wife'[257] and Eden treats his son no better, arguing with scant evidence, that Gilbert was materialistic and brutal in his love affairs and that his marriage with Lucy was no romantic love match; not my impression of the crustily charitable Gilbert Senior, nor the drily romantic young Gilbert.[258] Eden arrived too late for inclusion in Professor John Bush Jones's *WSG - A Century of Scholarship,* a representative collection of English-American studies from 1869 –1969, but not too late for Andrew Crowther[259] who has published studies of Gilbert as a dramatist , and who takes exception to Eden's view, as indeed does this writer, and it is certainly an opinion both unusual and extreme today.

Yet in 1869, the *Bab Ballads* attracted a fair share of rotten eggs; 'The dreariest and dullest fun we have ever met with:…no real humour, nor geniality…they are wooden, both in the verses and in the illustrations…the jokes are entirely destitute of flavour'. And although 'The *Bab Ballads* do not contain a single thread of interest, nor a spark of feeling', a certain truthfulness of workmanship does after a time disclose itself to those who will look at them more than once.[260]

A contrasting view came from Max Beerbohm, himself a humourist and fantasist with pen and pencil, who loved them, delighting in the triumph of their sheer silliness, their 'high-spirited invention' and their artistic spontaneity.[261] Beerbohm believed that to appreciate humour, one must be born in the era it was written – or very soon after, which might qualify the views of Walter Sichel in 1911 and Edith Hamilton in 1927, both of whom linked Gilbert to Aristophanes. Sichel's hyperbolic prose makes difficult reading but we grasp his almost limitless admiration for one who created 'the mirage of a masquerade, a borderline between the empyrean and the too-solid earth, and a welkin ring with laughter'. Edith Hamilton regrets Gilbert's loss of freedom compared to Aristophanes, noting the Ballads' pictures of dishonesty, sham and ignorance in high places but she is mindful of their differing worlds – a safe and comfortable England in contrast to a bitter and defeated Athens.

Beerbohm's view that the magic of the Ballads would not be magic if it did not defy analysis, was shared by G.K. Chesterton who described Bab as 'the utterance of a less inhibited personality with the unguarded ability of youth' moreover arguing that every single Savoy Opera was a spoilt Bab Ballad.[262] For Chesterton, mixed-up babies which constitute important plot elements in *HMS Pinafore* and *The Gondoliers* are actually better served by the *Ballad of Private James*. The real joke is not the muddled infants but the

---

[257] 'The Task of Filling up the Blanks'. Review of Eden by anonymous critic, G&S News.

[258] Eden, p.102

[259] Andrew Crowther 'Ages Ago – Early Days of Gilbert and Sullivan'. G & S Internet Archive, Boise State University, accessed 21.05.007.

[260] Anonymous and 'MB' Reviews of the BB's. Quoted in John Bush Jones, *WSG: A Century of Scholarship.* New York University Press, 1970. p3

[261] Ibid. p64

[262] Max Beerbohm 'G & S in the 1880s'. *Essays by Fellows of the Royal Society of Literature*, ed. Walter de la Mare, London. 1930.

outrageous abruptness with which brooding James mentions an intuition that,

> 'a glimmering thought occurs to me
> Its source I can't unearth
> But I've a sort of notion we
> Were cruelly changed at birth'.

JE, p93.

Chesterton declared that to be 'as pure as spirit of Nonsense: that divine lunacy that God has given to man as a holiday of the intellect, especially to Englishmen'. He linked Gilbert's fantasy figures to the clowns and policemen of the *commedia del'arte*, noting that the limelight shone on the player. For Gilbert, the play was not the thing – what mattered were the players and the consequent possibility of ultimate incongruity.[263] The key to Gilbert's writing always lay in the nature of the individual character.

Chesterton's perception and analyses of Gilbert and the Ballads in the 1930s was ahead of its time. During the decades which followed, writers on Gilbert (Leslie Baily and Hesketh Pearson in particular) presented lively and discursive accounts of a largely straightforward and uncritical nature. Baily's *Gilbert and Sullivan* grew from a series of radio programmes first produced by the BBC in 1947 and broadcast worldwide. The book is evenly divided between appreciation for Gilbert and Arthur Sullivan and features

---

[263] Gilbert's influence on the Nonsense of Chesterton might serve to convince waverers in the acceptance of Gilbert as a Nonsense writer; in *The Man Who Was Thursday,* Chesterton's anarchical Policeman explains that 'burglars and bigamists are essentially moral men…they accept the essential ideal of man, they merely seek it wrongly. Thieves respect property. They merely wish the property to become their property that they may more perfectly respect it'. *The Essential Chesterton*, OUP, 1987, p150

reproductions of historic programmes, photographs and portraits. Baily usefully reminds readers that Gilbert, Sullivan and D'Oyly Carte saved the musical theatre from the tawdriness and vulgarity of the mid-nineteenth century, from the vice and indecorum described by Dickens and the smell of orange peel and lamp oil with an undercurrent of sawdust. Baily sees Gilbert as 'under the clown, the moralist and behind the satirist, the sentimentalist' with a weakness for a pretty face as, 'even in the most savage of the Ballads, a young woman is inevitably comely'. [264]

A theatrical focus marks the two studies by Hesketh Pearson whose essential view of Gilbert was as a 'strong, full-blooded, impatient and irreverent Englishman'.[265] His *Gilbert and Sullivan* first appeared in 1935 but a more concentrated version *Gilbert – his Life and Strife* was published in 1957, and is of particular note for the transcriptions of personal correspondence. Pearson was a young actor in the company of Beerbohm Tree and had first-hand knowledge of plays and players: his choice of biographical subjects reveals a taste for the highly theatrical – Sydney Smith, Oscar Wilde, G.B. Shaw and Benjamin Disraeli.

Modern literary criticism discovered Gilbert in 1975 with Professor Max Keith Sutton of Kansas University whose landmark study presented the full range of WSG's considerable output.[266] The notion of Gilbert as a contemporary radical satirist is supported with credible evidence, although the professor's imagination at times rivals that of his hero. Sutton believes that among themes detected in the *Bab Ballads* are Darwin's theories of evolution echoed in the Victorian mania for competition and illustrated by Bab as cannibalism.

'King Borria Bungalee Boo
Was a man-eating African swell
His sigh was a hullaballo
His whisper, a horrible yell - his whisper, a horrible yell'.

JE, p90.

(This may have some relation to Mrs. Jellaby, Dickens' nightmare philanthropist in *Bleak House* ,1852, whose passion for the inhabitants of Borrioboola-Gha takes over from the care of her own family.)

Less controversial and more helpful for the present enquiry are Sutton's theories concerning Gilbert's awareness of political shenanigans which surface in Bab's frequent allusions to class struggles; 'They show how obsessively people rely on systems to give life the semblance of order and thereby neglect

---

[264] Leslie Baily, *Gilbert and Sullivan*, London, Cassell & Co, 1952, p44/45

[265] Hesketh Pearson, *Gilbert and Sullivan*. London, Hamish Hamilton 1935. p30

[266] Max Keith Sutton, *W.S.G.* Boston, Twayne Press. 1957. A distinguished fellow-American literary critic to follow where Sutton led was Harry Levin whose *Playboys and Killjoys*, OUP, New York, 1987, discussed Gilbert as a writer 'who subjected the leading professions to self-exposure', p.58/59.

the possibility of living freely…trapped by their sense of propriety'.[267] Our understanding that this is so endows readers with their own possibility of being free. Sutton describes how the *Ballad of Captain Reece* illustrates two ethical doctrines that were controversial in the 1860s: one was the utilitarian injunction to create the greatest good for the greatest number and the other was the application of Ruskin's Golden Rule[268] to political economy.[269] He admires the captain's 'impressive foolishness with a touch of Don Quixote's comic sanctity, who stays uncontaminated by the self-help morality of a competitive world'.[270] Sutton understands Bab's suggestion that vice is virtue and virtue vice (inspiring GBS among others) and his lesson to the Victorians, who put their faith in moral absolutes, was that the world might actually be morally relative.

Professor Alan Fischler takes his lead from Sutton and takes Gilbert's Nonsense seriously. In his study of the Savoy Operas he concentrates on the libretti and sets forth a closely reasoned argument proposing that the operas succeeded not because they demonstrated particular contemporary controversy, but because they did not: he maintains that Gilbert's popularity was based on a simple illustration of existing bourgeois values, abandoning the more astringent tone of the Bab Ballads and Gilbert's earlier stage efforts.[271] It is precisely this earlier and more combative Gilbert with which this study is concerned: a spirit written out from most of the entertainment inherent in the eventual operettas. Alan Fischler believes that Gilbert's topsy-turvydom was never designed in 'the punitive spirit of corrective satire'[272] but as a catharsis by laughter: that the educated classes of the 1860s needed help in coming to terms with science's destruction of their cherished faith in a God who had given order and meaning to their lives; 'Gilbert's comic method constituted a response to this need: he offered his audiences imperfect law as a replacement for perfect providence, yet simultaneously encouraged them to laugh at this substitute and purge their reservations about its inadequacy'.[273]

Policemen for priests? Arnold and Ruskin were explicit in their proposals that the void left by God required filling with culture or art, and although it seems awkward to accept that Gilbert consciously replaced the Deity with temporal authority in order to fill the Savoy Theatre, there is the fact that Christian providence is conspicuously absent from the libretti. (Less so in the *Bab Ballads*.)

Jane Stedman and James Ellis who cut their teeth on Gilbertian doctorates, provide contemporary debate and discussion on the *Bab Ballads*. Stedman

---

[267] Sutton, p.46

[268] Ruskin's Golden Rule held that the imaginative understanding of the nature of others and the power of putting ourselves in their place is the faculty on which virtue depends.

[269] Ibid, p38

[270] Ibid, p39

[271] Alan Fischler, *Modified Rapture: Comedy in W.S. Gilbert's Savoy Operas.* Charlottesville; London. University Press of Virginia, 1991.

[272] Fischler, p 50

[273] Ibid, p51

describes how 'tight metrical structures and rhymes give Bab's personages a frame to burst out of, and in this respect, they are like figures in a farce. Their energy results in frequent, parodistic violence which is regularized into laughter by the rules of etiquette…and the ridiculous names of the characters involved'.[274] Dr Stedman believes that, through all the laughter, Bab was satirising human nature in 'its inconstancy, greed, egotism, self-interestedness. hypocrisy, credulity and ultimately, its mortality'.[275] Perhaps reasonably, given the title, Stedman only offers the reader a few pages on Bab and devotes the majority of her long and immaculately researched study to Gilbert, the dramatist. In contrast, James Ellis has become a Bab scholar, responsible for the latest collected edition of the Ballads, and the author of an illuminating *Introduction*.[276]

'The Babs provided Gilbert with the challenge to compound, light and explode ingenious little crackers of topsy turvy adventures. The improbable conditions unimpeachable logic and unexpected denouements…irresistibly successful in the Ballads.'[277]

Yet neither have provided more than an outline of the multi-layered context which lies behind the inspiration of the *Bab Ballads,* and no writer in the last few years has updated an understanding of the magic, power and fun of Gilbert's Nonsense verses. I shall give Sir William Gilbert the last quotation, if not the last word.

'The Bab Ballads are not, as a rule, founded on fact. The pictures in particular are beyond criticism. They defy it. Yet because while they are certainly quite as bad as the Ballads, I suppose they are not much worse'.[278]

Gilbert's very typical self-abasing comments were for his benefit, not ours. He pretended not to take his Nonsense seriously, as if the success of so incidental an art somehow made a lesser man of him, but we are not quite fooled. Nonsense, like Gilbert, operates on the premise of conventional coherence. Gilbert's whole persona was that of a distinguished, upright English gentleman yet under his watch chain and waistcoat lay a world of wordplay that constantly frustrated any expected significance. The Nonsense of the *Bab Ballads* ruined forever the chance for a judge to be taken wholly seriously, for a policeman's authority to be without question and for a clergyman's moral integrity to be beyond reproach. The jester nodded his cap, tinkled his bells and the world laughed.

'Tell me, Edward, dost remember
How at breakfast we,

---

[274] Jane Stedman, *W.S.Gibert: A Classic Victorian and His Theatre*. OUP, 1996. p26

[275] Ibid. p27

[276] W.S. Gilbert *The Bab Ballads*. Editor, James Ellis. Cambridge, Massachusetts. Belknap Press, Harvard University. 1970. 3rd Printing, 2003.

[277] Ellis, p 23.

[278] Author quote from Sidney Dark and Roland Grey, *W.S. Gilbert His Life and Letters*. London, Methuen, 1932, p24.

Put our bacon in the teapot
While we took and fried our tea?

How we used to pocket ices
When a modest lunch we bought
Quaff the foaming Abernathy
Masticate the crusty port?

How we cleaned our boots with sherry
While we drank the blacking dry
How we quite forgot to pay for
Articles we used to buy

How a ruffian prosecuting
Who'd been swindled, so he said
We appeared at The Old Bailey
And were done ourselves instead'.

JE, p65.

GILBERT, BIOGRAPHICAL
1) London

In contrast to Edward Lear and Lewis Carroll, Nonsense only inspired William Gilbert when he was a young man. The *Bab Ballads* were written in the 1860s when Gilbert was in his twenties and so it is this first period of Gilbert's life that we shall be concerned with. Nothing Gilbert ever wrote later would match the mayhem madness of the Ballads but such was never his intention: it was as if their magic otherworldliness caught him by surprise between the demands of his journalism, the wit of his burlesque and the ambition of his serious drama. An older Gilbert pinned them down, cut, pared and adapted them for comic opera libretti, all the while resisting the fame of their invention. Like Pagliacci – or his own Jack Point[279] – sometimes, the jester cried to be taken seriously.

William Schwenck Gilbert was born in 1836 in the home of his maternal grandparents, No. 17, Southampton Street, Strand and London remained his hearth, his heart and his home for almost all his life.[280] The area lay some miles from the country village of Lear's birthplace in Highgate, but was not intensely developed until the Great Fire of 1666. By 1840, the Strand had become one of the most desirable areas in London, encompassing elegant terraces with sloping gardens down to the Thames, each with private jetties and adjacent to the original vast palace which Edward Seymour, Duke of Somerset, first built in 1549.[281]

The year of Gilbert's birth proved to be a significant year for London: London Bridge Railway Station opened with a new line to Greenwich, Charles Darwin joined the Royal Geological Society in Kensington, King's College, Strand, was added to London University and the first performance of Donizetti's *L'Elisir d'Amore* was given at the Lyceum. Railways, genetic discoveries, education and opera were to become grist to the Gilbertian mill. In the following year, 1837, Princess Victoria was crowned Queen, for which event James Robinson Planché wrote a small review of English Queens, and Edward Stirling staged the first public reading of a Dickens' novel, *The Pickwick Papers* at The City of London Theatre, Bishopsgate.

Gilbert spent his boyhood in London, attending school first at Brompton

---

[279] *Yeoman of the Guard.* 'They don't blame you as long as you're funny'. C.A. G&S. p819

[280] WSG bought a country estate, Grims Dyke, near Harrow in 1900.

[281] The first Somerset House had been homes to Elizabeth 1st, Anne of Denmark, Henrietta Maria of France, General Fairfax and Catherine of Braganza. It was HQ to Fairfax', 'model army'.

and then at Great Ealing School,[282] a remarkable establishment for a time considered the equal of Eton and Harrow. He appears to have enjoyed a close and affectionate relationship with his father Gilbert Senior who declares that 'cynicism' was far more the effect of an education than natural tendency; that 'memories from my earliest childhood recall that the ridiculous has thrust itself into every action of my life. I have been haunted through my whole existence by the absurd without the slightest power on my part to avoid it'. [283] We know, too, that Dr Gilbert was an Honorary Secretary of the Society for the Relief of Distress, that he was anti-Catholic, anti-Church of England, anti-vivisection and philo-semitic and that he believed poverty, not innate depravity, was the ultimate cause of crime.[284] Leslie Baily describes the legacy of 'viewing the world upside down through his legs as an impish gift from father to son'.[285] Other gifts to his only son included strong opinions and a consequential intolerance.

During the family travels on the continent, the baby Gilbert was 'captured' by Italian bandits near Naples who demanded a ransom for 'dis lofly bambino'. An irate Dr Gilbert redeemed his son for £25, a bargain for posterity who inherited the legend in both *The Gondoliers* and *The Pirates of Penzance*. Gilbert briefly attended school in Boulogne and caught a glimpse of Napoleon III and his wife, Empress Eugenie, in procession. It inspired his first comic rhyme and a curiously undying fascination for France's most unlikely hero.

'When the horses white with foam
Drew the Empress to her home
From the place where she did roam
The Empress, she did see
The Gilbert familee
To the Emperor, she said
'How beautiful the head
Of that youth of gallant mien
Cropped so neat and close and clean
Though I own he's rather lean'.
Said the Emperor, 'it is!
And I never saw a phiz
More wonderful than 'is'.[286]

What the boyhood verse does illustrate are two aspects of Gilbert's Nonsense which were to be significant: a pleasure in the perils of an exaggerated rank and a cavalier disregard for conventional spelling when confronted with the imperative of a rhyme. The faintly unrealistic 'Emperor'

---

[282] Thomas Henry Huxley and John Henry Newman were alumni; THH's father was a Junior Master under the revered headship of Dr Nicolas.

[283] William Gilbert, *Memoirs of a Cynic*. London, Tinsley Bros. 1880. p36

[284] Stedman, p8

[285] Leslie Baily, *The Gilbert and Sullivan Book*, London. Cassell & Company. 1952. p3

[286] Mrs Francis Carter, Gilbert's niece, recalled this family anecdote to Leslie Baily. (The Gilbert & Sullivan Book, p12)

and 'Empress' (Queen Victoria was yet to agree with Disraeli's suggestion that she become one herself, but the English had good reason to be nervous of French Emperors) found an echo in Gilbertian Admirals, Mikados and Lords High Everything Else. The King of Barataria in *The Gondoliers* is dismayed to discover that 'everyone is somebody municipal' and to learn that 'when everyone is Somebodee, then No One's Anybodee'.[287]

Two concerns of primary interest to Gilbert, the theatre and publishing, were primarily London based. The theatre's focus on London, according to Rowell, 'dated from the close-knit society of the Restoration which found its theatrical entertainment at the London playhouses rather than in its country seats and for the next hundred years, the only acting visible in the provinces came from the strolling players who eked out a furtive, even persecuted existence'.[288] *Fun* – like *Punch*, the *Illustrated London News* and four-fifths of nationally distributed periodicals in the 1850s–1860s was published in Fleet Street, London: a thriving **provincial** newspaper business had no echo in the more significant and longer-lasting magazines.

Many of Bab's characters bounce around London, notably in the City or South Kensington where Gilbert and Kitty lived, first at No. 24, The Boltons, and subsequently at No. 39, Harrington Gardens, a house whose astonishing design of jumbled vernacular motifs from every country in Northern Europe remains to be marvelled at today. The 'hearty flamboyance, perfectly suited to its owner'[289] of No. 39 was designed for Gilbert by the architectural practice of Ernest George and Peto, and their highly individual development of Harrington and Collingham Gardens in the Alexander Estate remains unequalled in London town houses.[290] No. 39 presents a façade of great stepped redbrick gables in nineteen stages. The model ship, which controls the broad front, alluded to Gilbert's believed descent from Sir Humphrey Gilbert, a noted Elizabethan seafarer and not, as one innocent supposed, to H.M.S.Pinafore. Gilbert retorted that he did not put his trademark on his house. (Humphrey Gilbert drowned off the Azores saying as he did so, that he was nearer to heaven by sea than by land.) Inside, an oak-panelled hall includes a floor to ceiling chimneypiece in carved stone and a blue-tiled inglenook in which Gilbert hung his hams. Here also are panels of Holbein-esque painted glass, but the stamped, leather paper by Jeffrey and Company has gone. The doors to the ground floor rooms still display whimsical mottoes: the drawing room door proclaims:

'and those things do best please me,
That befall preposterously',

---

[287] G&S, p937

[288] George Rowell, *The Victorian Theatre*. CUP, 1978 p5

[289] Hermione Hobhouse, ed. *Survey of London*. The Athlone Press, for the GLC. 1986 p189

[290] Wonderfully appropriately, the entire house is occupied by Haskoll, an architectural practice. (info@haskoll.com) The mottoes above the doors remain, so do the ham hooks in the fireplace and the first floor window from which Gilbert threw sweets down to various children below.

and the dining room door announces, with Dante,

'All Hope Abandon Ye Who Enter Here'.

Was late Victorian cooking that bad?

The population of London in Gilbert's boyhood was over two million and rose to nearly four million in 1871. In 1836, it was the largest city in the western world but one of contrasts and extremes as sharp as anything fancifully presented by Gilbert. Grim industrial quarters of railways, black factories and cholera-struck hovels grew in stark opposition to Tennyson and the Pre-Raphaelites, whose fantasy life moved in fairy landscapes of blossom-rich fields, shining white towns, dusky forests between magician's towers and milky lakes darkening with enchantment. Much of London presented bitter struggles with poverty, dirt, death and disease and the ostentatious dazzle of a new-rich West End was in a frightening opposition to the dockland degeneracy of the East.

The theatre in Gilbert's boyhood may not have been as disreputable as an East End slum, but it certainly did not belong to the glitter of the West End. Only Drury Lane and Covent Garden were socially possible venues, despite the new Queen's interest in the theatre and support for Charles Kean. Dozens of minor theatres, homes of melodrama, pantomime and burlesque were left to the fast and to the raffish. Refinement, respectability and religious zeal all kept the audiences away and the theatre suffered, because, as Matthew Arnold suggested, it did not attract an audience representative of the society of its day.[291] Opera alone retained a social cachet, partly on a belief in the elevating effect of serious music and partly due to the Victorian pleasure in ostentation. Even performances of Shakespeare were only a draw if a celebrated actor or actress was involved. Yet in both the East and the West End of London, improved housing, cheaper public transport and factory employment produced a new large audience hungry for entertainment: 'People mutht be amuthed, Thquire' said Mr Sleary in Dicken's *Hard Times*,[292] 'they can't alwayth be a'workin', they can't alwayth be a'learning'. In mid-Victorian London, they began to be amuthed at the theatre which, together with the novel and the printed periodical, began to displace religion in the battle for hearts and minds.

---

[291] Matthew Arnold, 'Letters of an Old Playgoer', quoted by Cecil Price in the *Sphere History of Literature*. Vol. 6. Ed, Arthur Pollard, London. 1970. p387

[292] Charles Dickens *Hard Times* Penguin Classic Edition, 1969, p82. First published 1854.

GILBERT, BIOGRAPHICAL
2) The theatre

Gilbert was born backstage. His father was a drama critic and personal friend of Charles Kean: colleagues of Dr William Gilbert Senior included Dion Boucicault, James Robinson Planché, Charles J. Mathews and Mrs Vestris. The family lived between Covent Garden and the Haymarket surrounded by what Planché describes as 'the smell of gas lamps and orange peel'.[293] Gilbert wrote plays at school, acted in them and painted sets. Had his father been more of an actor, there is every likelihood that Gilbert would have followed suit: theatrical dynasties have long been particularly strong, bonded by unsocial working hours and the need to form supportive artistic coteries of their own. The intercommunion between mid-Victorian painters, musicians, poets and writers did not extend so much to the stage and the comradeship such as existed between Tennyson and Edward Lear, or the romantic partnerships between George Eliot with G.H. Lewes and Franz Liszt with Marie d'Agoult [294] had significantly fewer theatrical equivalents.[295] Tennyson wrote a commendatory sonnet on the career of William Charles Macready[296] (1793–1873) but there is no evidence of a meeting, much less a friendship. Young Gilbert's one recorded appearance on the professional stage inspired John Hollingshead to comment that Oliver Cromwell in the part would not have been worse.

In the early years of the nineteenth century, the stage neither aimed nor aspired to provide original entertainment. Adaptation of French novels, such as Dion Boucicault's celebrated *Corsican Brothers*[297] or variations on[298] Shakespeare were the lifeblood of the business. Touring companies, reliably represented by Dickens' Vincent Crummles and his terrible troupe in *Nicholas Nickleby,* rehashed the classics and mangled the parts even if most did not possess an 'Infant Phenomenon' to bring the curtain down.

The confident familiarity with Shakespeare was demonstrated by endless travesties but original drama for the English theatre in the 1820s and 1830s

---

[293] John Russell Stephens, *The Profession of the Playwright.* CUP.1992

[294] This genuine friendship was cemented by the marital 'irregularity' of both couples.

[295] Dickens, Bulwer-Lytton and Macaulay were friends.

[296] Ernest Reynolds *Early Victorian Drama.* Cambridge, W. Heffer & Sons, 1932. p150

[297] 1852: Queen Victoria saw it five times and sketched scenes from it in her journal.

[298] Dr T.Bowdler,1818, published expurgated versions of Shakespeare which omitted 'delicate' passages, but Nahum Tate's 17thc. sentimentalised versions were much more destructive. Tate even altered certain tragedies to give them happy endings…

barely existed at all.[299] Successful drama demands that the creative personality becomes submerged in the creation of character, in an artistic climate of rigorous condensation and restraint, qualities more associated with the classical era of the eighteenth century and conspicuously lacking in the Victorian mania for growth and expansion. The Victorians seemed to set a special value on voluminousness for its own sake, and size and scale formed part of a culture of sensation from which no endeavour in the mid-nineteenth century was entirely free. The Great Exhibition of 1851 was merely one manifestation, as were the 'loose baggy monster'[300] three volume novels, Ruskins's encyclopaedic *Modern Painters,*[301] and the Midland Hotel at St Pancras Station.

Bab spends a great deal of time in the theatre. He observes with a cynical detachment how actors fool both audiences and themselves, how the clown is invariably tragic and what Nonsense most reality turns out to be.

'An actor sits in doubtful gloom
His stock-in-trade unfurled
In a damp funereal dressing room
In the Theatre Royal, World'.

JE, 137.

(The verses continue to recount a skeleton's 'Father Christmas' costume which hides both the bones of the 'actor' and the real misery felt by many during the 'festive season'.)

What filled the stage in the early nineteenth century was a motley mass of melodrama, extravaganza, burlesque, pantomime and even equestrian drama supplied by resident dramatists or non-resident hacks for a largely middle or working class audience and a handful of connoisseurs. Forbidden by the Licensing Act (repealed in 1843) to offer 'legitimate drama' theatre managers proved ingenious in offering burlesque, melodramas, farces, operattas, pantomimes and performing animal acts – theatres were in danger of becoming little more than a circus. Impresarios vied for audiences by mounting increasingly spectacular combinations of straight theatre with singers of the calibre of Malibran, virtuosi such as Paganini and dancers like Taglioni. Drama was in danger of disappearing completely in the 1830's as 'the spread of less literate forms of entertainment threatened to engulf the stage in a torrent of spectacle, farce and extravaganza'.[302]

The all-classes Elizabethan audience had deserted the playhouse by the beginning of the nineteenth century. A Puritan ban on theatrical entertainment and the forcible closure of all theatres during the Commonwealth was

---

[299] Edward Bulwer Lytton's creative partnership with William Macready began with *Richelieu* in 1840.

[300] Henry James' famous description appeared in his Preface to *The Tragic Muse*, Vol VII, 1890.

[301] The first of the five volumes appeared in 1843.

[302] Michael Baker, *The Rise of the Victorian Actor.* Croom Helm, 1978.

reinforced by a religious revival of the 1830s, and religion, which fostered drama in its early days, now worked to prevent the building of theatres and the social recognition of actors. Refinement, religious zeal and respectability kept the educated audience away and opera alone retained a social cachet. Queen Victoria herself was a keen theatre goer and encouraged the work of Charles Kean and the Princess Theatre but baleful elements within the Church hamstrung the theatre until the late nineteenth century.

In a patter which burlesques the recitative of 'serious' opera, Bab notes that English Opera does not always fit the bill.

> 'there's that fickle Covent Gardin, promised operas retarding,
> And perhaps for aye discarding in their love of dividend.
> But they've failed in English operer, and wisely think it properer
> By pantomime tiptoperer their balance sheet to mend'.
>
> JE, p66.

A clerical assumption was that actors risked damaging their personal characters by regularly assuming fictitious ones. Actresses came for even more opprobrium than their masculine counterparts: the tools of an actress' trade are her emotions and her physical body, two attributes young Victorian women were not encouraged to flaunt. The intensity of the theatrical taboo 'took root in the profound anxiety of contemporaries that the traditional moral order was the target of exceptional assaults...nowhere was this concern more deeply felt than in the sphere of sexual morals'.[303] Rumours of links with prostitution had always accompanied the stage, a situation exacerbated by the claims of young women apprehended soliciting to be 'actresses'.[304] Adaptations of French novels were seen as encouraging adultery and divorce. Religious strictures were reinforced by the censorship of the Lord Chamberlain's office which imposed codes of behaviour unknown elsewhere: the press might be as scurrilous as it liked and painters presented tableaux that would have been banned on stage - yet even Shakespeare was not immune from prudish alteration. Theatres were obliged to close on religious feast days, Ash Wednesday and during Holy Week. Lewis Carroll was deterred from taking Holy Orders on account of a Church ban on theatricals.

Bab has fun with a phantom 'curate' whose pleasure in the theatre, Punch and Judy, croquet and operatic quartets finally allows a strict Bishop to relax.

> 'One evening, sitting at a pantomime,
> (Forbidden treat to those who stood in fear of him)
> Roaring at jokes sans metre, sense or rhyme
> He turned and saw immediately in rear of him
> His peace of mind upsetting and annoying him
> A curate, also heartily enjoying it'.
>
> JE, p69.

---

[303] Michael Baker, *The Rise of the Victorian Actor*. London, Croom Helm, 1978 p 48
[304] Ibid.

But matters were changing and when young Gilbert attempted to join Kean's company in 1860, the evangelical and earnest drive for self-improvement which so characterised the early years of Queen Victoria's reign was being overtaken by the notion of recreation for its own sake. The theatre exists to meet the needs of its audience and no proselytising manager could have relied upon Greek tragedies or comedies of wit and manners to fill his auditorium satisfactorily in 1840.

This study is not concerned with Gilbert as a dramatist, but a certain cognisance of his theatrical influences is required as a vital context to his Nonsense verse: first must come the encouragement of Tom Robertson whose dramas 'began the slow shift away from the broad effects of melodrama and farce towards a more subtle realisation of everyday life upon the stage[305] 'and whose social comedies introduced a note of contemporary awareness wholly lacking on the Victorian stage. In *Caste* (1865) and *Society* (1867) 'there is a faint attempt to escape from the mechanical formulations and standard sentimentalities of earlier nineteenth century drama'.[306]

We have been briefly introduced to James Robinson Planché, the scholarly actor with a passion for historical accuracy, modern direction and adherence to the script, but as notional godfather to WSG, he deserves a moment more of our attention. In addition to hundreds of plays, libretti, revues and burlesques of classical mythology, Planché wrote travelogues, children's books and magazine articles – as drama critic of the *Morning Herald,* he must have known Gilbert's father, although there is no recorded meeting. Planché led an exemplary private life with his wife, the actress Elizabeth St George and deserves a better fate than survival in scholarly footnotes. Posterity can only mourn *The Burghers of Calais*, a libretto Planché wrote for Felix Mendelssohn and which, despite years of planning, correspondence and work, was never completed and any musical remnants have disappeared. It would be almost impossible to chart all the direct influences of Planché on Gilbert's work: the soft-hearted pirates who cannot pillage orphans[307] as they are foundlings themselves, is a state of affairs identical to that of Planche's Massaroni in *The Brigands* (1829) and *Faint Heart Never Won Fair Lady*, Planché's one-act comedietta which ran at the Lyceum during 1857 is far too obviously the inspiration for the trio sung by the Lord Chancellor, and Lords Mountararat and Tolloller in *Iolanthe,* Act lll.[308] But Planché's influence was not merely his ideas. Wit, grace and learning improved the quality of both serious drama and the parodic burlesque – his *Golden Fleece* earned Planché a reputation for scholarship even in the Universities and it requires a classical education not generally available today.

Gilbert was influenced in different vein to the extravanganzas of Planche

---

[305] Cecil J.Price, essay, 'The Victorian Theatre' in *The Victorians*, Editor, Arthur Pollard, London, Sphere Books, 1989, p388

[306] David Daiches, *Critical History of English Literature*. New York, Ronald Press. 1970. pll00

[307] 'Do you mean orphan often, or orphan ACTUALLY' became a Victorian catchphrase in the 1880s and I still use it.

[308] G & S, p433

by the farces of H.J. Byron, founder and first editor of *Fun* and credited with being the first to spot the promise of genius in the young writer. Byron was ingenious in his use of familiar material and undeniably clever, but 'his humour was mean, his plots at once complicated and puerile, and his characterisation purely theatrical'.[309]

Gilbert may not have been introduced to Lewis Carroll, but he knew something about him. Almost inevitably, they were attending the same theatres during the 1850s and 1860s and Lewis Carroll considered approaching the Gilbert of the *Bab Ballads* as an artist to illustrate some of his work.[310] Carroll records a visit to The Adelphi Theatre for a charity performance of the operetta *Cox and Box* adapted by F.C.Burnand from J.Madison Morton's original play and set to music by a young Irish composer, Arthur Sullivan.[311] Carroll met the cast, almost all of whom were on the staff of *Punch* – Shirley Brooks, Tom Taylor, Bernand himself and Mark Lemon. Gilbert <u>must</u> surely have been in the audience, if not backstage later. Carroll's three little Liddells were among a number of little maids he wrote verses about: in August, 1869, he inscribed a copy of *Alice's Adventures* to three Miss Drurys.[312]

'Three little maids, weary of the rail
Three little pairs of ears, listening to a tale
Three little hands, held out in readiness,
For three little puzzles, very hard to guess.
Three little pairs of eyes, open wonder wide
At three little scissors, lying side by side
Three little mouths that thanked an unknown friend
For one little book he undertook to send.
Though whether they'll remember a friend, or book or day
In three little weeks, is very hard to say'.

In the same year, Carroll took the little Drurys to German Reed's Gallery of Illustration for the safely proprietoral evening's entertainment provided by Gilbert's *Happy Arcadia*[313] writing later to remind them of the play:

'Three little maids, one winter day
While others went to feed
To sing to dance, to laugh to play
More wisely went to Reed's'.

Did Gilbert borrow Carroll's three maids for Yum Yum, Peep Bo and Pitti

---

[309] *Cambridge History of English Literature*, Vol. 13. Editor, Sir A.R. Ward. CUP, 1932. p273

[310] Sir Joseph Noel Paton, 1821-1901, was another possibility.

[311] May 11, 1867, Carroll Diary entry.

[312] Stuart Dodgson Collingwood, *Lewis Carroll*. p419

[313] *Happy Arcadia*, Gilbert's one act opera premiered in 1872, music by Frederick Clay, became the basis for *Iolanthe* considerably augmented by business from various *Bab Ballads*.

Sing's trio in Act 1 of *The Mikado*,1885?[314] (Later, a priggish Carroll recorded his horror at Gilbert's use of the word 'damme' in *H.M.S.Pinafore*.)[315]

No dramatist, not even William Schwenck, escaped the influence and ideas of William Shakespeare. In *An Unfortunate Likeness*, Bab acknowledges his debt with the story of a contemporary lookalike whose unmistakable Shakespearean face, features and haircut attract attention, not all of which is welcome. Behind the nonsensical tale lurks the notion that Bab – and the dramatist Gilbert – borrowed more from Shakespeare than mere physiognomy.

'Oh sir, I said, 'a fortune grand
Is yours, by dint of merest chance
To sport <u>his</u> brow at second hand
To wear <u>his</u> cast-off countenance

To rub <u>his</u> eyes when e'er they ache
To wear <u>his</u> baldness ere you're old
To clean <u>his</u> teeth when you're awake
To blow <u>his</u> nose when you've a cold!'

JE, 206.

We shall meet both H.J. Byron and F.C. Burnand again in later chapters dealing with Gilbert's contributions to national periodicals in the 1860s. Gilbert's entry as a young dramatist in the theatre is not the point of this study: by the time he had begun to attract critical attention for his plays, the *Bab Ballads* were largely compiled. Curiously, WSG never wrote either a serious verse drama, nor a Nonsensical play. His nonsense verses, adapted to the Savoy opera libretti, remain the only successful examples of their kind in the English theatre.

---

[314] G & S, p577
[315] Jean Gattegno, *Lewis Carroll*. New York, Crowell. 1976. p272

GILBERT, BIOGRAPHICAL
3) The Army

Foiled in his attempts to become an actor, Gilbert searched for another gladiatorial arena.

The tensions inherent in a creative personality required expression and release: if not with the glitter and greasepaint of the stage, where better than the battlefield? There is a shared iconography, heightened by the nearness of tragedy, drama, life or death. The soldier, like the actor, fights a battle that is not of his making, nor of his choice: he will achieve death or glory for someone or something else. Gilbert was not the soldier-poet Byron, passionate with doomed chivalry in support of Greek independence, nor yet a sensitive Sassoon whose moral courage struggled against perceptive melancholy and damaged health. He was a robust and trenchant Englishman with a highly competitive streak, likely to support an opposing view and certain to support the underdog. It is unlikely that he understood the politics of the Crimea in 1854 – few did. Britain was fighting for Turkey, a country that had refused mediation against Russia who had accepted British terms. Lord Aberdeen and his cabinet were against conflict. Gladstone did not support the notion of an 'heroic' Turkey, but believed that the power of Russia needed to be checked.

In 1854, England seemed to need the energising action of war. There had been peace for forty years. According to J.B.Priestly: 'The upper classes welcomed the Crimean war as a glorified large scale picnic in some remote and romantic place. The Black Sea was open to tourism. Commanders' wives insisted on going along, accompanied by their maids. Various civilians cancelled holidays to follow the army and watch the sport; to admire stern-looking infantry, and cavalry in brilliant uniforms'.[316] The *Illustrated London News* sounded a warning note;[317] 'Despite the excitement for all anticipating the approach of hostilities, there are points to which those, most ardent in the cause never had attention directed. Troops marching with flying colours, bayonets glistening and martial music thrilling the spectators cannot fail in stimulating a patriotic enthusiasm. But whilst the columns moving through the streets loudly respond to the acclamation of their countrymen, few of the lookers-on care to analyse the real position of the gallant fellows quitting home to serve the national honour'. The anonymous reporter, possibly William Howard Russell of *The Times,* knew that the army was only a decorative remnant of Wellington's forces in the Peninsula campaign. Its officers tended to be adventuring aristocrats with a good seat in the saddle, who had purchased their commissions and who would never be a match for the trained

---

[316] J.B. Priestley, *Victoria's Heyday*. London. Heinmann, 1977. P147
[317] *Illustrated London News,* 21st May, 1854

professional soldiers of France or Prussia.

Into the valley of death rode the gallant young men by the score. Complete annihilation was only avoided because the Russians seemed even more incompetent than their invaders. Sebastopol, Balaclava, Gallipoli, Inkermann, Alma, became household names as England read dispatches from the front every week: it became the most reported war in history. The *Illustrated London News* carried reports from Russell, loudly praising the British soldiers' 'acts of heroism worthy of every age and every nation , earning themselves immortal renown and the gratitude of every lover of justice and freedom'[318] but castigating the 'officers who furnished many illustrations of their want of the essential qualities of good soldiers, the power of undergoing hardship and fatigue without murmuring – they have shown themselves much inferior to their men'.[319] This, too, spurred Gilbert into the lists. A keen sense of justice, along with a long memory for a quarrel, remained a life-long trait, and, aged just twenty, Gilbert began to read for the examination to achieve a commission in the artillery. Competitive examinations were a novel introduction in the 1850s and afforded the older and safer Gilbert much harmless fun. (Reasons for them will be explored in a later chapter.) Even if he could have afforded to buy a commission – a Lieutenant in a regiment of line infantry would cost £700.00 in the 1850s, a captain would require £1,800.00 – it would have been impossible for the Artillery where officers could only rise through ability in gradual seniority up the ranks. Although artillery was employed at the siege of Calais in 1377, artillerymen were not royally instituted until 1741 and they alone held distinction for practical soldiery in the 1850s. 'The British Regiment of Royal Artillery ranks pre-eminent among that branch of military organisation attached to European armies. It does not equal our continental neighbours in number, but as regards efficiency and discipline it is unrivalled'.[320] Their curriculum was demanding: cadets required knowledge of mathematics, surveying, reconnoitring, practical geometry and mechanics: theory and practice of gunnery, construction of batteries, pontoons and fortifications: drill and evolutions of the infantry, together with sword, carbine and lance exercises. 'Every branch of this splendid service merits high eulogium – not alone as reflects the untiring assiduity of the officers to attain the closest to perfection in the science of gunnery, but equally as regards the men when in the execution of their duties'.[321]

Gilbert was never able to achieve his commission as peace was suddenly and unexpectedly declared in 1856. In a fragment of autobiography for *Theatre*, he admitted that 'among the blessings of peace may be reckoned certain comedies, operas, farces and extravaganzas which, had the war lasted another six more weeks, might never have been written'.[322]

War as a spectator sport ended in the Crimea. No longer would faraway conflicts resonate with the dash and derring-do of military glamour to the same

[318] *Illustrated London News*, 6th January, 1855
[319] *Illustrated London News*, 20th January ,1855
[320] *Illustrated London News*, January 28th, 1854.
[321] Ibid.
[322] Roland Dark and Sidney Grey, *WSG – wife and Letters*. London, Methuen, p5

extent.[323] Reports from Meerut, a little-known Indian town, forty miles north-east of Dehli, concerning the difficulties experienced by the British East India Company of maintaining order in May, 1857, did not touch the same chords, nor arouse the same instant call to arms. England felt a little scarred and a little battle-weary: Roger Fenton's Crimean photographs spoke of a different battle to the picturesque adventures expected by the ignorant, and only the foolhardy continued to believe that war was a game.

'When I know what progress has been made in modern gunnery
When I know more of tactics than a novice in a nunnery
In short, when I've a smattering of elemental strategy
You'll say a better Major General has never satagee!'

Pirates of Penzance,
G & S, p219.

Was the young Gilbert unconsciously aware that many of his ideas required a transformation of identity? Army uniforms with their instantly recognisable badges of rank and status were one very useful device. Uniforms of all kinds – clerical, theatrical, legal, aesthetical, naval – were a boon. Changing dress was shorthand for changing character, not always merely for comical effect but as an idiosyncratic method of dealing with human emotion. Transference enabled Gilbert to express the follies of ambition and misplaced affection in terms acceptable through fun. It was a throwback to pantomimic characters with their recognisable costumes of a *commedia dell'arte*. The love philtre of *The Sorcerer*, Gilbert's first collaboration with Sullivan, is the initial 'magic lozenge', Gilbert's particular brand medicine for transferring identities but every subsequent opera plot involves a metamorphosis, often chaotically and nonsensically across a class divide. Bab's characters are almost invariably dressed up in clothes, costumes or uniforms which tell a story before one word is read – and which often defy any 'logic' of the text.

In 'General John', Bab tells the story of Private James who, completely arbitrarily, announces to Major General John that he believes they were switched as babies. The changeling identity motif, as well as the instant acceptance of the idea, was a basis for dozens of *Bab Ballads* as well as the plots of both *H.M.S. Pinafore* and *The Gondoliers*.

'I've a strange idea that each other's names
We each of us here got on'.
'Such things have been' said Private John
'They have!' sneered General John.

'My General John, I swear upon,

---

[323] Perhaps this is wishful thinking, and memories were short: the military careers of Lords Roberts and Kitchener were to inspired patriotic fervour and idiotic gallantry, often against ludicrous odds in Afghanistan, Abyssinia, Egypt, Africa and France during the period 1870 - 1914.

My oath, I think tis so' -
'Pish', proudly sneered his General John
And he also said 'ho, ho!'

JE, p93.

More inarticulate army officers feature in Bab's *The Scornful Colonel* who teaches his men how to sneer with six hours of sneering drill each day. Gilbert himself may have smarted under an alien authority: when the Scornful Colonel's celebrated sneer fails to frighten an Ottoman Sultan, he is packed in a sack and drowned in the Bosphorus

Now, to your right, prepare to 'whish!'
Come all at once, and smartly 'pish!'
Prepare to 'Bah!' by sections 'Phew!'
Good! At three hundred yards, 'pooh, pooh!

JE, p264.

Sullivan resisted transferring identities as theatrical plots. His aims were to set stories of human interest and probabilities: he preferred realism to romance. Unlike Gilbert, Sullivan had some notion of actual soldiering from his Army bandmaster father and a Sandhurst family background. Gilbert knew showy, colourful hussars in their tight purple trousers and short jackets: he watched redcoats and bearskins guarding the palace: he could never resist the lure of costume, nor its metaphorical potential.

'When I first put this uniform on
I said, as I looked in the glass.
It's one to a million
That any civilian
My figure and form would surpass.'

Patience, Act One.
G & S, p289.

But as the Colonel puffs out his chest, he knows he is beaten. Even the splendour of his uniform cannot rival 'the peripatetics of long haired aesthetics' and that 'not even one beauty would feel it her duty to yield to its glamour at once'.[324]

Foiled by peace, Gilbert consoled himself with the militia. Initially, he entered the Civil Service Rifles, later known as the Third Battalion of the West Yorks, Light Infantry, the Prince of Wales' Own, followed by enlisting on the July 7th 1868, as a captain in the Royal Aberdeenshire Highlanders, which became the 3rd Battalion of the Gordon Highlanders. He retired with the rank of Honorary Major in 1878. Aged sixty-three, he did his duty and volunteered for service in the South African war against the Boers. Ian Bradley comments on Gilbert's 'fondness for the Army', noting that the Afghan and Zulu wars were just finished when *Patience,* 1881, was first performed and that 'military characters appear in nine of the thirteen Savoy operas.'[325] Twenty four of the *Bab Ballads* feature uniformed soldiers and sailors.

The concept of duty loomed large in Gilbert's consciousness, often inextricably connected with the services. Various *Bab Ballads* extol it in various utterly nonsensical fashions, mostly taking the idea to absurd extremes. In 'Lieutenant-Colonel Flare*',* the punishment meted out to military miscreants seems not quite to fit the crime.

> 'He always hated dealing
> With men who schemed and planned
> A person harsh, unfeeling,
> The Colonel couldn't stand…
> For men who'd shoot a sparrow
> Or immolate a worm
> Beneath a farmer's harrow
> He couldn't find a term.
> Humanely, aye, and knightly,
> He dealt with such a one
> He took and tied him tightly,
> And blew him from a gun.'

JE, p196.

---

[324] *Patience.* Bradley, G & S, p291
[325] Bradley, p276.

And famously in 'Captain Reece', (1868), Gilbert's naval captain believes it his duty to marry all his cousins and his sisters and his aunts to (unmarried) members of his crew as well as marrying the boatswain's widowed mother himself.

Volunteers, variously and subsequently known as Militia, the Territorials, the Home Guard or Dad's Army, were stay-at-home soldiers trained to protect the domestic front whilst the regular troops were engaged overseas. During the 1850s when British troops were stretched to the utmost in India, Abyssinia and the Crimea and when it was believed that Napoleon III had inherited plans from his uncle to invade England across the Channel, additional defences were required. *The Times* reported that over 170,000 young men had volunteered by 1860, of whom nearly half were Londoners. 'Every young man should join – it gives him healthy recreation, soldier-like habits and a feeling that he is a son of our common Mother-fine Old England, the land of the brave and the free'.[326] This particular panegyric continued to explain that 'those connected to the fast life tell us that the falling off of the attendance of young men at the casinos is something very remarkable: the reason is that they are engaged and interested in their drill'.

Yet the volunteers were almost strangled initially by ridicule and a certain comedic element still remains. 'Fireside soldiers – dare not go to war' was the street urchins' gibe as the rifleman marched to the armoury.[327] Pearson describes Gilbert as 'an efficient and picturesque officer on parade and only drawing the line at personal discomfort'. On one occasion, he had led his men in a straight line back to their firesides rather than follow a circuitous route through a sodden Highland assault course, explaining that there was no pleasure in tramping up hills through a Scotch mist.[328] Apparently, he enjoyed wearing the kilt and dancing Highland Reels which might militate against his later, defensive innocence of music. (Far more likely was a competitive awareness of a field in which Arthur Sullivan reigned undisputed champion.) In his history of Gilbert's Highland regiment, G.A. Raikes describes how they marched to 'fifes and drums and occasionally to the bugles, a French fashion

---

[326] Ibid

[327] Frederic W. Walker, *Building an Army*, 'The Romantic Rise of a Territorial Force' *Cassell's Magazine* May 1st, 1909.

[328] Pearson, p22

lately imported from the Crimea.'[329]

Bab has fun with McPhairson Clonglocketty Angus McClan whose truly terrible efforts on the bagpipes lead to divided loyalties when the Sassenach Pattison Corbay Torbay, infuriated beyond reason, cuts him in half.

'hech gather, hech gather, hech gather around
And fill a'yer lugs wi'the exquisite sound
An air frae the bagpipes – beat that if yer can
Hurrah for Clonglocketty, Angus McClan!'

JE, p153.

Despite Bab – and Gilbert's – fascination with military glamour, Bab was never fooled into thinking that officers – military, naval or policemen – were anything other than the usual mix of human frailty dressed up. In *The Two Majors*, the inappropriately christened Major La Guerre and his rival Major Makredi Prepare, decide not to fight for the hand of pretty Fillette. After all, why should Makredi be obliged to eat La Guerre, moustachios and all, or splash the parade ground with blood? With much trumpeting threats and ill-disguised relief, the two Majors abandon La Fillette to a Corporal Jacques Debette.

'He married her then: from the flowery plains
Of existence the roses they cull.
He lived and he died with his wife and his brains
Are reposing in peace in his skull'.

JE, p243.

The situation of two cowardly rivals for the hand of a simple maid who decide not to fight for her after all has its counterparts in *Iolanthe* and, even more closely, *Utopia, Ltd.*

Gilbert's engagement as a volunteer helps demonstrates the significance of the movement in the early years of the nineteenth century: further proof was supplied by an army of fictional part-time soldiers. Captain Donnithorne comes closest to our perception of a gallant, thoughtless aristocrat dressed up as a soldier.[330] George Wickham is worse and a marriage to Lydia serves him right.[331] Rawdon Crawley and Becky Sharp[332] do not spoil a couple and only perhaps Captain Stubbs paints the movement in shining colours. One of Trollope's most endearing creations, the red-haired, strikingly plain Stubbs is a man of shining principle and unswerving devotion who finally wins the beautiful, if ever-so-slightly silly Ayala.[333]

---

[329] Captain G. A. Raikes, *Historical Records of the lst Regiment of the Miltia*. London, R.Bentley & Son. 1876.

[330] George Eliot, *Adam Bede,*1859, but set earlier c.1800

[331]Jane Austen, *Pride and Prejudice,* 1813.

[332] W.M. Thackeray, *Vanity Fair,* 1847.

[333] Anthony Trollope, *Ayalas Angel,* 1881.

Charles Dickens complains that 'we are rather at a loss to imagine how it has come to pass that military young gentlemen have obtained so much favour in the eyes of the young ladies of this kingdom'.[334] Boz describes a swaggering 'Colonel Fitz-Sordust' of the resident militia who takes his young officers to the theatre where they talk of nothing but charming girls and their patriotic honour, 'crowing over the lower classes whom they treat with a little gentlemanly swindling.' Dickens' irritation with the fascination that redcoats held for young women equalled Gilbert's stance over clergymen.

But in 1859, it was possible that the militia might serve a serious purpose. Regular troops remained in India, the Crimea and there were rumours of an involvement in the American Civil War. (One of Prince Albert's forgotten achievements was the inhibition of this possibility.) Napoleon III fulfilled his pledge to Cavour and invaded Italy to expel the Austrians in a war that precipitated Prussia's assistance to the other German power and appeared menacingly expansive. Palmerston believed that when Napoleon[335] denounced the treaties of 1815, he meant to revive his great-uncle's plans to invade England and the War Office was alarmed by a rapid programme of building armoured ships by the French navy and fortifications at Cherbourg. The volunteers stiffened their sinews: if they believed Palmerston, invasion was imminent in 1860 and even Egypt and India were threatened by de Lessep's construction of the Suez Canal.[336]

Gladstone prevented England from being drawn into an essentially European conflict by a masterly policy of free trade. The power of his oratory convinced his unwilling audience into a conclusion that sensible men could do nothing else – powerful additional support came from the liberal minds of Macaulay and J.S. Mill. Gilbert and over 150,000 volunteers drilled over Salisbury Plain and cleaned their rifles: they continued to view Napoleon lll with circumspection and young children were frightened into good behaviour by being told that 'Boney' might get them if they didn't eat up their sprouts or go to bed on time. Boney III haunted Gilbert, just as he haunted the volumes of *Punch* and even if Gilbert never actually wrote 'The Lie of a Lifetime' an inordinately tedious joke polemic in heroic couplets aimed at the Emperor which ran for sixteen instalments in 1864 and totalled over one thousand lines, he did illustrate the first six rounds. The Emperor, caught between romance and reality, remains one of history's more unlikely heroes, a character summed up by the trenchant view of veteran statesman Adolphe Thiers: 'France made two mistakes: the first when she took Louis Napoleon for a fool and the second when she took him for a genius'.

If Napoleon stirred the blood of the Volunteer Movement, he was a gift to

---

[334] Charles Dickens, *Sketches by Boz*, 1836.

[335] Napoleon III was the son of Josephine de Beauharnais' daughter Hortense, and Napoleon I's younger brother Louis. He looked like a deformed pirate, and his wife, Eugenie de Montijo was Spanish, glamorous and unsuitable. First impressions of Napoleon III were always disastrous, but he possessed a certain charm and eventually even Queen Victoria succumbed.

[336] Historical facts and further information from Keith Feiling *A History of England*. Book Club Associates, 1974.

Gilbert just as he was to every cartoonist of the 1860s. We shall find emperors, with and without their clothes throughout the Nonsense of Bab and the opera libretti.

GILBERT, BIOGRAPHICAL
4) The Civil Service

There were perhaps only two explanations why an energetic, extrovert actor manqué such as William Gilbert should have elected to join the Civil Service in 1857. First and foremost lay the possibility of rising through the junior ranks to become a Member of Parliament, a career choice of immense status in the 1850s–1870s and secondly, if in apparent opposition, the new system of entry via competitive examination which offered preferment on ability,and *appeared* to throw over the inequities of aristocratic patronage and privileged connection. Gilbert, who liked a battle, would always choose confrontation in contrast to collusion. But the timing of his entry was unpropitious; he had selected a government administration raw with reforms initiated by Northcote and Trevelyan and smarting from the whip hand of Ralph Lingen. There is a third reason, only recognisable with hindsight, and that pertains to the inspiration of Nonsense which lay close to the surface of all formulaic, masculine mid-Victorian institutions. Gilbert's collection of them, however significant to posterity, might have appeared a touch arbitrary at the time – and his appointment as a Clerk in the Education Department of the Privy Council was not only random but frankly uncongenial. He was paid £120 a year, 'the worst bargain any Government ever made'.[337]

Readers who are familiar with Dickens' Circumlocution Office in *Little Dorrit* will have some idea of government departments in the 1850s, institutions viewed as 'wholly abominable and bedlamite'[338] and represented by characters as worrying as Sir Titus Barnacle. True, some Civil servants were dishonest, many were indolent and most were discontented: how could they not be when the plums of the department were invariably presented to place seekers with no qualifications save the support of powerful ministers, connections with an aristocratic house or a new fortune? Another equally dispiriting portrayal of the mid-Victorian Civil Service came from Trollope in *The Small House at Allington,* (1862), in which Johnny Eames struggles with his position as a lowly clerk in Somerset House (on seventy pounds a year) and battles with Adolphus Crosbie, a clerk whose connections, office in Whitehall and the chance to win the hand of Lily Dale make him a 'swell'. Trollope, a former official in the Post Office, knew whereof he wrote and we must take his First Commissioner, Sir Raffle Buffle (or Huffle Scuffle, as his impudent juniors called him behind his back) entirely seriously.

Bab is not often found on an office stool, but he tilts at the windmills of

---

[337] Baily, p18

[338] Charles Dickens *Little Dorrit*. 1855-57. OUP Edition, London, 1982. Vol.2, Chapter viii. p433

useless class distinction and mocks privilege founded on birth as opposed to ability. In the nonsensical world of Bab and Gilbert, for example, pirates, (who are well-to-do) are much more gentlemanly in their behaviour and conduct than kings, (who have some dirty work to do.) Clerks, like Matthew Wycombe Coo, are lowly and struggling forms of life, whatever their age;

'Good Pasha Bailey kept a clerk
(for Bailey only made his mark)
His name was Matthew Wycombe Coo
A man of nearly forty two'.

JE, p169

There <u>were</u> men of principle and purpose in the Civil Service when Gilbert joined it, and most particularly, in the Department of Education, a burgeoning institution whose Herculean task was to realign emerging state intervention with voluntary bodies. This political punch-bag involved reform relating to factory children, sectarian education, teacher-training and government funding: then, as now, it may be described as a 'hot potato'. Sir James Kay-Shuttleworth, described by *The Educational Guardian* as 'a large minded philanthropist whose aim was to promote education rather than give an easy berth to the employees of Downing Street' had run the Department since 1839 but overwork undermined his health and he was obliged to accept premature semi-retirement.[339] Kay-Shuttleworth protested in 1857 against the argument that England's commercial pre-eminence was dependent upon cheap labour and that therefore education must be subservient to its demands. Another idealistic champion against the exploitation of children was W.Cowper, political head of the Education Department, who wrote in 1858 that 'so urgent and permanent were the demands for child labour he despaired of seeing any measure adopted that would induce the working classes to keep their children at school long enough to acquire a complete education.'[340]

Whilst Gilbert lay 'fettered to an office stool'[341] around him raged the religious conflicts relating to the control of education by the Church of England. The teaching of the Church was a bulwark of the state: it taught due obedience to laws, and to public authority: it taught the wealthy to be philanthropic and to assist in the religious education of the poor. But in the 1850s, its influence was weakened by growing divisions, initiated by Wesleyans and Methodists and followed by Tractarians (or Puseyites) and Roman Catholics. We shall see how the idea of established authority confronted with energetic and powerful resistance is demonstrated by several of Gilbert's *Bab Ballads* in a later analysis. Unfortunately for Gilbert, Sir

---

[339] A.S. Bishop 'Ralph Lingen, Secretary to the Education Department'. *British Journal of Educational Studies* 16, No 2, (1968) 138–163.

[340] Quoted in Eric E. Rich, *The Education Act* 1870. Longmans, London. 1970. p51

[341] From HMS Pinafore: the celebrated satire on W.H. Smith who was promoted to First Lord of the Admiralty. 'If your soul isn't fettered by an office stool – Be careful to be guided by this golden rule – Stick close to your desks and never go to sea – And you all may be rulers of the Queen's Navee'.

James Kay-Shuttleworth was succeeded as Secretary of the Department of Education to the Privy Council by Ralph Lingen, who had acted as his *locum tenens* in 1849, and who became full Secretary in 1854. Lingen, a scholar in classics with a penchant for penning Greek verse, was a brilliant but abrasive character for whom the letter of the law reigned supreme. Even his devoted pupil, Matthew Arnold, whilst supporting Lingen's undoubted commitment and energy, could not commend his chief's lack of humanitarian feelings. *The Educational Guardian* in November, 1862 criticised this 'prince of red tapists' as being 'animated by no popular sympathy, ignorant of, or sceptically disregarding, the powerful sentiments by which communities are influenced and moved only by considerations of official convenience and statistical uniformity'.[342] The Secretary's legal training produced minutes that *The Times* found 'obscure, imperfect and repugnant to each other. Nothing was more difficult to the uninitiated than to find the rule that was wanted except to understand the rule when it was found'.[343]

Lingen, almost single-handedly, lost all the existing goodwill between the Education Department, professional educators, their employers, their advisors and the press and it is due to Lingen that the nation lost a chance, in the winter of 1867, to provide itself with an integrated and comprehensive educational system: A.S. Bishop believes that the Liberals were determined that middle class education should not fall under the control of a department in which the majority of educators had no confidence and no respect. We cannot know whether Gilbert himself, was like the noble statesmen in *Iolanthe*

'who do not itch
to interfere with matters which
they do not understand.'

G & S, p419

but even the lowliest clerk in the Department of Education would have found his stool an uncomfortable place to be sitting on in 1859.

Gilbert's chaffing at his 'hated thralldom' and 'baleful office'[344] were in no small part due to the arrogance and high handed manner of Ralph Lingen. Even the reforms presented to Parliament in November 1853 by senior civil servants Sir Charles Trevelyan and Sir Stafford Northcote or the Newcastle Commission could not assuage his irritation and impatience. Northcote and Trevelyan envisaged a public service recruited and organised on principles so novel that they were furiously debated for a generation before they won overall acceptance. An earlier belief that the report was a response to pressures from rising middle classes, well-educated but allegedly short of work has been convincingly quashed by Asa Briggs. Briggs demonstrated the aristocratic orientation of Trevelyan and proved that his report aimed *to weaken* the

---

[342] A.S. Bishop 'Ralph Lingen'. *British Journal of Educational Studies*, 16, 2(1968)138-163
[343] Quoted in *The Educator*, July. 1860. In Bishop, as above.
[344] W.S. Gilbert, fragment of Autobiography. Quoted in *Theatre*, April, 1882

capacity of the middle class to penetrate the upper reaches of the Civil Service, thereby strengthening the hold of the landed classes on administrative power.[345]

This would have been of no consequence to a young clerk reading for the new competitive examination introduced by Northcote-Trevelyan as the main means of Civil Service recruitment. Gilbert duly sat the examination which required proficiency in English composition, precis-making, some law and bookkeeping. He would have been required to provide character references and demonstrate a level of physical fitness. The Civil Service had attracted those in delicate health. 'It may be noticed that the comparative lightness of the work and the certainty of provision in case of retirement owing to bodily incapacity furnish strong inducements to the parents and friends of sickly youths to endeavour to find them employment in the Government'.[346] The competitive examination re-appeared in *Iolanthe* as a suggestion from the Fairy Queen that it should be extended for entry into the peerage.

Earldoms shall be sold apart – daily at the auction mart.
Yes, peers shall teem in Christendom
And a Duke's exalted station – be attainable by com-
Petitive examination!'

G & S, p407.

And yet again for the incorrigible Sir Joseph Porter, KCB, who 'wore clean collars and a brand new suit/For a Pass Examination to the Institute'.[347] (Which did so well for he, that now he is the Ruler of the Queen's Navee.)

In a series of pen-portraits for a periodical entitled *The London Society*, (1868),[348] Gilbert presented his view of a selection of London characters with his own lively illustrations to accompany the text. His 'Foreign Office Clerk' comes the closest to his own painful experiences in Somerset House even if his drawing of a very dapper youth with far too careful a toilette and no chin at all is not a self-portrait.

If Ralph Lingen was sharpening his pencil – so was Gilbert. His experience at the Department of Education was part of <u>his</u> education, a four year course in human nature, put to excellent use in the Nonsense which we shall be examining in some detail in later chapters. We shall meet several Gilbertian characters who;

'Always voted at their party's call

---

[345] Peter Gower, 'The Origins of the Administrative Élite.' *New Left Review*, 1 (1987)162.

[346] From the Trevelyan Report, quoted in G.A. Campbell *The Civil Service in Britain*, London, Duckworth. 1955. p27

[347] *HMS Pinafore,* Act l. G & S, p135

[348] http://web.ukonline.co.uk/ajcrowth/babliophile.htm Accessed 29/l/2008

And never thought of thinking for themselves at all'[349]

But Gilbert realised that politics and the law require stereotyped behaviour to exist.

Nothing could be more difficult than;
'The prospect of a lot
Of dull MPs in close proximity.
All thinking for themselves, is what
No man can face with equanimity'. [350]

Iolanthe, Act Two.
G & S, p413

Gilbert's term of employment in the Civil Service was abruptly concluded when he was presented with a legacy of four hundred pounds from an aunt. In later days, he looked upon his release as 'the happiest day of my life'.[351] The unexpected windfall paid for a call to the Bar – of which <u>much</u> more later.

---

[349] Sir Joseph Porter, KCB, aka Pinafore Smith, from Act l of *HMS Pinafore*.

[350] Private Willis' song from sentry duty in Westminster. *Iolanthe,* Act ll.

[351] Baily, p20

BAB – BEGINNING AT THE BAR

The legacy which released Gilbert from the Education Department in 1860, enabled him to pay the hundred pound fee to become a student in the Inner Temple, a hundred pounds to be accepted as a pupil in the chambers of Mr Charles James Watkin Williams, (afterwards a judge in the Queen's Bench Division of the High Court, 1880) and one hundred pounds to set himself up in chambers in Pump Court, Middle Temple. Pump Court lies between Middle Temple Lane and the cloisters leading to Temple Church in a still-surviving network of medieval lanes, gardens and courts. Arthur Pendennis, anxious to win 'one of those prodigious prizes which are sometimes drawn in the great lottery of the Bar'[352] joined the real-life occupants of the Middle Temple: notably Charles Dickens, William Blake (No. 3. Fountain Court from 1821–1827, although nothing to do with the law) and Henry Fielding who had lived at No. 4 during his sojourn as Chief Magistrate of Westminster with particular responsibility for curbing the proliferation of gin parlours (1740–50).

Gilbert shared his chambers with fellow barristers Horace Penditton and Felix Polter, 'a property clerk who did nothing and a practical laundress who did everything'. In an article for *The Cornhill Magazine*[353] Gilbert describes 'the communion of interest in teacups and razors – which, as none of us were well supplied with the necessities of life but each happened to possess the very articles in which the other was deficient – was incumbent. We had all embraced the higher walk of the legal profession: we were patiently waiting for the higher walk of the legal profession to embrace us'. In the interim, Felix Polter wrote farces and Gilbert begat Nonsense.

The presumption that Gilbert was using the professions as a time-honoured English option of social mobility sounds pejorative, but it has a basis in reality, a situation mirrored by Thomas Hardy in *A Pair of Blue Eyes*[354] when Elfride's affections are all too swiftly transferred from lowly clerk to promising barrister. Gilbert's father did not wish his son to enter the disreputable world of the theatre but he had not sufficient money to purchase advancement for him elsewhere. Gilbert must find his own straight and narrow way which initially involved four depressing years as a clerk in the civil service. The legacy which opened the Bar to him promised the status, privilege and possibilities inherent in that most English of English institutions.

---

[352] C.M. Thackeray, *The History of Pendennis*, Chapter 29.

[353] 'My Maiden Brief'. *Cornhill Magazine*, December, 1863. This features the real Penditton and Polter, poor things, as hapless legal apprentices involved in a hopeless case.

[354] Thomas Hardy, *A Pair of Blue Eyes*, 1873.

Metaphorically, Gilbert could win a pair of blue eyes.

'Attorneys are we
And we pocket our fee
Singing so merrily, trial la law!
With our merry ca sa
And our jolly fi fa
Worshipping verily, trial la law!'

JE, p157.

Gilbert could not have been unaware of a theatrical element in law, nor perhaps the potential for comedy, satire and nonsense that ritual inevitably inspires. The word 'ritual' in this context requires closer examination.

'Archaic society rituals contained at the outset all the elements proper to 'play' – order, tension, movement, change, solemnity, rhythm and rapture'.[355] As these elements became incorporated into solemn societal adult functions related to law, religion and marriage, they inevitably lost the aspect of 'play'. But the need to play remains a basic human instinct and if our original rituals have been taken over by the institutions of society, we childishly mock their new clothes in impotent fury at our loss. It was our game – we want it back. Gilbert's spell at the Bar was to provide crucial ammunition in the business of recovery.

Although Gilbert never lost his interest in the law, it cannot be said that the law ever took much interest in him. His legal career remains distinguished only for the few faintly comic courtroom scenes well-documented by Hesketh Pearson in which Gilbert's clients invariably got the better of him. He practised for four years, averaged about five clients in a year and earned seventy five pounds. In the hours spent waiting for briefs, he began to write and illustrate articles for the new comic magazines.

The tradition of briefless barristers turning their pens to fictions other than

---

[355] Johan Huizinga, (translated by R.F.C. Hull.) *Homo Ludens*. London, Routledge & Kegan Paul. 1949, p17.

those required by law was time-honoured.[356] Thackeray was a pupil in the Middle Temple in the 1840s whilst contributing humour to periodicals under a string of pseudonyms including Fitz-Boodle, C.J. Yellowplush, Esq and Michael-Angelo Titmarsh. Wilkie Collins entered Lincoln's Inn before the publication of *Antonina* in 1850. Most significant of all is the career of another Gilbert – Gilbert Abbott a Beckett – who began his professional life as a barrister before becoming a metropolitan magistrate and then launching in 1813 an illustrated comic journal entitled *Figaro in London*. Beckett conducted *Figaro* for three years, finding time among other ventures for *The Wag* and *The Comic Magazine*. Links with comic journalism and the Bar persisted in the career of Tom Taylor, a learned and eloquent scholar who became a barrister in 1846, secretary to the Board of Health and editor of *Punch* for six years from 1874. He shared a set of chambers with Thackeray at No. 10, Crown Office Row, immortalised by Thackeray's commemorative ode on their unsalubrious quarters;

'They were fusty, they were musty, they were grimy, dull and dim
The paint peeled off the panelling, the stairs were all untrimmed
The flooring creaked, the windows gaped and doorposts stood awry
The wind whipped round the corner with a wild and wailing cry
A dingier set of Chambers no man need wish to know –
Than Tom's and my old quarters at 10, Crown Office Row!'[357]

Gilbert's Lord Chancellor was Gilbertian. Henry Peter Brougham, first Lord Brougham, was a doughty remnant of the Georgians who made his name with a spirited defence of Queen Caroline in 1820. Brougham was a Scottish barrister of brilliant brain, boundless capacity for hard work (and hard liquor) and possessed of an inquiring mind. 'No subject was too small, too complicated, or too abstruse for his notice and on all alike he was ready to pour out a fluent, discursive stream of eloquence, bitter sarcasm, invective and occasional extravagant banter'.[358] He became an expert on slavery, Bonaparte, military hierarchy, and foreign and colonial trade. The French, whom knew him as a frequent visitor for tea with Louis Philippe at the Tuileries and as the instigator of tourism at Cannes, were captivated by his genius, versatility and eccentricities. 'He ruled more by fear than by love, but when envy and rivalry did not interfere, his amiable qualities shone out: he was obliging and actually *friendly.*'[359] A highly susceptible Chancellor?[360] Brougham himself died in

---

[356] Less well known are the links between the Bar and the Victorian Stage: an ex-actor named John Cooper welcomed apprentice barristers at his training school and two lights of the Victorian Bar, Charles Wilkins and Edwin James began life as strolling players. Herman Charles Merivale, whom Trollope put up for the Garrick in 1864, combined both professions and entitled his Autobiography *Bar, Stage and Platform.* London, Chatto & Windus, 1902.

[357] Hugh H.L.Bellot *Inner Temple Legal, Literary and Historical Association,* London, Kessinger Publications, (paperback) p81.

[358] Beresford Atlay, *Victorian Chancellors.* London, Smith Elder, 1909. p189

[359] Ibid, p181

1868, just as Gilbert was perfecting his Nonsense ballads in the guise of Bab, but he lived on in *Punch,* as part of the cover illustration for the *London Charivari* – his tall, disjointed frame, strong bony limbs and Wellingtonian nose were a caricaturist's delight.

Gilbert's pupil-master was cast in different vein. Charles James Watkin Williams 'seldom led and was seldom ambitious of leading ...relied upon logicality and clearness of statement rather than rhetoric or declamation, but he was remarkable for a certain dry humour and was quite indifferent to hostile criticism'.[361] Watkin Williams wrote legal textbooks during his reign in the Middle Temple before becoming a circuit judge in 1873. Of the certain interaction between Watkin Williams and his pupil Gilbert, no evidence is believed to exist but a certain tension may well have arisen over the Prisoners Counsel Act of 1836.

This important new and controversial piece of legislation enabled barristers to address the jury on behalf of prisoners charged with felony. (Provided the defendant could afford to be represented.) Previous trials relied upon the accused providing his own defence, regardless of illness or illiteracy, in a legal theory known colloquially as 'the accused speaks'. The new Act gave barristers the right 'to create a persuasive narrative from the fractured facts'[362] and overnight the barrister became an actor. But just as barristers were enabled to present facts and felons in a particular light, so novelists and writers, (particularly those with a legal background) were similarly inspired. Charles Dickens, Edward Bulwer-Lytton, William Harrison Ainsworth and William Makepeace Thackeray argued over the ethical implications of the representation of criminality in fiction. As Schramm relates; 'The press castigated both authors and barristers for expressions of inappropriate sympathy towards violent criminals – the crux of the dispute was the extent to which the influence of a text may move a potentially transgressive agent to action.'[363] Watkin Williams declared that nothing less than an Act of Parliament should ever induce him to deprive a prisoner of the right of making a statement to the jury of facts not given in evidence. On the occasions of which we have evidence, Gilbert would have fervently desired precisely the opposite.

> 'Barristers we
> With demurrer and plea
> Singing so merrily, trial la law!
> Bewigged and begowned,
> We rejoice at the sound,
> Of several syllables, trial by law!'

JE, p157.

---

[360] *Iolanthe,* G &S, p447

[361] Dictionary of National Biography, 1909. p384.

[362] Jan-Melissa Schramm, 'The Anatomy of a Barrister's Tongue: Rhetoric, Satire and the Bar in Victorian England.' VLC, 32:ii (2004)285-303

[363] Ibid.

Bab has no hesitation in speaking up for a Ballad character - but neither does he have any difficulty expressing his own opinion. As third person narrator of many *Ballads*, he is drily objective, frequently employing the rhetoric and jargon of the law courts and always enjoying the nonsense of the surprise against the expected or the arbitrary against the logical. Gilbert believed that conflict, symbolised by law, is part of the human condition: it was certainly a powerful part of his personality and we shall examine how this manifested itself later in the book. Adversarial aspects of Gilbert's character remained very much in evidence all his life, long after he left the Bar proper, and long after success might have watered down a tetchy temperament. Hesketh Pearson describes his extreme sensitivity to personal injustice whereas Sutton gives Gilbert credit for a wider perspective, arguing that 'Gilbert's concern with legality is only part of his larger concern with the unwritten laws of social and literary convention'.[364] Neither Gilbert nor Bab set out to challenge the existing order – their aim was to make fun of it. GBS believed that one purpose of drama was to force the public to reconsider its morals: one purpose of Nonsense is to demonstrate what the morals are.

Another consequence of the Prisoners' Counsel Act was the broadcast of sensation. Variations on ''Orrible Murder. Read All About it' kept the broadsheets, popular periodicals and even the quarterly journals busy. Thackeray, in a column for the *Cornhill* described an infamous murder in Northumberland Street, arguing that the incident was a greater sensation drama than the most celebrated of the genre, Dion Boucicault's *The Colleen Bawn*, (1860). As Jan-Melissa Schramm points out 'the deployment of rhetoric by legal and literary advocates in the service of felons – a discursive and narratological defence of violence – fed a 'murder-mania'.[365]

Ineffectively disguised as 'Snarler' Gilbert entered the lists. Snarler is 'Our Own Correspondent at A Murder Trial'[366] and 'exploits his avowed deficiency in sympathy to stir the reader's compassion for a murderer and to arouse disgust at the frivolity of the spectators.'[367] Practised in the use of his pen and newly entered into the courts of the law, Gilbert took up arms against the sensation industry of the murder trial and at one remove, the sensational novels of Wilkie Collins and Mary Braddon. It is at this point that the dual careers of William Schwenck Gilbert converge. The idealistic barrister almost imperceptibly grows into the journalistic knight: initially, at least, his champions and his victims are the same.

'I do not think I ever knew
A man so wholly given to
Creating a sensation.

---

[364] Sutton, p20

[365] As in Note 10.

[366] *Fun*, April 14th, 1866.

[367] Max Keith Sutton, p30

Or p'raps I should in justice say
To what, in an Adelphi play
Is known as 'situation'.

JE, p155.

BAB – THE PEN IS MIGHTIER THAN THE SWORD

Gilbert's career in journalism began, according to his own account in 1891, when H.J. Byron, founder and editor of *Fun,* is supposed to have asked him for a contribution. 'He asked me to send him a column of stuff with a half page block every week. Well, I didn't think it possible to get fresh ideas week by week, but I accepted it and continued writing and illustrating for six years, although at the end of every seven days, I felt written out, just as I do now.'[368] But we have learned not always to accept Gilbert's own version of events and perhaps a more truthful account of his beginnings as a writer is contained in the unfinished fragment of *Autobiography*[369] in which Gilbert describes the labour and anxieties invariably involved in sending unsolicited manuscripts to editors and journals.

His first contribution was a quasi-humorous poem entitled 'Satisfied Isaiah Jones' which did not satisfy the editor of *Once a Week* because it was too long, but it was pronounced clever and amusing. Encouraged, Gilbert persisted and was eventually accepted as a regular contributor to the new magazine *Fun*, whose publisher Charles MacLean has been credited as the first to spot the promise of genius in WSG. *Fun's* first editor, H.J.Byron launched himself into Nonsense on September 21st 1861 with a comic journal that actually survived forty years, although its success owed as much to *Punch* writers F.C. Burnand and C.S. Calverley as to Byron himself.[370]

Gilbert failed in an attempt to solicit regular employment on the permanent table of *Punch*. Editor Mark Lemon was careful in the early years to superintend the weekly contents page and keep out anything thought brutal or improper. He refused to print *The Yarn of the Nancy Bell* on the grounds that cannibalism was offensive. 'Punch keeps up by keeping to the gentlemanly view of things and it being known that Bohemians don't write for it'.[371] It is difficult for us to regard the whiskery and wealthy dramatist as a bohemian, but such was the young Gilbert's reputation in the early 1860s, a view reinforced by his tendency for practical jokes, membership of risqué London clubs, and theatrical burlesque. The testy relationship between Gilbert and *Punch* was never resolved. *Punch* mercilessly criticised Gilbert's dramas,

---

[368] Harry How, Interview with WSG for *The Strand Magazine.* July-December 1891. No. 4.

[369] Published in *Theatre,* 1-2 April, 1883.

[370] Stedman describes Byron as a 'kind of burlesque James Joyce', (Stedman, WSG, p11) but I cannot resist the lure of a showman whose operatic parodies included *Ill Treated Ill Trovatore*, 1863. How much did the Marx Brothers owe to Byron?

[371] Susan & Asa Briggs, *Cap and Bells*. London, MacDonald. 1972. pxvi

referring to Gilbert's own favourite composition *Broken Hearts* as *Broken Parts,* and accused Gilbert of plagiarism[372]. Pearson describes a typical sally between Gilbert and Lemon's successor, F.C. Burnand. 'Do you ever receive good jokes from outsiders?' Gilbert carefully inquired. 'Oh, often' Burnand replied. 'They never appear', Gilbert grunted.[373]

At 3d an issue, *Punch* was more expensive than either *Fun* or *The Tomahawk* and appealed to the middle classes of society 'who spent six times as much on periodical literature as the rest, per head, of population.'[374] *Punch* occupied a unique position among its many competitors as a familiar and reliable point of reference with an active and influential position in contemporary opinion: it offered a coherent and workable medium for the dissemination of both its own and a wider public view with a mediatory status which straddled interiority and the external.[375] *Fun,* a comic paper of no pretention (even with illustrations by E.G. Dalziel) appealed to the lower to lower-middle classes, was politically to the left of *Punch*, and cost 1d.

Gilbert began to use pseudonyms – A. Dapter, R. Chimedes, Snarler and The Comic Physiognomist – whose masks enabled the illustration of particular ideas or satires to be presented in abstract form. The interest from these pseudo-reporters lay in their point of view – their self-importance, their ironic misanthropy or their capricious playfulness. To Gilbert, all the world was a stage, and all the men and women merely players. 'Bab', the Gilbert family pet name for their eldest son, was adopted following the fashion set by Phiz, Spy, Ape and Boz for single syllable disguise.[376] Slowly through the columns of *Fun,* Bab began to emerge as a distinctive voice, and the Ballads to assume a certain recognisable and collective identity. Bab – the Precocious Baby – featured a logotype of a baby bashing a piano keyboard with the subtitle 'Much Sound and Little Sense' which indicated Gilbert's faint hope that he will not be taken seriously. (Gilbert was never entirely reconciled to his fame as a writer of comic verse.) The reader learns to anticipate Bab's voice as one not yet civilised into cynicism, nor drilled into deceit. An authorial voice validates the incredible and because we are told nonsense firmly, and in rhyming couplets, we momentarily believe it. The dramatised subjectivity of the Ballads, and the interfering and summarising authorial voice, are crucial factors in the dissemination of their Nonsense.

Bab is a child who sees life with clear sighted reality and accepts that some elderly women are plain, that clergymen can be boring, that criminals may have a sense of decency and that policemen are no better than anybody else. Bab does not have romantic illusions. (I think his creator did.) Happy

---

[372] James Ellis, Introduction to the *Bab Ballads*. p8-9

[373] Hesketh Pearson, *Selected Bab Ballads*. Introduction. Private Printing, 1955. (A fascinating detail is that the Sussex Library edition of these belonged to Bishop Bell of Chichester, 1929–1958.)

[374] Alvar Ellegaard, *The Readership of the Periodical Press in Mid-Victorian Britain* .Goteborg, 1957. p37

[375] Therie Seebrook Hendry, 'Unpacking Punch'. Sussex D. Phil thesis, 2002.

[376] Hablot Knight Browne, Leslie Ward, Carlo Pelligrino and Charles Dickens, respectively.

endings may be desirable, but happy endings are usually romantic manipulation and cannot impress the reader as true.

Bab's tale of three sons of Mr Jasper Porklebay (of Porklebay and Brown), who attempt to become, respectively, an actor, novelist and artist but succeed to a fortune because their wealthy father dies before he can disinherit them, contains elements of both autobiography and wishful thinking.

> 'The second, Donald, would insist
> On starting as a journalist
> And wrote amusing tales and scenes,
> In all the monthly magazines.'

JE, p246.

We have some idea of Gilbert, the embryonic journalist, from fictional portraits by Annie Hall Thomas, a prolific and professional novelist described by Jane Stedman as a 'popular writer who wrote for money and earned a comfortable sum'[377] and whose work has been compared to that of Mary Braddon and Florence Marryat. Annie Thomas could never have been the model for the 'lady novelist' on Koko's little list: Gilbert fell in love with her and proposed marriage sometime during 1866. It appears that his suit was rebuffed by Annie's widowed mother, perhaps because of his bohemianism and increasing connection with the stage.[378] The proposed alliance with a young woman of equal spirit and ability reveal Gilbert to be a modern man attuned to feminist ambition and possessed of sufficient confidence to feel unthreatened by it.

> 'Mighty maiden with a mission
> Paragon of common sense.
> Running font of erudition,
> Miracle of eloquence!'

Princess Ida,
G &S, p483.

Gilbert treated women on entirely equal terms and it is difficult to believe that he would not have whole-heartedly supported John Stuart Mill's unsuccessful attempt to secure the woman's franchise in 1867. Both he and Annie contributed to *The London Society*, edited by James Hogg: the latter character fictionally presented in one of Annie's novels as paying more in politeness than in coin. Gilbert's working life involved close association with the only profession in which men and women achieved parity in the 1860s – the theatre.

In *Only Herself*,[379] Annie's hero, 'Bertie Carlyon,' is a struggling young writer. 'Starting in his London life with a sound constitution and a perfect

---

[377] Jane Stedman, *WSG, A Classic Victorian and His Theatre*, OUP 1996 p43-50

[378] Stedman, p45

[379] Tinsley Bros, London 1870.

physique, he retained both by never resorting to stimulants which he did not need. Consequently, for him, there were no tomorrow mornings of burning eyes and shaking hands and muddled brains'.

Annie paints a portrait of a talented and hardworking man with a touch of brilliance behind an engaging and lighthearted façade. Her 'Bertie' took great pains to conceal the work behind his art; in modern parlance, Bertie regarded visible effort as uncool.

'Most people thought that he resembled the lilies of the field in the matter of taking no need for the morrow and of not toiling. And most people belied him hideously.'

If 'Bertie Carlyon' is a picturesque poseur concealing his ability to work extremely hard, 'Roydon Fleming' represents another aspect of Gilbert as a humorist with a brusque manner and better brains than most.[380] 'Roydon' dreams of having a burlesque produced in the theatre: he has the happy knack of wording nonsense epigrammatically even though he is a poorly paid clerk at Somerset House.[381] 'Roydon' is six feet tall, wears a Highland plaid with authority, and, although not conventionally handsome, commands attention from women.

Bab affects mock horror with the contrast between creator and created in 'Disillusioned'. (1867).

'The novelist, whose painting pen
To legions of fictitious men
A real existence lends,
Brain -people, who we rarely fail,
Whene're we hear their names, to hail,
As old and welcome friends;

JE, p98.

Gilbert wrote ballads and plays, articles and humour but he did not attempt the novel form: the competition was formidable. Between 1858–1862, Dickens produced *A Tale of Two Cities* and *Great Expectations*, George Eliot wrote *Mill on the Floss, Silas Marner* and *Romola*, Trollope published *Dr. Thorne, The Three Clerks, Orley Farm* and *Framley Parsonage*, Wilkie Collins created a sensation with *The Woman in White* and *No Name*, and Victor Hugo (*Les Miserables*) and Turgenev (*Fathers and Sons*) could be read in translation.

Improved printing technology, distribution from the new rail network, W.H.Smith's railway book stores and relief from print and paper taxes contributed to the boom in cheap publishing of the 1860s, as did the growth in literacy of a rapidly increasing urban population. The periodical in particular threatened to overwhelm society by sheer weight of number, variety of interest catered for and tub-thumping moral messages. In 1864, the total circulation of monthly periodicals of a Christian nature published in London was almost two million and many a clergyman made more money from publishing sermons

---

[380] Annie Thomas *Played Out.* London, Chapman and Hall. 1866. p107
[381] Stedman, p44

than from delivering them.[382] Moral and respectable became synonymous in the 1860s: even Tennyson's *Merlin and Vivien* was regarded as indelicate and not suitable for reading out loud. 'The test applied in such cases was that of Podsnap in *Our Mutual Friend:* 'would it bring a blush into the cheek of the young person, namely poor badgered Georgina Podsnap? If so, the highest class of literature and poetry must be excluded'.[383]

Illustrations for the journals were provided by artists who drew on boxwood wooden blocks which were then engraved for letterpress printing: some cartoonists were crude and lacking in subtlety, some enjoyed a contemporary success and have since been forgotten. Like Edward Lear, Gilbert illustrated his own comic verses and this study will be examining his drawings in some detail. Some – notably John Tenniel, (the only British artist to be knighted by Queen Victoria), John Leech and Dicky Doyle – produced images that defined politics, religion and social issues into visual symbols: an instant iconography of comic effect.

The more widely read periodicals such as *The Cornhill Magazine, Fraser's,* and *Household* Words attained an enormous circulation: *The Illustrated London News,* founded in 1842 soon sold 60,000 copies per issue, rising to 130,000 in 1851 after the paper published Caxton's designs for the Crystal Palace and reached 200,000 copies a week with the sensational photographs from Roger Fenton of the Crimean War. By 1863, over 300,000 copies a week were regularly passing over the newsvendors stalls, a figure only equalled by *All The Year Round*, a general readership magazine established in 1859, then serialising *A Tale of Two Cities.*

Comic journals *Judy, Toby, Banter, The Bat, The Porcupine, Tomahawk* and *Mirth* were poorer imitations of *Punch* and mostly shortlived. *Figaro in London* (1831–1839) was a godfather *to Punch* and reached a peak weekly circulation of 70,000. The life of most of these journals was as brief as the flare of a gaslight but they provided a platform for Gilbert and his fellow conspirators who dominated the popular literary and journalistic world of London in the 1860s and 1870s: Tom Robertson, C.S. Calverley, G.R. Sims and Augustus Sala. In 1879, Gilbert's friend Edmund Yates, 1831–1894, founded *Time: A monthly Miscellany of Interesting and Amusing Literature* and Gilbert agreed to provide a new series of Bab Ballads (Yates, known as the original gossip columnist, was also involved with *Town Talk, Comic Times* and *Train* for which Lewis Carroll wrote a contribution.) In the event, Gilbert only wrote two, 'Jester James' and 'The Policeman's Story', both of which lack the bite of the ballads for *Fun* in the 1860s. Gilbert in 1879 was richer, older and staider. His Nonsense had become a touch predictable.

Augustus Sala's *Temple Bar* journal launched in December 1863, initially resembled *The Cornhill* but drifted into sensation and popular stories.

'As for politics, there will not be any…the dominant tone of our journal will strive to incalculate thoroughly English sentiments – respect for authority,

[382] Christopher Hibbert, *A Social History of England*. Grafton Books, London. 1978. p627

[383] Amy Cruse, *The Victorians and Their Books*. George Allen, London. 1935. p224

attachment to the Church and loyalty to the Queen'.[384]

John Chapman launched the *Westminster Review* in 1851, as a radical campaigning journal but it never quite became the tool that Chapman envisaged; radical political roistering has never sat comfortably with the English psyche.[385] *Punch's* collective identity was operated by individual models of social stereotype. Certain stock characters 'Sweet Girl Graduate' 'Lady Doctor' 'Fast Woman' offered the then current perception that men and women occupied different spheres. Inevitably, this meant marriage was a battle between the sexes which became 'a source of endless merriment' to the writers of *Punch* – all of whom were men. But the journal's – indeed the Victorian – preoccupation with identity met with no greater challenge than Darwin. Into the scientist's theories of evolution could be read divisive consequences of race and class. *The Descent of Man* could even be taken to denigrate the women's movement through a confirmation of patriarchal attitudes, one result of which was women becoming seen as less fit in the struggle for survival.[386] The actor Gilbert unconsciously devised his own transformation of identity through ritual, pantomime and stylistic mask which we shall examine in connection with Gilbert's Nonsense in later chapters.

---

[384] Peter Blake, *The Paradox of a Periodical: Temple Bar magazine under the editorship of Augustus Sala.* Unpublished Sussex MA thesis, 2006.

[385] *Private Eye* comes close but the French *Le Canard Enchaîné* remains a model of its kind.

[386] Posterity has read this into Darwin subsequently: it may not have been much considered at the time.

BAB AND THE BISHOPS

The Victorians were religious. In 1868, there were approximately 21,500 clergymen, two Archbishops and twenty eight Diocesan Bishops for a population of sixteen million souls in England and Wales.[387] (The Church of Ireland fielded two Archbishops, ten Bishops and two thousand clergy before disestablishment in 1870: Wales became disestablished in 1920.) Today, there are around 25,000 clergymen for a UK population of nearly sixty million.

In his classic study of *The Victorian Church*, Owen Chadwick describes how Victorian scholars brooded over metaphysics and argued over moral principles, and how 'authors, painters, architects and poets seldom forgot that art and literature shadowed eternal truth and beauty, legislators professed outward and often accepted inward allegiance to Divine law, and all men of Empire ascribed national greatness to the providence of God and Protestant faith'.[388] It is precisely on account of our national religious character in the mid-nineteenth century that so many awkward questions arose and so much energy was expended on religious controversy: faith mattered. To Gilbert, faith, with all its institutional accoutrements, mattered both in particular and in general. Bab's nonsensical bishops offer harmless mockery, but there is a certain bite to the portraits of bland, boring and ineffective clerics, almost certainly demonstrating Gilbert's keen sense of personal grievance over the loss of Annie to the Rev. Pender Cudlipp.

In October, 1867, Gilbert wrote *The Rival Curates,* a Bab Ballad for *Fun,* a nonsensical tale of two curates who competed to be recognised as the milder. A fierce struggle took place between Mr Clayton Hooper of Spifton-extra-Sooper and the Reverend Hopley Porter at Assesmilk-cum-Worter before Hopley Porter was fatally corrupted by the temptation to smoke, play croquet, wink at girls and wear scent. It was one of the *Bab Ballads* the idea of which Chesterton believed to have been spoiled by *Patience,* the opera which it inspired: for Chesterton, the seed of sublime nonsense lay in the notion of men ferociously competing as to which of them is the more insipid. *Patience* altered Bab's clerics to two aesthetes, 'Bunthorne, a fleshly poet and Grosvenor, an idyllic poet'.[389]

The germ of Gilbert's joke lay in the nonsense of an intense rivalry between men, be they aesthetes or clergymen, whose nature and calling is not to have intense rivalries at all. For months, Gilbert seesawed over the choice of

---

[387] *Crockford's Clerical Directory.*

[388] Owen Chadwick, *The Victorian Church.* Vol. 1. London. A & C Black, 3rd edition, 1981. p1

[389] Original cast description for *Patience,* 23rd April, 1881.

Church or Grosvenor Gallery for his operatic protagonists. The very public debates which raged during the previous decade over Papal aggression, Tractarian influence, Evangelical Bishops and the contested authority of the Liberal or Broad Church understanding of the nature of the national Church offered almost limitless scope for fun. Clerical schisms had been seized upon and accentuated by the new mass market press which enjoyed airing doctrinal differences, then as now: nothing entertained so much as the spectacle of highly educated men in furious debate and controversy over matters which most of the population barely understood. Moreover, a kinship between the abilities required for the pulpit and the stage made clerics a natural subject for satire – clergy themselves may be seen as an extreme example of maintaining artifice, and operating devices closely related to pantomime, masque and ritual. Aesthetes had already been castigated by the *Punch* contributor Gerald du Maurier,[390] whereas a gentle clerical mockery along the lines of *All Gas and Gaiters*[391] or *Father Ted*[392] lay a hundred years distant when the fires of religious controversy had died down to a warm glow. In Gilbert's uncompleted clerical opera,[393] the Revd. Lawn Tennison[394] would attract a devoted chorus of female parishioners, contrasted with a troop of manly soldiers. The men sing, hopelessly:

'They all prefer this excellent but very prosy clergyman?
Now is this not ridiculous and is this not preposterous,
And is this not to suicide enough to urge a man.
Instead of rushing eagerly to cherish us and foster us
They all prefer this excellent and prosy clergyman'.

G & S, p282.

The maidens sigh, 'gentle vicar, hear our prayer, Twenty love-sick maidens, we'   and so on and such forth, including a tantalising couplet later in the opera featuring those essential High Church accoutrements 'The glitter ecstatic/Of cope and dalmatic'.

But Gilbert realised he was on shaky ground. In an 'Author's Note' for the American edition of *Patience,* he wrote: 'while I was engaged on the construction of this plot, I became uneasy at the danger I was incurring by dealing so freely with members of the clerical order and I felt myself crippled at every turn by the necessity of protecting myself from a charge of

---

[390] Du Maurier invented an aesthetic family, the Cimabue Browns who lived in 'passionate Brompton' and wore medieval clothes in a series of drawings for *Punch* during 1877.

[391] Celebrated BBC sitcom which ran from 1966–1971 and which featured an easy-going Bishop, an accident-prone curate, a tiddly Archdeacon and a starched Dean.

[392] Channel 4 sitcom from 1995–1998 which again featured an alcoholic layabout priest, Father Jack, a simple minded Father Dougal and Father Ted. The show won a BAFTA for Best Comedy in 1996.

[393] Ian Bradley. *The Complete and Annotated Gilbert and Sullivan.* OUP. 1996. p282

[394] Pun borrowed by Joyce in *Finnegans Wake.*

irreverence'.[395] In a letter to Arthur Sullivan in November, 1880, Gilbert described how 'I don't feel comfortable about it. I mistrust the clerical element. I feel hampered by the restrictions which the nature of the subject places upon my freedom of action'.[396] Gilbert returned to his original inspiration, perhaps subconsciously aware of a linking medievalism significant to both Pre-Raphaelite aesthetics and High Church Tractarians. The Pre-Raphaelite Brotherhood adopted biblical or medieval themes and illustrated them with minute attention to detail: Tractarians wished to return to the early pre-Reformation church unhampered by state interference; to a tradition of ecclesiastical law which offered the comfort and safety of ultimate authority on doctrinal matters.

No such doubts assailed Bab. Over twenty ballads feature clergymen: bishops, in particular. The Bishop of Rum ti Foo (distinguished in Bab by a rare sequel in which he danced the Cutch chi boo and married a native girl) ate scalps served up in rum but refused to hop holding his ankle in one hand. The Reverend Rawston Wright fanned an aesthetical flame and sang to pigs at night, the Rev. Georgie's High Church antics infuriate his Fairy Mother and Barnaby Payle, B.A., empties the church with boring sermons. Bab's sketches complete a picture of measly curates, bouncing bishops, prosy parsons and sanctimonious sermons. Gilbert, passionately objected to the affectation of parsons and their unaccountable attraction for women. Bab tells a lightly autobiographical tale of John and Freddy who dance in competition for Mary Anne.

'Decide', quoth they, 'let him be named
Who henceforth as his wife may rank you'.
'I've changed my views', the maiden said,
'I only marry curates, thank you'.

JE, p100.

And, adding insult to injury, a clergyman who disliked the stage. Several Ballads deal with the clerical strictures concerning theatre-going. One of Bab's evangelical bishops finds a curate in the stalls behind him.

'One evening, sitting at the pantomime
(Forbidden treat to those who stood in fear of him)
Roaring at jokes sans metre, sense of rhyme
He turned and saw immediately in rear of him
His peace of mind upsetting and annoying it
A curate, also heartily enjoying it'.

JE, p70.

But the curate is a phantom, the Bishop's silent conscience of his ascetic humourlessness and when the Bishop allows his clergy to watch the play, the curate vanishes, never to be seen again. Most popular entertainment on the

---

[395] James Ellis. *Complete Bab Ballads.* HUP, 1970. p333
[396] Bradley, p268.

stage was amusing and frivolous rather than instructive or ennobling. Churchmen in particular were concerned about the low educational potential that this implied, fearing harmful consequences for what was rapidly ceasing to be an essentially illiterate audience. 'In some quarters, these fears went yet deeper with plays stigmatised as directly subversive of religion, the rule of law and parental control'.[397] In a tradition dating back to the seventeenth century Nonconformist and dissenting Christians in particular disapproved of theatrical presentation, partly through a puritanical belief that acting was incompatible with earnestness and sincerity of purpose and partly in fright lest entertainment offer the mass audiences a rival attraction for hearts and minds. But the narrow piety and blanket disapproval of certain evangelicals lost them credibility. They even castigated secular literature for which they have been amply repaid by monstrous portrayals such as Charlotte Brönte's Mr Brocklehurst at Lowood, by the painful earnestness of missionary St John Rivers in *Jane Eyre* and the joyless intensity of Trollope's Josiah Crawley.

Bab's own evangelical cleric, Micah Sowles, thunders hellfire and brimstone from the pulpit in a sermon bought from London for half a crown.

> 'His armour he has buckled on to wage,
> The regulation war against the Stage
> And warns his congregation all to shun
> The presence chamber of the Evil One!'

JE, p160.

His Bishop enquires if Micah has ever actually been to the theatre and gives him a ticket for Drury Lane. Micah is confronted by 'a dreary person on the stage, who mugged and mouthed in simulated rage / Who growled and spluttered in a mode absurd /And spoke an English Sowles had never heard'. Micah is penitent.

> 'I thought I was a dreary thing
> I thought my voice quite destitute of ring
> I thought my ranting could distract the brain
> But oh, I hadn't been to Drury Lane!'

Hesketh Pearson relates how WSG once found himself in a hotel which was hosting a theological conference. 'I should think, Mr Gilbert, you must feel slightly out of place in this company' remarked a divine. 'Yes,' replied Gilbert. 'I feel like a lion in a den of Daniels'.[398]

Soon after Gilbert's birth in 1836, the Church of England began to lose its position as the 'one respectable, politically dominant creed with a virtual monopoly of higher education and intellectual life'[399] with the defection to Rome of John Henry Newman and some of those associated with him in the Oxford Movement. Despite the fact that Newman and his friends were deeply

---

[397] Michael Baker *The Rise of the Victorian Actor*. Croom Helm, London. 1978. p46

[398] Hesketh Pearson, *Gilbert and Sullivan* London, MacDonald, 1935. p126

[399] A.O.J. Cockshut, *Anglican Attitudes*. London, Collins, London. 1959. p9

spiritual men whose original aims were to preserve the sanctity and holiness of Christian practice from an increasingly liberal society and growing rational thought, they attracted a nervous and panicky opposition. No doubt it was their use of very word 'Catholic' with its resonance of papal pother which rang alarm bells – Gilbert *père* particularly distrusted what he believed to be popish interference, a prejudice passed neat to his son. In 'The Fairy Curate', a Broad Church fairy is delighted with her son's ambition to become a clergyman but he shows worrying signs of becoming 'very foolish, Papal rule-ish'.

'Time progressing, Georgie's blessing
Grew more Ritualistic.
Popish scandals, tonsures, sandals,
Genuflections, mystic.
Gushing meetings, bosom beatings,
Heavenly ecstatic.
Broidered spencers, copes and censers'…etc.

JE, p288.

Eventually, Georgie becomes a Mormon in outraged reaction against a passing Bishop who has difficulty comprehending George's ethereal maternity. Newman's eventual conversion to Roman Catholicism in 1845 was a logical reaction to concerns over State intervention in ecclesiastical matters but it is difficult for us now to understand the depth and violence of the reaction against it. New converts to Rome were called 'perverts' and when three of the evangelical Christian William Wilberforce's sons became Roman Catholic, the remaining Anglican, Samuel Wilberforce, Bishop of Oxford, wrote of his brother Henry's defection 'his broken vows and violated faith weigh heavily on my soul. May God forgive him'.[400]

No such mistrust attended the advent of the Evangelical Movement in the early nineteenth century. Traditional Anglicans might not share the crusading zeal of Methodist preachers, foreign missionaries and Christian social workers, but none could deny their reforming sincerity. Their preference for personal biblical study as opposed to an involvement in Church politics appeared to make them an unthreatening religious body and, by 1860, their compassionate work for the less privileged, specifically campaigns for anti-slavery, and popular education in slum districts, had won them acceptance, if not widespread support. Queen Victoria and Prince Albert acknowledged their Christian principles and aristocratic support came from Lord Shaftesbury who shared with Palmerston considerable influence in Church appointments. Owen Chadwick quotes Queen Victoria's *Journal* in 1838: Melbourne told her that 'Dr. Pusey and Mr. Newman were very violent people of the High Church character, that William Wilberforce and the evangelicals were enthusiasts, that all Quakers were sly, that Luther was a very questionable man, that all hermits were rogues and commonplace sermons were better than wild sermons'. No wonder the new young Queen loved a Prime Minister who could tell her that

---

[400] J.W. Burrow, 'Faith, Doubt and Unbelief.' In *The Victorians*, Ed., Laurence Lerner, London, Methuen & Co, 1978. p154.

'bishops should be young – or they go off directly and don't learn anything. Obstinate dogs, those bishops, always poking themselves into everything'.[401]

The Broad Church, or Liberal Anglicanism, represented the traditional spirit of English compromise. Their anxiety was that educated men were turned away from traditional beliefs by an inflexible, literalist approach to the Scriptures; their solution was to allow individuals their own interpretation of the Bible, trusting in the ultimate moral guide of the New Testament. Archibald Campbell Tait, Bishop of London in 1862, commented famously that the Liberals were deficient in religion and the religious were deficient in liberality.

But the real threat to all religions lay in a growing agnosticism. As one modern commentator has noted, 'most Victorian agnostics held two convictions very strongly: one was that religion, in the sense of doctrine and worship was rapidly and inevitably dying and the other was that the Christian religion, especially in its Protestant version, contained a vital core of moral truth which Christians themselves had undervalued or ignored and which nineteenth century agnostics separate out from a debilitating husk of dogma and miracle'.[402] Agnostics were plainly men and women of intellectual power and sincerity, working with the new knowledge which might make divine revelation redundant and blessed with the hallmark of progressive thought.

Gilbert was either too careful or indeed too spiritually unattached to ally himself with any one particular Victorian religious movement. His subversive nature would not have encouraged alliances with any authority, spiritual or temporal, in complete contrast to Sullivan, the young Church chorister, and *soi-disant* godchild of Mendelssohn, who happily wrote oratorios and hymn tunes.[403] Bab's priest Sir Macklin could, in every action, show, some sin and who could doubt him? He argued high, he argued low and argued round about him. In similar vein, Bab explains how Mr Blake, that hardened sinner who only went to Church two or three times a week and who;

'was quite indifferent to the kinds of dresses
That clergymen wore at the Church where he used to go to pray
And whatever he did to relieve a chap's distresses
He always did in a nasty, sneaking, underhanded, hole in the corner sort of way'

JE, p212.

Mr Blake's supremely Christian 'good by stealth' actions subvert Victorian Church mores in yet another example of Bab upholding convention by nonsensical reversal.

---

[401] Chadwick, p160

[402] A.O.J. Cockshut, *Anglican Attitudes* .London, Collins, 1959. p24

[403] Sullivan's Oratorios include 'The Prodigal Son,' (1869) with a scriptural libretto, and 'The Golden Legend' (1886) with text adapted from a Longfellow poem concerning the fall of Lucifer. Hymns include tunes for 'Angel Voices Ever Singing,' 'Love Divine All Loves Excelling' and 'Crown Him with Many Crowns'.

Max Keith Sutton has written that 'Bab's sense of nature's unconcern leads to a deeper implication: that no Providential force cares for the rights and wrongs of human action'.[404] In fact, Bab's position is that of a detached and ironical observer, tolerant of and amused by, all religious extremism. (The plot sketch for *Utopia Ltd.* includes plans to abolish religious differences and put all clergymen out of work.[405]) Bab's stance is one of pragmatic realism confronted by topsy-turvy morals. When Sir Herbert and a policeman illustrate the science of phrenology on a burglar, they discover that;

'Just here the bump appears, of innocent hilarity,
and just behind his ears, are Faith and Hope and Charity!
He, of true Christian ways, a bright example sent us.
This maxim, he obeys – *sorte tua contentus sis'.* [406]

JE, p290.

Sir Herbert, you will by now expect, has a head
'that teems with inhumanity,
with Murder, Envy, Strife, propensity to kill any'.

Bab might not align himself with a specific religious creed or group – but he did believe in moral duty, an outlook closely linked to justice and fair play and related to Christianity. Christian morals are based either on the life, death and resurrection of Jesus or the Jewish Torah as exemplified by the Decalogue, or Ten Commandments. Bab is conscious of a Jewish tradition of learning which might occasionally prove superior to a workaday Anglican cleric:

'In an otherwise empty pew
Sat a respectable Jew
His starting eyeballs glistened
Despite dissent, with best attent

---

[404] Max Keith Sutton, *WSG*. Boston, Twayne, 1975. p34
[405] Baily, p201
[406] In translation; 'be content with your lot'.

That Hebrew person listened'.

JE, p172.

The tedious Reverend Barney Payle drones on, ultimately providing the thoughtful Hebrew person with a clerical caricature. We do well to remember the philosemitism of Gilbert *père* and the fact of Jewish emancipation in 1858. Bab offered an ambivalent attitude towards Judaism with the stock cliché of an hairy and richly schnozzled,

'Jew, who drove a Putney bus
For flesh of swine, however fine,
He did not care a cuss'.

JE, p104.

After seven years of bullying by a proselytising Bishop, the Jew converts to Christianity and marries the Bishop's daughter. Equally bent on saving souls is Bab's Reverend Simon Magus,

'A Jew' said Simon 'happy find!'
I shall purchase this advowson mind.
My life shall be devoted to
Converting that unhappy Jew'.

JE. p279.

But it is the notion of duty which inspires one of Bab's most celebrated Ballads. In 'Captain Reece', the gallant sailor goes to extraordinary lengths to make his crew happy.

'By any reasonable plan, I'll make you happy, if I can
My own convenience, count as nil, it is my Duty and I will'.

JE, p143.

The captain orders currant wine and ginger pops, library books, warm slippers and hot water bottles. Finally, he agrees to marry his own family to various crew members and marries the boatswain's mother himself, even though,

'My daughter, that enchanting girl
Has just been promised to an Earl
And all my other familee
To Peers of various degree.'

JE, p143.

Duty calls and Bab pays heed, acknowledging the one supreme achievement of the established Church in the mid-nineteenth century – the alliance of two words not inevitably or invariably connected: Christian Duty. This concept was underlined by education. The new wave of Public Schools, or 'Elevated Grammar Schools' was largely instigated by clerics and almost entirely staffed by them. Nathaniel Woodard, banned from his curacy in Bethnall Green, for 'Romish' views, planned an ambitious series of boarding schools with a strong religious emphasis which would encompass the entire country; eleven, including Lancing and Hurstpierpoint were actually established.[407] G.E.L. Cotton, D.D., Master of Marlborough in 1852 (a young master in *Tom Brown's School Days,* set in the 1830s but published in 1857) was celebrated for his sermons, many of which were published, setting a new fashion in Victorian literature. Through school sermons, the public judged the tone of the school and the Church estimated the headmaster's suitability for preferment.[408] Virtually all secondary and tertiary educational institutions in the United Kingdom were originally founded to train clergy for the Established Protestant Church. Dean Farrar, author of the 'feverishly earnest' [409]*Eric or Little by Little*, was a Housemaster at Harrow in 1858. (For Kipling's irreverent schoolboys in *Stalky and Co,* 'Ericking' became a synonym for

---

[407] J.A. Mangan, *Athleticism in the Victorian and Edwardian Public S*chool. CUP. 1981. p36

[408] Ibid.

[409] Norman Vance, *The Sinews of the Spirit: The Ideal of Christian Manliness in Victorian Literature and Religious Thought*. CUP 1985. p169

pious twaddle.)[410]

Gilbert was aware of the social implications that religion involved: he knew that the leaders in all classes not only respected religion but identified with it. Although the indifferent masses rarely went to Church, suffering from a belief that Christian religion was a middle and upper class preserve, most working class leaders believed that the mission of Christianity was to bring them freedom and social justice. The only question remaining was how this object could be promoted?[411] In one sense, the established Church was a bastion of class privilege and the idea that it operated social distinction was founded on fact. Clergymen with well-endowed rectories and vicarages ranked with the gentry in socio-economic status.[412] (Even if notably less wealthy). Some succumbed to the additional temptation to become JPs or commissioners. Bab's Reverend Simon Magus is careful not to appear too grasping about his rectory.

> 'A poor apostle's humble house
> Must not be too luxurious.
> No stately halls with oaken floor
> It should be decent and no more'.

JE, p278

Ambitious young men could gain instant social acceptance as clerics: all doors opened to the sons of gentlemen if they possessed education and learning even without wealth or influence. Humanity and compassion were the acceptable equivalents of money and status – but there was sufficient real charity to prevent the Anglican Church from being wholly identified with privilege during the 1860s. Ambition, never an easy trait to reconcile with Christianity, might carry a clergyman into a bishop's palace and into the comical costume and mores beloved of Gilbert and his accomplice in clerical nonsense, Bab.

Real bishops in the 1860s sat uncomfortably between the established Anglican Church and the State. They were no longer appointed for blatantly political reasons but 'a prime minister would naturally not promote a man who would oppose him'[413] and Palmerston, influenced by the evangelical Lord Shaftesbury, took care to appoint sober Evangelicals of no particular bias and no great distinction in learning who would put their Sees before their politics. The scholarly merit of many bishops was not necessarily accompanied by great originality of thought, which, combined with a never-ending workload, made it all too likely for their efforts to be reduced to the humdrum activities of a public official. Their quiescent leadership encouraged Bab to mock the twenty eight bishops as ineffective and slightly ridiculous figureheads, more

---

[410] Vance, p193

[411] Desmond Bowen, *The Idea of the Victorian Church*. Montreal, McGill U.P. 1968. p253

[412] Anecdotally, primogenitural families organised sons into the army, the navy and the church.

[413] Crowther, p141

concerned with maintaining appearances and overseas missions than with leading their flocks or challenging doctrine. (Patently unfair when most bishops were old, the roads were bad and travel to outlying parishes on horseback was awkward.)

The Bishop of Rum Ti Foo plays the tum and eats scalps served up in rum. He learns to dance to please the Rum Ti Foozleites but refuses to learn to hop. Bab's colonial cleric in 1869 echoes the English Bishop Colenso of Natal who incurred establishment wrath by a liberal interpretation of the Scriptures, particularly in connection to polygamy. Colenso, a wise and learned missionary, dealt flexibly with some unsettling questions from native Africans and championed Zulu codes and conducts for which he was excommunicated by Bishop Grey of Cape Town in 1863. (We shall meet Colenso again in Section Three of this thesis, as the author of the Beaver's arithmetic homework in Carroll's *The Hunting of the Snark,* p79)

'No', said the worthy Bishop, no, 'that is a length, to which I trow
Colonial Bishops cannot go.
You may express surprise, at finding Bishops deal in pride
But if that trick I ever tried, I should appear undignified
In Rum ti Foozle's eyes.'

JE, p127.

Later, the Bishop dresses the natives in his old gaiters and meets them half way by 'dressing up in cowries rare and wearing feathers in his hair'. Most mid-nineteenth century bishops struggled to find an acceptable compromise amidst secular liberalism, materialistic industrialism, sceptical empricism, Tractarian rigidity, evangelical purity, Broad Church flexibility and working class indifference. Maybe cowrie shells were the answer after all.

BAB AND JOHNNY FOREIGNER

B ab's frequent engagement with foreigners concentrates on just three ideas: France, Africa and the Orient. None of his Nonsense features Indians, Americans, Australians, or the Chinese; not even stock music hall stereotypes such as German baker, Italian tenor, Russian tailor, or Polish Count lurk in Gilbert's contributions to *Fun, Punch* or the *London Graphic* during the 1860s. Superficially, Bab deals in cliché. The French are beautifully dressed cowards, Africans are naked savages and all Turks are bloodthirsty heathens, familiar ideas designed for the reassurance of a middle class English readership in a comfortable armchair. Even the occasional Scotsman predictably wears a kilt, plays bagpipes badly and mangles English. Gilbert's ideas about 'abroad' come from periodicals and pantomime: unlike Edward Lear, he never travelled and apart from a boyhood spell in Boulogne, never crossed the Channel.

The Ballads contain none of the ironical, xenophobic extremism found in Gilbert's libretti for the Savoy Operas.

'He might have been a Roosian,
A French, or Turk or Prussian
Or perhaps Italian!
But in spite of all temptations,
To belong to other nations,
He remains an Englishman'.

HMS Pinafore, Act 11.
G & S. p171

Russians, Frenchmen, Turks, Prussians and Italians would have been the most familiar foreign countries and concepts for all Englishmen during the 1850s and 1860s. Newspaper reports of the Crimea dramatised Russia and Turkey: the King of Prussia was Queen Victoria's son-in-law: King Louis-Philippe of France had been usurped by a new Bonaparte in 1848, and Italy battled towards unification.

Just as Bab's more pungent ridicule of the clergy was made possible by the selective readership of *Fun*, Bab was allowed to endorse certain foreign ethics and standards which a popular audience in the theatre might have found unacceptable. In fact, they are only 'foreign' by the merest cliché symbolism, just as every 'Japanese' official in *The Mikado* belongs to the English Civil

Service. Real Japanese drama, news of a minor revolution in Japan when the Daimos revolted and made the Mikado prisoner would never be reflected by Gilbert.[414] Both Bab and Gilbert are allowed a theatrical liberty to ridicule the English for their snobbery, materialism and hypocrisy, but Bab has a deep and inviolable love of his country, reflected in Lord Montararat's Handelian hymn in *Iolanthe* or Koko's victim 'who praises with enthusiastic tone/Every century but this, and every country but his own'.[415] Iolanthe's rousing patriotism seems make an ironic virtue of the English mistrust for intellectual ability.

'When Britain really ruled the waves
(In Good Queen Bess's time)
The House of Peers made no pretence
To intellectual eminence
Or scholarship sublime.
Yet Britain won her proudest bays
In good Queen Bess's glorious days!'

Iolanthe, Act II.
G & S, p417.

Bab actually believes that the human condition transcends national boundaries and humanity, a condition about which he *pretends* not to have illusions. In fact, corruption, cowardice and hypocrisy are to be found everywhere. 'Brave Alum Bey', a foreign potentate, swears never to take off his cork clothes in an oath to remain faithful to Backsheesh and when his ship founders in a hareem, he floats to safety, refusing to share a cork with his English travellers who drown. Eventually, they are fished up by the anchor, more or less alive. 'Sir Guy The Crusader' loves Leonore, a Saracen Maiden:

'Brunette, statuesque,
The reverse of grotesque,
Her pa was a bagman from Aden
Her mother, she played in burlesque'.

JE, p95.

But gallant Sir Guy fails to prevent 'the turbaned old Turk' from regularly hitting his daughter with a carpet beater and is obliged to run away to London, leaving Leonore to marry the stage prompter. The tale is based on the legendary Guy, Earl of Warwick whose exploits included an adventure-filled expedition to the Holy Land.[416]

The geographical isolation of England cannot isolate the English from sharing the same decency – or snobbery – as the 'Three Kings of Chickeraboo'. Three black Africans, Pacifico, Bang-Bang and Porkchop establish their territories on beer barrels and give themselves Royal Rank which entitles them to the limitless respect of Rear Admiral Bailey Pip.

---

[414] *Illustrated London News*, February 22nd, 1868

[415] W.S. Gilbert, *The Mikado*. G & S, p573

[416] Ellis, p328

'Great Britain's Navy scours the sea
And everywhere her ships may be
She'll recognise our rank, perhaps
when she discovers we're Royal Chaps'.

JE, p139.

Royalty is the ultimate British weapon and no matter what custom, creed or country, all are susceptible. In 'The King of Canoodle-Dum' a wandering sailor persuades Calamity Von Peppermint Drop, an African Chieftain, that he is William IV from the North of England. (A sensible impersonation: William was known in his old age as the Sailor King)

'Calamity Pop most wisely
Determined in everything
To model his Court precisely
On that of the English King'.

JE, p236.

Whereupon, the Canoodle Dums chew tobacco, dance the hornpipe, swear carefully, shiver their timbers and drink rum. All is undone when Admiral Chickabiddy lands on the island and William 1V is unmasked and carried off in chains. An African King 'Borria Bungalee Boo', one of Bab's fantastical names which derives from simple and perjorative English roots – bore, bungle and boo - proves immune to the feminine wiles of Queen Tippity Wippity Tol the Rol Loo with her enticing Amazon maidens and eats them for dinner. The English, says the Nonsense of Bab, came, saw and conquered Africa: regardless.

Neither Gilbert nor Bab could be unaware of the opening up of the African continent during the 1860s. David Livingstone crossed the continent from Zambezi and discovered the Victoria Falls in 1855; three years later, Richard Burton and John Speke journeyed into Africa to discover Lake Tanganyika and Victoria Nyanza which Speke believed to be the source of the White Nile. Livingstone's fourth expedition lasted four years. His believed disappearance captured the imagination of the nation and when Henry Stanley found him on the shores of Lake Tanganyika in 1871, their opening encounter passed into history. More intrepid English adventurers who made headlines for their exploits in Africa included James Brooke, the British White Rajah of Sararwak, and Richard Burton, appointed Consul of Fernando Po, an island off Africa's West Coast in 1868.

Richard Burton achieved fame in the 1870s with a complete English translation of *The Arabian Nights*. Some were reproduced in *Fraser's Magazine* during the 1860s, but the tales Scheherazade told to save her life from the Sultan had existed in chapbook form since the 1750s and had become a childhood staple for educated families. The simple plots became pantomime fodder – *Sinbad the Sailor, Aladdin and His Magical Lamp* and *Ali Baba and the Forty Thieves*. Bab tells a Nonsensical version of one of them in 'Prince Agib', (1868). In the real Arabian Night version, Prince Agib's fate resembles something dreamt up by Gilbert. He accidentally kills a young man with a knife he was trying to eat a melon with and is forced to escape revenge by hiding in a sheep's skin: a great rok carries him away to various adventures but ultimately his insatiable curiosity causes him to lose the sight in one eye. The ballad is written in seventeen limericks, a most unusual construction for Bab and one which may relate to Edward Lear's second *Book of Nonsense* in 1871. Gilbert knew Lear's limericks and wrote a parody: this ballad could be a competitive demonstration of a master lyricist and composer of ever more imaginative flights of fancy. Nonsense based on an Arabian fantasy is a potent combination. Bab's Agib, Prince of Tartary, is a musician visited by minstrels, the 'ouaits'.

'They played him a sonata, let me see,
Medulla oblongata, key of G.
Then they began to sing
That extremely lovely thing
Scherzando! Ma non troppo, ppp'

JE, p164.

Agib feeds them beer and eggs and sweets and tin before they reveal a different identity but the narrator who is listening through a keyhole, is whipped with a cat-o'nine-tails and never knows what happened.

Bab's violent Turks are a delightful stereotype whose terrifying illustration can confound expectation. Armourer Ben Ouseff in 'The Sensation Twins' is a peaceful soul forced to oblige the twins by cutting them in half. 'Simple James' is actually a 'gay Mongolian dog' as Bab cannot pronounce Turkish names: he cannot invent them either as 'Pasha Bailey Ben' derives from the 'Old Bailey' and 'Big Ben' and the brave Alum Bey is named after a rocky islet off the Isle of Wight.

Gilbert spent part of his boyhood in Boulogne where he attended a junior school. The town had belonged to the English during the reign of Henry lll and remained a popular holiday location for English travellers. Bab wrote a sensible Ballad about it in 1868.

'Of all the snug places where the hardworking races rush off every summer, a crop of 'em,
I think that you will own that delightful Boulogne may be said to stand quite at the   top of 'em.
It's conveniently near and it's not overdear so your purse won't need much reimbursing,
You can sit on a park bench and learn how to speak French just from hearing the natives conversing.'

JE, p187.

The metre is an unusual one for Bab and has a direct descendant in Ogden Nash. Undoubtedly, Gilbert spoke French and possibly better than 'Lorenzo di Lardy' in his Nonsensical courtship of the Dam du Comptore, alias Mademoiselle de la Sauce Mayonnaise. The tale is based on two Victorian clichés that probably still exist: firstly, that poverty-struck rank can command rich women and that Frenchwomen symbolise heartless and opportunistic flirtation.

'Coraline Celestine Eulalie
Houp la! je vous aime, oui, mossoo,
Combien donnez moi aujourd'hui,
Bonjour, Mademoiselle, parlez-vous'.

Coraline's English is worse.

'Oh my, pretty man, if you please,
Blom boodin, biftek, currie lamb,
Bouldogue, two franc half, quite ze cheese
Rosbif, me spik Angleesh, godam'.

JE, p102.

(Just in case a modern reader imagines that Franglais was invented by Miles Kington.) *Punch* felt similarly inspired on December 11th 1869 with an account of 'Lamparatreece Eujayneee's Tour of the East' in which the inveterate correspondent pronounced himself 'meal paradong mong share, song meal parrdong.Voo nayte par trrompay par mwaw. Dewtoo, dew too'. Several Bab Ballads feature Boulogne for which Gilbert clearly retained an affectionate memory. Although he was as English as any man that ever lived, he did not share a view, common to many of his countrymen, that *Punch* expressed in July 24th 1869;

'Give me an English dinner, plain.
Substantial roast and boiled for me
French toys and kickshaws I disdain
Says many a man, and no fool he'.

Queen Victoria came to the Pas de Calais in 1843 when Gilbert would have been seven. One can only speculate that the Royal procession to legitimise the Orleans dynasty (Queen Victoria's first cousin Victoria of Saxe Coburg and Gotha married Louis Phillipe's second son, the Duc de Nemours) would have stopped in Boulogne and been welcomed by cheering schoolchildren, Gilbert amongst them. His devotion to Victoria – we LOVE our Queen[417] – appears heartfelt and genuine.

We have seen that Bab's view of abroad was limited by circumstance, informed by cliché and wholly subjective. 'Foreigners' are only the English dressed differently – or, if they are African, not dressed at all. Their costumes and habits are a distraction to what Bab's Nonsense is really about: infinite, unvarnished reality, sometimes in mirror image as in the monstrous appetites of the savages which match the colonising greed of nineteenth century Westerners, sometimes in the straightforward prostitution of Delilah de Lardy whose money persuades the noble Lord to marry her instead of the young French Mademoiselle de la Sauce Mayonnaise he so plainly prefers. (Who, in the event, is represented as not caring a farthing about whichever suitor comes her way.)

Gilbert could not escape the Victorian view of England as the centre of the world nor the arrogant superiority with which Bab observes 'Johnny Foreigner'. But we need to remember that in the 1860s–1870s , England was an empire upon which the sun never set (the reason cited was that God didn't trust the English in the dark) and that the map was pink from Cape to Cairo. Few could have foreseen the collapse, disgrace and dishonour of a postcolonial world a century ahead: it is ironic that Bishop Colenso, once castigated for native sympathies, should now be revered and Cecil Rhodes should be exposed as a butchering raider. Bab, 2008 version, would be delighted.

---

[417] *Pirates of Penzance*, Act ll. G & S, p261

The British Character; Adaptability to Foreign Conditions. Pont, (Graham Laidler), Punch, April 4th 1934.

BAB AND THE WOMAN QUESTION

Gilbert's education in an all-boys school, followed by short stints in the civil service and at the Bar, combined with a lifelong attendance to the militia and various masculine clubs might have been expected to inhibit feminine comprehension: certainly any understanding beyond the most respectable conventions would seem unlikely, if not impossible. Mitigating circumstances were three younger sisters, his love affair with a 'lady novelist' and a theatrical career with actors of all sexes.[418] In fact, Gilbert enjoyed the company of women 'especially intelligent ones' and was attractive to them.[419] He was handsome and upright - the very model of a modern man of action and his marriage to Lucy Blois Turner was long and happy. (Sullivan belonged to the H.L. Mencken school of bachelors who understand women far too well to marry them.[420])

Yet Gilbert has traditionally been criticised for his 'heartless' portrayals of plain older women by those perhaps unaware that Gilbert's critical principles did not allow a male comedian in drag to portray the older woman in farce.[421] Gilbert saw life as it was, and not as either the audience for his theatrical burlesques or posterity might wish it to be. Today, the primness of political correctness enters the arena – no doubt Katisha and Little Buttercup would be described as 'visually challenged' rather than elderly and tough. (Interestingly, 'heartless' Ballad portrayals of older, plainer, sillier men have not attracted the same reactions.) Nonsense operates in the *Bab Ballads* as a cloak for some uncomfortable realities, even as a nod towards feminism and the independence of women beyond being groomed for servitude and slavery. Bab does more than mock conventional sexual mores: he presents alternative scenarios in shorthand for nearly a third of the ballads. A patriarchal society in 1850 might attempt to commodify women for the marriage market but Gilbert suggests that women have choices and may make them, even in opposition. Contemporary heroines in literature achieved status for similar declarations of independence – Dorothea Brooke does not marry Sir James Chettam, neither did Jane Eyre marry St. John Rivers.[422] The modern reader also needs to be aware that Gilbert worked in one of the only professions during the 1860s

---

[418] Included by WSG in Koko's little list of society offenders who never would be missed. *The Mikado*. G & S, p571.

[419] Stedman, p41

[420] Mencken was a great admirer of Gilbert, writing in *The Baltimore Evening Sun*, May 30th, 1911, that WSG was a worthy successor to Aristophanes and Rabelais.

[421] Stedman, p.78.

[422] Dorothea marries the 'great bladder to rattle dried peas in' and Jane marries an older widower with one eye and a shady past.

where women and men met on equal terms – the stage.

With hindsight, it appears that the mid-Victorians found gender issues just as complex and insoluble as we do. A simple conception of male patriarchy as defined by images of powerful facial hair and large passive families belongs to *The Monarch of the Glen* and Prince Albert. The truth was inevitably far more various and troubled.

'Oh, that my soul, its gods could see
as years ago they seemed to me
when first I painted them;
invested with the circumstance
of old conventional romance;
exploded theorem!'

'Disillusioned.' JE, p98.

The expressions 'gender politics' and 'homosexual relations' may not have existed in 1850 but the concepts were real enough. The 'separate spheres' of development, principally caused by industrialisation in the late eighteenth century, removed women from the workplace and men from the family. Both men and women searched conscientiously for new roles in a changing world where former certainties had vanished along with horse-drawn transport and the domestic loom: both sexes suffered equally in the new national and collective ethos of application to progressive tasks with the single aim of furthering industry and making money. This concentration of ability towards commercial concerns was most particular in nineteenth century England, and herein lies one clue for the Nonsense of the 1850s–1870s: society needed a jester to wave his cap and bells at the Nonsense which put commerce first and civilisation second. [423]

Yet feminists in their idealistic ambition to become acknowledged and accepted as the intellectual and professional equals of man, disinherited themselves at a stroke from traditional bastions of female power. In *Victorian Heroines*, Nicola Humble reminds us that 'the feminine ideal was empowering as well as enfeebling and the Victorian woman who wanted control over her body, her health and the size and wellbeing of her family had much to gain from a cultural construction which made her sexually remote'.[424] Frances Mary Buss, Sophie Jex-Blake and Barbara Bodichon 'were all driven by the conviction that, given the appropriate training, women might aspire to levels of success in academic and practical life on a par with those achieved by men'.[425] Men, in their desire to escape the thralldom of a petticoat nursery, a period of

---

[423] Lord Chesterfield wrote to his son in 1749 that 'commerce was the enemy of English culture' and as such it probably remains.

[424] Nicola Humble and Kimberley Reynolds, *Victorian Heroines*. New York, Harvester Press, 1993.

[425] Carol Dyhouse 'The Role of Women', *The Victorians*, edited by Laurence Lerner, London, Methuen. 1978. p178

feminine influence extended by education and later marriage, evolved elaborate initiation rites of schools, clubs, armies, colonies and professions. This lent them a spurious masculinity but one which divided them from womankind in all but the most necessary or the most trivial concerns.

'The Woman Question' began to occupy the minds of mid-Victorian reformers, (most notably J.S. Mill) and to address issues of marriage, property ownership, the franchise and external employment: combining marriage and employment outside the home was scarcely seen as a possibility for an aspiring bourgeoisie in 1860.[426]

'The Man Question' was seldom debated in similar terms, yet Victorian masculinities were beset with as many quandaries as those suffered by women. (A growing body of work has developed over the past decade to redress the balance.[427]) An inherent tension existed between the desire to achieve middle/upper class status 'as manifested in the amassing of wealth, in marriage as an elegant domesticity and in the new nineteenth century formation of masculinity, the professional man' and the romantic ideal of the male artist/writer as a detached observer.[428] Further complications ensued with a new romantic attitude to the dignity of physical work as machines removed craft from life and vice versa. Ford Maddox Brown spent ten years from 1856–1865 on the monumental canvas *Work,* an elaborate allegory on the contrast between mental and manual labour. It depicts muscled diggers watched by Thomas Carlyle, who 'seems to be idle, but is engaged upon a work which shall be the cause of well-ordained work and happiness in others'.[429]

Carlyle's theories of male bonding and powerful masculine role models might appear dangerously close to homo-social and homo-erotic boundaries, the state of affairs in *Past and Present* (1843) where a monk represents Carlyle's heroic ideal of a celibate who disciplines desire, and whose power derives from a knowledge and understanding exclusive to his brotherhood.[430] Religion and gender might make uneasy bedfellows but they remain inseparable: 'friendships in Christ stimulated masculine intimacy in a disembodied fashion' and a focus on the beauty of the transcendent body of Christ resolved many a more personal masculine desire.[431]

Bab duly mocks the accepted practices of mid-Victorian marriage in the middle and upper-middle classes 'the decorative packaging of consumption

---

[426] Until the Married Women's Property Act of 1882, all a woman's money and property belonged automatically to her husband unless prior settlement had been made.

[427] Donald E.Hall, in particular, with titles including *Fixing Patriarchy: Feminism + Mid-Victorian Male Novelists,* 1996, and *Muscular Christianity: Embodying the Victorian Age.* 1994. Joseph Bristow has joined the debate as Editor of the *Cambridge Companion to Victorian Poetry,* 2000.

[428] Herbert Sussman, *Victorian Masculinities.* CUP, 1995. p114

[429] Lionel Lamborne, *Victorian Painting.* London, Phaidon. 1991,p 241

[430] Sussman, p38

[431] Richard Dellamora, *Masculine Desire and Sexual Politics of Victorian Aestheticism,* University of North Carolina Press. 1990. p46/47

goods for display'[432] and the desperate desire to marry rank and title. In 'The Periwinkle Girl', Mary's considerable allure, nonsensically represented by the quantity of winkles that admirers are obliged to eat, makes

'both high and low and great and small
fell prostrate at her tootsies
they were all Noblemen and all
Had balances at Coutts's'.

But when Periwinkle Mary realises that Duke Bailey and Duke Humphy can only offer her the guilty splendour of an unwed liaison, she is forced to consider a third suitor,

'a man of lowly station
A miserable, groveling Earl
Besought her approbation.
He'd had, it happily befell,
A decent education.
His views would have befitted well
A far superior station'.

JE, p141.

Mary cuts her losses and marries the Earl, memorably remarking 'come Virtue in an earldom's cot, go Vice in ducal mansion!' Sir Barnaby Bampton Boo,[433] last of a noble race, who is coming to woo at the deuce of a pace, knows that for a 'a baronet, dears, you would cut off your ears' and is thus able to marry the 'terribly pert and vain' instead of Milly, 'the good and the plain'. Even Gregory Parable, LL.D., a grave and learned scholar he, is not immune from father's duty to his child.

---

[432] Dyhouse, p.177
[433] Ellis, p185

'To see his daughters richly wed
To dignitaries of the earth.
If possible, of noble birth…
And failing that, to wed her to, a Boucicault or a Baring which
Means anyone who's very rich'.

JE, 193.

(Note the alliterative pairing of playwright and banker, both allegedly wealthy, and both familiar names in Victorian society.) But an Earl he has in mind thinks they are drunk and sends them packing, whereupon the lodger who captured the heart of his daughter whilst Parable was engrossed thus, with the vocative of *filius*,[434] turns out to be the Duke of Gretna Green.

Gilbert subverts conventional gender-based expectation in a selection of *Bab Ballads* in which women choose their mates, prefer eating to sex, rule the roost, marry burglars, or pretend their husband is a budgerigar. Worst of all, women might behave just like men: very badly indeed. Female independence is given an airing, no less effective for being Nonsensical as well as being something that Gilbert had painfully encountered himself. Choice is illustrated by the Ballad of 'Old Paul and Old Tim' who are equally wealthy and equally old, equally timid and equally bold and whom neither are a suitable match for Emily who declares;

'She told them she'd marry whichever might bring
Good proofs of his doing the pluckiest thing'.

JE, p299.

And settles for Paul who has boxed little boys' ears instead of Tim who struggles to make Frenchmen 'in scores who ought to be guarding their cities and shores', an ironic comment on the failure of the French soldiery to rally to arms. In 'The Way of Wooing' a pretty girl sits in a window spurning elegant compliments and finally selects the gallant 'suitor poor with homely face who rode up at a startling pace' illustrating Gilbert's constantly re-appearing mantra that 'faint heart never won fair lady'.

Bab tells the tale of John and Freddy, two brothers competing for the hand of Mary Ann who declares she will marry whichever of them dances longest. Here is a recreation of the medieval trials undergone to prove love, an idea familiar from Schikenader's libretto for the *Magic Flute* when Tamino must go through fire and danger to win Pamina, or even from nursery rhymes which suggest that kissing frogs or scaling thorn bushes are necessary trials of purpose to win handsome mates. Despite Freddy and Johnny's commitment and energy, they are pilloried by a passing curate who,

'trembles for each dancing frater
Like unregenerated Clown
And harlequin at some the-ayter'.

JE, p100.

---

[434] Norman Vance explains that the awkward 'filie' is often contracted to 'fili'.

Freddy and Johnny pass out with exhaustion and Mary Ann marries the curate, leaving Bab to suggest pragmatically that when she's buried <u>him</u>, she will return to either Freddy or Johnny. In 'To My Bride' Fortune sings to Bab's 'bachelor of two and thirty, and when you're intimate, you call him Bertie'. We have met Bertie Carlyon the hero in one of Annie Thomas' novels supposedly based on Gilbert. Bab's 'Bertie' is more than a touch autobiographical. He is,

'working mildly at the Bar
After a touch at two or three professions
From easy affluence extremely far
A brief or two on Circuit – soup at sessions.
A pound or two from whist and backing horses
And say, three hundred from his own resources.
Quiet in harness, free from serious vice,
His faults are not particularly shady
You'll never find him shy – for once or twice,
Already he's been driven by a lady who parts with him,
Perhaps a poor excuse for him - because she hasn't any further use for him.'[435]

JE, p86.

Bab affects scorn concerning those aspects usually considered important in a bride.
'Oh, bride of mine – tall, dumpy, dark or fair
Oh, widow – wife, maybe, or blushing maiden...
Say, must I wait til husband number one
Is comfortably stowed away at Woking?[436]
How is her hair most usually done?
And tell me, please, will she object to smoking?'

JE, p87.

Another trial for love is demonstrated by the 'Ballad of Ferdinando and Elvira' where Ferdinando must prove his affection and make Elvira chose him instead of 'noblemen in coronets and military cousins, and captains by the hundreds and baronets by dozens' not by enduring 'polar bears or hot volcanic grottoes, but finding out who wrote those lovely cracker mottoes'. Eventually, a pastry cook 'who chirped and sang and skipped about and laughed with laughter hearty, he was wonderfully active for so very stout a party' declares himself to be the author of the cracker jokes and enables Ferdinand to win Elvira.

Bab's Fanny and Jenny enjoy solitary dinners in competing restaurants,

---

[435] Aaaah... Bab in unfamiliar victim mode.

[436] The London Necropolis Company burial ground was established between Brookwood and Woking in 1850, and sanctioned by Act of Parliament in 1852. Special trains ran direct from Waterloo.

Jenny 'ordering beef and potatoes as well, and cut off the joint until senseless she fell' whilst Fanny, with an airier taste, swallowed plum pudding all day. Anxiety over reactions from the restaurants makes both women decide that

'such youth and such beauty as both of us own
Are safe in the walls of a convent alone'.

JE, p108.

and they retire to a nunnery. Appetites of all kinds were unseemly in certain Victorian households, and the strict and fashionable corsets made them almost impossible. Whilst the ballad tells one story, Bab's illustration tells another: both women pictured tucking into vast plates of dinner are stick thin.

In 1865, Ruskin published a series of lectures he gave in Manchester to aid the foundation of a library at the Rusholme Institute and to help raise money for additional schools in the slum districts of Ancoats. Entitled *Sesame and Lilies*, the book proved to be his most popular and enduring publication – and a minefield. The most familiar quotations concern the role of women as ministering angels, wise not for self-development but for self-renunciation and whose place remains glued to their husbands and their hearths. Yet read more carefully, Ruskin is contradictory. Women's power is for rule, not battle, he declared, stirring up a hornets' nest that has buzzed ever since. Ruskin's own failed marriage and descent into madness might invalidate his theories, but I doubt it, and so did Gilbert. Bab knew that frivolity was often a front; women not only rule, but they might do battle, too.

In *Babette's Love*, a French fisher girl ignores the suit of a Customs Officer at Boulogne and falls for a British sailor who hangs around the port. His captain declares the tar must act in honour and marry Babette.

'Not so, unless you're fond of strife.
I have an able-bodied wife
awaiting me at Wapping stairs.
If all this here to her I tell,
She'll larrup me and you as well
the other sailors of the crew
They always calls her 'Whopping Sue'
'Oho, the Captain said,' I see,
And is she then so very strong?
She'd take your Honour's scruff,' said he,
'And pitch you over to Bolong'.
'I pardon you' the Captain said,
'The fair Babette you needn't wed',

JE, p106.

Another battle-axe is, literally, employed by 'a skilled mechanic, who was famous in his day – a gentle executioner whose name was Gilbert Clay'. In the ballad 'Annie Protheroe' (1868), Bab tells the story of Clay's love for Annie, and his sadistic pleasure in the knowledge that he is to decapitate her former swain, Peter Grey. But when Annie watches him lacerating the edge of the axe with sulphuric acid, she produces a reprieve with a flourish, saves Peter and marries him instead. Woman's power is limitless, warns Bab, impugn it at your peril. The Ballad of 'Gentle Alice Brown', (1868), is about another young woman with a murky past who has,

'helped Mamma to steal a little kiddy from its Dad
And assisted dear Papa in cutting up a little lad
I've planned a little burglary and forged a little cheque
And slain a little baby for the coral on its neck'.

JE, p166.

A kindly curate with a fondness for the real business of saving burglars, knows that Alice is promised to another young robber and that her partiality to a young Customs Sorter must be dealt with;

'The worthy priest he up and drew, his cowl upon his crown
And started off in haste to tell the news to Robber Brown
To tell him how his daughter who was now for marriage fit
Had winked upon a Sorter who reciprocated it'.

The sorter is summarily chopped up and dissected leaving Alice to marry the burglar and live happily ever after at everyone else's expense. (The pleasure of her father at the match is Bab's joke at patriarchal control.)

The reader never meets Mrs Bagg but understands from 'Baines Carew, Gentlemen', that his legal skills and personal sympathy are powerless to protect Captain Bagg from the calumny of his wife.

'Domestic bliss has proved my bane
A harder case you've never heard
My wife, in other matters sane,
Pretends that I'm a dicky bird!'

JE, p131.

Bab's drawing of Captain Bagg gives Mrs. Bagg a certain leeway, but it is clear she goes too far.

'She places sugar in my way
In public places calls me sweet
She gives me groundsel every day
And hard canary seed to eat.'

The case convulses the sympathetic Attorny Baines whereupon the gallant Captain toddles off to a tougher lawyer.

Bab's anti-hero 'Lorenzo De Lardy' abandons love for money, the young officer in 'Tempora Mutantur' forgets his girl in the excitement of army life, 'Sir Guy The Crusader' flees from his actress girlfriend's Turkish father and Constable John gets rid of a rival by arresting him on the Derby racecourse. But in 'First Love', little Ellen chooses the disgraceful and very plain Reverend Bernard Powles and marries him for money instead of his very good, if myopic, curate whose only fault was playing the harmonium. Bab affects surprise:

'I often, often wonder what
Poor Ellen saw in him
For calculated he was not – to please a woman's whim'

JE, p238.

But Powles is 'cursed with acres fat, a Christian's direst ban – and gold. Yet, notwithstanding that, poor Ellen loved the man'. As Miss Rice Davis might put it in court during 1963, she would, wouldn't she.

The chapter on Bab and the Woman Question may be the only chapter in which to briefly mention Gilbert's one known alleged venture into pornography. His *Sods Opera*, written in collaboration with Arthur Sullivan, featured a cast including a certain Count Tostof, Miss Tess Tickle, the Brothers Bollox and Scrotum, a wrinkled old retainer. Details are impossible to verify further, but a copy apparently existed for many years in the Guardroom of St James's Palace. No new authoritative record exists of this remarkable creation…

BAB, MUSIC AND ART

The Ballads take no consistent shape, form, metre or rhyming pattern. There are limericks, sonnets, epigrammatic couplets, stanzas, tercets and quatrains. There is often a repetitive chorus, a reminder that 'ballad' actually means dancing song. Some ballads were designed to fit popular airs, in the manner of burlesque. They are musical in the sense of possessing rhythm and metre even if Gilbert claimed, defensively, not to have a musical bone in his body. Adrian Welles Beecham, (Mus.Doc, Durham, 1926, and eldest son of Sir Thomas Beecham, Bt) wrote musical settings to 40 of the *Bab Ballads* during the 1930s. Beecham searched for Gilbert's own suggested 'airs,' 'An' Orrible Tale' for 'Thomson Green and Harriet Hale' (JE, p145) and 'The Whistling Oyster'[437] for The Precocious Baby. (JE, p129) 'I was able to trace the first, quite a good second rate kind of tune at that time but the other, to quote Gilbert, was when the world was guilty of such a ballad three ages ago, and is now not to be found. However, I experimented with putting tunes myself to some of the Ballads and I found I got quite a lot of fun playing and singing them over the exquisitely funny words'.[438]

Ellis claims that the Babs are eminently recitable, with 'their tongue-twisting alliterations and consonances, and their reverberating syllabics but they are not singable'.[439] It is worth remembering that not all the libretti in the Savoy Operas are, strictly speaking, singable either: the 'Nightmare Song' of John Wellington Wells in *The Sorcerer* or General Stanley's 'Model of a Modern Major General' from *The Pirates of Penzance* belong to the 'singspiel' category of semi-sung comic patter as opposed to lyrical ballad.

Bab never mocked music, nor musicians. (I do not count Scottish bagpipes or pipers in either category.) 'Prince Agib', that strange survivor of *The Arabian Nights* inspires a musical introduction, utterly nonsensical.

'Strike the concertina's melancholy string,
Blow the spirit stirring harp like anything.
Let the piano's martial blast,
Rouse the echoes of the past,
For of Agib, Prince of Tartary, I sing!'

JE, p164.

---

[437] *The Whistling Oyster has* become a generic name for sea food restaurants in Australia…
[438] Adrian Welles Beecham. *Introduction to the Collected Bab Ballads*. Two Vols. London, Hutchinson, 1930.
[439] Ellis, p22

Various troubadours strum mandolins, play harmonia or blow clarions in the cause of love, but there are no fat ladies singing, no amateur keyboard wizards and no young Miss Bennetts delighting their audiences enough. Neither does Bab anthropomorphise in the manner of both Lear and Carroll with guitar playing cats or singing turtles.

Gilbert invented words to fit a rhyme – nobilitee, strokery pokery; occasionally just invented words for fun – bratticed wrackers, outhribbled; and mangled French – 'vous etes trop scraggy pour Babette'. He was a master of the English language, a requisite for a Nonsense poet: if one definition of Nonsense is a reversal of the familiar, the creation of it requires a more thorough understanding of the familiar than most of us are familiar with. Language enables an aim of Nonsense. 'It is by means of language to set before the mind a possible universe in which everything goes along serially, by one and one. This serial order must not be upset by indistinctness of the units or by fusion of the whole'.[440] Nonsense is a precise and ordered business. Nonsense is not necessarily comic – comic has less subversive relations with reality than Nonsense – and Nonsense is not satire or parody which are, generally and by their very nature, ephemeral and shortlived.

Gilbert, Lear and, initially, Lewis Carroll were all self-taught artists who illustrated their own work. Gilbert's drawings in particular have a wit and a punch – almost a savagery – which sets them apart, although a certain family resemblance exists between some Bab illustrations and Tenniel's sketches for Alice. This is due in some part to the Dalziel brothers (our acquaintance from Edward Lear) who engraved the blocks for both artists. George, Edward, Margaret and John Dalziel founded the Camden Press in 1857 and were responsible for both the range and quality of wood engravings of serious artists as well as the cartoonists and caricatures of the mid-nineteenth century. George Dalziel worked with John Leech for his *Punch* drawings and with Ford

---

[440] Elizabeth Sewell, *The Field of Nonsense*. Chatto & Windus, London. 1952. p56

Madox Brown's for the illustrations for the Routledge edition of 'The Prisoner of Chillon', (1875). Illustrations were customary in Victorian fiction as well as in the periodical press and the enduring partnership of, for example, Hablot Browne (Phiz) with Dickens created iconic images which modern film makers still respect.[441] The tradition appears to have been revived by the contemporary graphic novel.

Gilbert became dissatisfied with his first pictures for *Bab,* writing in the 1898 edition of *The Bab Ballads and Songs of a Savoyard* 'I have always felt many of the original illustrations of the Bab Ballads erred greatly in the direction of unnecessary extravagance. This defect I have endeavoured to correct and have designed more than 200 new drawings for this volume. I am afraid I cannot offer any further recommendation'. Readers familiar with the operas will recognise the 'earnest endeavour to correct.' Much of Gilbert's Nonsense was perfectly serious, 'a solemn business, maintaining the strictest of controls over both its inferences and its effects'.[442]

The 1898 drawings replaced about 70 of Bab's original drawings and 'the whole impression is one of unfortunate emasculation'.[443] Part of the problem lay in new methods of reproduction with line blocks which faithfully imitated fine pen strokes and which replaced the old wood engravings with their heavy blacks and strong contrasts. Max Beerbohm agreed that the original Bab illustrations 'erred gravely in the direction of unnecessary extravagance' adding further 'so did the Bab Ballads! To make these drawings equally right, Mr. Gilbert ought to have rewritten the poems. I am glad that his innate love for logic did not drive him to this double vandalism'.[444] George du Maurier was writing of the original illustrations in 1890 when he described the little pictures 'as a joy forever. They stick in the mind like charming tunes that won't allow themselves to be forgotten. Whatever may be the ultimate fate of the words, the cuts are truly marvellous creations'.[445] In a volume of devoted scholarship, James Ellis has restored the original drawings to his 1970 *Bab Ballads* and it is these which now appear in modern editions.

It seems to me that older, richer, staider Gilbert had lost Bab's earlier bite. The 'sweet, amiable, inoffensive and totally inappropriate drawings'[446] with their 'good manners and refined lines' of 1898 carried none of the impact of Bab's first appearances for *Fun* during the 1860's. A particularly revealing difference lies in the two illustrations for 'The Modest Couple'. In 1868, Gilbert draws himself as a moustachioed baby in a spotted jumpsuit and a theatrical feathered headdress, fearlessly confronting the reader head-on: thirty

---

[441] Christine Edzard's 6-hour filmed adaption of *Little Dorrit* in 1988 was extraordinarily faithful to the images of Phiz.

[442] James Rother, 'Modernism and the Nonsense Style'. *Contemporary Literature,* 15: 2. (1974), 187

[443] 'A Note on Gilbert as Illustrator', Philip James in *The Bab Ballads,* OUP, 1955.

[444] Saturday Review, 27th May, 1905. Quoted by Philip James, as above.

[445] George du Maurier, 'Illustration of Books.' Originally in *The Magazine of Art,* Cassell, London. 1890, adapted by George P. Landow for The Victorian Web Internet site. Accessed 25/2/2007

[446] Ellis, p4

years on, he becomes a booted and spurred Flagstaff, two stone heavier and with a comical air of judgement, worn slightly sideways.

Like the drawings of Edward Lear, Gilbert's strong small sketches exist with minimal background. Sometimes, only a shadow situates the figure on the ground: for a theatrical man, the lack of props and defining appurtenances can feel like a surprise, and certainly the situation was different in the Savoy Operas where complete ships sailed across the stage or Arcadian gardens with waterfalls occupied every inch of available space. The cartoon quality of Bab's figures gives them movement and impact. They do not constantly appear on their toes as Lear's figures are inclined to do, but the range of their movements is both varied and expressive. English characters, even Ogres, wear the clothing and costume of the mid-Victorian period. They sport colourful and elaborate uniforms, some of which Gilbert enjoyed wearing himself. Most men sport luxuriant whiskers unless they are boring clergymen in which case their absence of facial hair illustrates their lack of anything much else.

Occasionally, a drawing of Bab's women supports the fashionable theory that Gilbert was unkind. Milly de Plow is certainly wonderfully plain, but she is not so very much more upsetting than images of the budgerigar-featured Captain Bagg or the unappealing group of Sea Side Snobs.

BAB – IDENTITY AND TRANSFORMATION

Gilbert's 'serious baby' gave him the chance to remain a child. The creation of Bab allowed him to be 'sanguinary, mercenary or hedonistic'[447] with no fear of reprimand or redress. Ellis argues that Gilbert's construction of his eternal infant gave him liberty and that Bab might tackle in *Fun* those aspects of life which Gilbert found trying in reality – but disguises pose as many questions as they answer. Gilbert might never have been entirely certain who he was meant to be. The proliferation of ever-changing public persona from The Comic Physiognomist to Snarler, A Dapter, Desiderius Erasmus and A. Pittite as pseudonyms for his early journalism may all have indicated a desire to avoid the creation of a stable, private self, and his constant early career moves made identity through work impossible. Gilbert could not have escaped the Victorian creation of personal identity as a social construct rather than an absolute entity: despite his nonsensical approach to contemporary mores, he remained generally committed to the values they espoused. It seems likely that despite a wholly original mind, his true self-fulfillment lay in the achievement of socially sanctioned ambitions and ideals. Eventually, Gilbert became what Bab would surely have mocked: a country gentleman surrounded by his own acres, a Captain of the Volunteer Militia and a knighted Justice of the Peace.

James Ellis has written that 'from almost everything we know about Gilbert's life and personality, he was not one man, but two'.[448] The energetic, masculine and dominant soldier is in striking contrast to the perceptive writer, affectionate husband and gentle lover of children and animals. In this respect at least, he echoed Robert Schumann who created Eusebius and Florestan to illustrate the two contrasting aspects of his personality, a theory based on the writings of Johann Paul Richter (1763–1825) whose *Flegeljahre,* (1831) featured twins Vult and Walt to express dual identity. Eusebius is the feminine, softer and more poetic side of the vigorous and manly Florestan and both survive pianistically in *Carnaval* and *Davidsbundlertanze.* (Both conjoin as a March of David against the Philistines, or Schumann's idealistic crusade against commercial insensitivity.)

Alan Fischler believes that Bab's transformations are an expression of disgust at the prevailing 'anti-social soul of comedy' and he quotes Gilbert's own diatribe on the violence of pantomimic presentation and the impunity with

---

[447] Ellis, Introduction.

[448] Ellis, p17

which its perpetrators defy civic law.[449] Certainly, Gilbert was rough with unskilful impresarios and he disliked the plot tricks of sensation fiction but Bab's mill used any particular grist to hand, as indeed did the young dramatist WSG... methinks that perhaps the gentleman doth protest too much.[450]

Gilbert's ideas of transformation lay beyond mere dressing up – 'on with the motley, the paint and the powder'[451] – and beyond theatre as metaphor. He became obsessed with what became known as the 'magic lozenge' or fairy spell which could transform identity at the flick of a wand, or when taken with water before meals. A Gilbertian 'lozenge' appeared in his short story 'The Elixir of Love,'[452] whose nonsense featured an entire English village stricken with romantic love after swallowing Baylis and Culpepper's potion at 1/5d a bottle. The plot resurfaced in *The Sorcerers* where Gilbert's love-sick Bishop became Dr Daly of Ploverleigh and the old established firm of potion makers from St Martins Lane became the infamous Wells, Ltd.

'John Wellington Wells, I'm a dealer in magic and spells
In blessings and curses and ever-filled purses
In prophecies, witches and knells'.

The Sorcerer, 1877.
G & S, p69.

(Dr Daly is the only clergyman in the operas as opposed to dozens of clerics portrayed in the *Ballads*.) An earlier dramatic version of Gilbert's love philtre appeared in 1866 as a burlesque of Donizetti's *L'Elisir d'Amore* entitled *Dulcamara, or, The Little Duck and the Great Quack,* which involved a contemporary scandal involving an American Dr Hunter and his very dubious cure-all remedies. Apart from this topicality, Gilbert's travesty did not radically distort the original plot except for a final multiple revelation of identity in which the cast are all each other's long-lost relations, regardless of age or sex.[453]

Bab employs a reversal of the Donizetti parody with 'The Cunning Woman', (1868). Bill offers his sweetheart a mystic phial which will transform her from a fetching nymph to a coarse, plain and unkempt young woman to safeguard her from the attentions of an acquisitive Lord Pillaloo. It works – the noble Lord sneers in disgust and Bill's love and honour remain intact.

Sensational discoveries of hidden identity are very familiar from the operas; the aurally-challenged Ruth apprentices Frederick to a pirate, not a pilot in *The Pirates of Penzance* only to reveal that the pirates are 'all

---

[449] Alan Fischler, *Modified Rapture*. Charlottesville, University of Virginia Press, 1991. p38
[450] Stedman, p80, describes Gilbert's parody of sensation fiction in his Reed entertainment *A Sensation Novel.*
[451] 'On With The Motley' from Leoncavallo's *Pagliacci,* 1892 is the celebrated tenor aria in which the dying clown must still dress up in his costume and make the audience laugh.
[452] Written for *The Graphic*, Christmas Edition, 1876.
[453] Stedman, p36/37

noblemen gone wrong'. In Act 2 Buttercup is obliged to reveal that Captain Corcoran and Ralph Rackstraw in *H.M.S. Pinafore* were mixed up as babies, although the audience may long have suspected that 'the humble tar' had too much bearing to be credible and that a captain who never, ever swore at sea was unlikely.

Arthur Sullivan disliked Gilbert's lozenges and resisted all attempts to create an opera from such Nonsense. He would be obliged to accept the multiple identities of Pooh Bah as Archbishop, Paymaster and Lord Chief Justice, substituted babies in *The Gondoliers* and *H.M.S. Pinafore* and painted ancestors walking out of their frames in *Ruddigore* but transforming identities with magic pills and potions was a step too far. Eventually, Gilbert employed Alfred Cellier's lyrics for *The Mountebank* in 1892, a theatrical fantasy in which a liquid potion 'made everyone who drank it become what he pretended to be: the hypocrite became a man of piety, the swindler, a man of honour, the quack, a man of learning and the braggart, a man of war'.[454]

Bab enabled transformation of human identities without the lozenge. In 'The Phantom Head', a clergyman, doctor and clerk bewail their lack of distinguishing features. The clerk meets a solitary head in a churchyard, hanging around since an execution in 1668 and upon learning that there are three spare heads without accompanying torsos, each with dramatic countenance, they agree a swap.

> 'One handsome head each friend – assumed, and bore it thence
> But, ah, the fearful end! But ah, the consequence!
> For none would take a pew, in Mr Parks's church
> The Doctor's patients too, have left him in the lurch.
> The humble little clerk, has no companions when
> He rises grim and stark, to give his loud Amen!'

JE, p220.

A similar tale concerns 'A and B, or The Sensation Twins' In one of the Bab's most gruesome ballads, A and B are cut in half by a Turkish armourer to redress a dreadful inequality of physique and appearance. But the ultimate in surgical 'make-overs' creates new identities which cannot function.

> 'I only wish I knew how they,
> drain their unpleasant cup
> I only know that A and B
> were terribly cut up.
> Perhaps they lived in severed bliss,
> perhaps they groaned and died.
> Perhaps they joined themselves like this
> – and gave their legs a ride'.

JE, p124.

(They are also Gilbert: 'and for his benefit, I saw, who further knowledge

---

[454] Baily, p339.

seeks; The one had Civil Service pay, the other wrote critiques'.)

Occasionally, Bab's transformations occur with a dramatic revelation of switched babies. In 'General John and Private James' Private James suddenly exclaims

'A glimmering thought occurs to me,
its source I can't unearth
But I've a kind of notion we,
were cruelly changed at birth'.

JE, p93.

For Chesterton, Bab's fun lay not in the transformed identities, but the outrageous and arbitrary abruptness with which both agree the exchange, a situation mirrored by the unquestioning acceptance of the Bumboat Woman's baby-farming-swap story in *H.M.S. Pinafore*. Likewise, Paley Vollaire admits to dustman Frederick West in the Bab Ballad 'The Baby's Vengeance' that he was jealous of his mother's 'mangling reimbursing, with now and then (at intervals) wet nursing' aristocratic babies and changed places. But a switch to the upper class brought only disgrace and misery in contrast to the happily married dustman.[455]

The notion of a deliberate identity switch was familiar from contemporary fiction: in *The Woman in White* (1860) Wilkie Collins creates 'a conspiracy to rob one woman of her identity by confounding her with another, sufficiently like her to answer a wicked purpose'[456] and the identity of Esther Summerson is finally revealsed as Lady Dedlock's daughter in *Bleak House (*1851). The motif enabled a variety of uses, farcical or fabulous: Mark Twain breathed new life into the idea with *The Prince and the Pauper* in 1882 in a story which challenges assumptions concerning morality, social spheres and class distinction. Bab's 'Bob Polter' is offered a choice: would he like to be the demon of Drunken Sottery or its gleaming rival Total Abstinence? Bob sends them both packing, declaring 'I am who I am meant to be'.

Did dreams help establish identity? Bab's the Story of Gentle Archibald' relates how a polite small boy becomes a violent clown in a story that challenges assumptions as well as transforming identities. Archie's dream enabled the sub-conscious to dominate the identity of the conscious by volition. But the awakened consciousness proved to be a disaster.

'the change has really turned his brain
He boiled his little sister Jane
He painted blue his aged mother
Sat down upon his little brother
Tripped up his cousins with his hoop
Put Pussy in his father's soup
Placed beetles in his Uncle's shoe

---

[455] JE, p225

[456] Wilkie Collins, 'How I Write My Books,' *The Globe*, November 1887, quoted in Harvey Sucksmith's Preface to the OUP edition of *The Woman in White*.

Cut a policeman right in two
Spread devastation round and, ah,
He red hot pokered his Papa!

JE, p83.

Archie cheerfully proving the theory that the virtuous man is content to dream what a wicked man really does. But Archie wakes up, Eusebius succeeds Florestan and it is Eusebius who will fulfil a kind Papa's ambition for him to become a clergyman. It is difficult not to interpret Archie's dream as symbolising the repressive and authoritarian childhood of many a Victorian family and one from which escape was impossible.

Dreams are a crucial vehicle for Nonsense as they enable the rational to become the irrational, the logical, illogical and the real, surreal. Freud's belief that all dreams represent the 'royal road to a knowledge of the unconscious activities of the mind' and that wish fulfilment is the foundation of dream content was challenged in the 1960s by medical science which claimed that dreams were simply random neuron firings 'regulated by a lowly, elemental and physiological mechanism'.[457] However, recent research has narrowed the gap between the beliefs of psychologists and doctors, and the dream has been restored to a more central, valid position in explorations of the unconscious. Carl Jung held that dreams reflected the richness and complexity of the entire unconscious, personal and collective: conscious attitudes are compensated for, unconsciously, within the dream by their opposites.[458]

Bab himself alliteratively narrates 'My Dream' in which he finds he has come to dwell in topsy-turvydom, a kingdom greatly associated with Gilbert.

'Where vice is virtue, virtue, vice
Where nice is nasty, nasty nice.
Where right is wrong and wrong is right
Where white is black and black is white.'

JE, p280.

Elizabeth Sewell is another theorist of creativity through oppositional tension, suggesting that Nonsense is created by the mind's instinct towards order, playing against disorder.[459] Her ideas are given weight by the obsession with order and meticulous attention to detail which characterise Edward Lear, Lewis Carroll and William Gilbert, all of whom operated as two, often contrasting, personae. A dual identity enabled artistic integrity whilst simultaneously engaging with society – none of my three Nonsense writers were reclusive hermits or social outcasts.

Another dream of Bab is the nightmare of Leap Year when, ducking the

---

[457] Dr Mark Solms, St Bartholomew's Hospital, London. Internet site, accessed, 15th Jan, 2007.

[458] Anthony Storr, *The Essential Jung*. Selected Writings. James Hall, *Jungian Dream Interpretation*. Internet sites, accessed 15th Jan, 2007.

[459] Elizabeth Sewell, *The Field of Nonsense*. Chatto and Windus, London. 1952. p46

attentions of

> 'an elderly dame, she confessed to a flame
> though she's older by far than my mother, my mother.
> Which dreading my jeers for a number of years,
> she had struggled but vainly to smother, to smother.'

JE, p39.

Bab wakes up in time.

Elderly women wooing younger men was an idea that Gilbert found irresistible and variations on Bab's dream occur throughout the Savoy Operas, notably concerning Frederick and Little Buttercup in *H.M.S. Pinafore* and Katisha and Nanki-Poo in *The Mikado*.

The ultimate transformation is not only a switch of identity, but swallowing that identity whole. 'The Yarn of the Nancy Bell' is one of Bab's most celebrated Ballads, partly through Mark Lemon's prissiness in rejecting it for *Punch,* and partly from the unapologetic nature of the cannibal story. Max Keith Sutton believes this ballad represents 'the common Victorian theme of social competition and the struggle for personal advancement leads towards this brutal image...of all the images of human exploitation, cannibalism is the most explicit, there being no more literal way to treat a person as an object than by eating him'.[460] In the Ballad, an elderly naval man recites his doleful history to a passing stranger.

> 'Oh, I am a cook and a captain bold, and the mate of the Nancy brig.
> And a bo'sun tight and a midshipmite and the crew of the Captain's gig'
> The Nancy Bell foundered on a reef.
> 'For a month, we'd neither wittles or drink,
> till a'hungry we did feel
> So we drawed a lot and accordin' shot,
> the Captain for our meal.'

JE, p76.

Eventually, there is but one survivor who has become, gastronomically speaking, the entire crew.

Sutton's ingenious interpretation might seem a step too far: but it is relevant to my ideas on identity and chimes in with Bab's frequent desire to become something – someone – some people – different. In Bab's 'The Pantomime Super to His Mask' it is the stage again which symbolises the nightmare loss of identity for an actor who is 'swallowed' by a role he is forced to inhabit. The actor 'swamped in thine own preposterous nonentity, credited for the smile you wear externally / I feel disposed to smash thy face externally' but finds he cannot. The mask subverts conventional assumptions

---

[460] Sutton, p36

about precisely who is becoming who: or perhaps 'they'. It challenges the actor in a parody of Hamlet.

'Art thou aware of nothing there
Which might abuse thee as thou are abusing me?
A brain that mourns thy unredeemed rascality?
A soul that weeps at thy threadbare mortality
Both grieving that their individuality, is merged in thine?'

JE, p74.

BAB DEALING WITH COMPETITION, HIERARCHY AND SNOBS

R ivalry and competition are strategies for survival. They have been recognised since time began and their impact and import on every facet of civilisation cannot be adequately dealt with by any one philosopher, economist, scientist or even Bab. Every age has competition as a mainspring in some form, at least in Western culture: in contrast, Eastern philosophy and Buddhist Noble Truths teach that competition produces unhappiness and 'dukkha', an untranslatable concept relating to the misery of Western materialism. But the spirit of competition in mid-nineteenth century England, with a liberal government, free market economy, growing industrial might and colonial expansion, flourished as never before. Religious rivalries, sexual duels, professional jealousies and social climbing: all were grist to the Nonsense mill of Bab.

'where lawyer, patriot, soldier, author, finds his game, he strikes it.
For oh, we live in a wicked world where dog eats dog and likes it'.

'The Thief's Apology',
JE, p309.

Until Charles Darwin published *The Origin of Species* on November 24th 1859, very little competition existed for God. Powerful institutions in England promoted and upheld the widespread acceptance of a Divine Creator, and those who questioned divine authority risked charges of heresy with terrifying consequence. German university teachers enjoyed a freedom of speculation in philosophic and religious study which was the envy of Broad Churchmen in England[461] – it was German rational thinkers who began to argue that a supernatural revelation was both irrelevant to faith and incompatible with reason: that the Bible was valuable as an explanation of spiritual truth but not itself an object of devotion nor was criticism of it necessarily a critique of religion. Competition simmered among those academics and intellectuals who could understand German theological discourse, a process greatly aided by George Eliot's English translations of Strauss' *Leben Jesu* in 1846 and Feuerbach's *Wesen des Christenthums* in 1854.

Darwin's theories seemed to be in direct contradiction to a literal reading of the Genesis account of creation. Evangelical believers in Biblical

---

[461] M.A. Crowther, *Church Embattled: Religious Controversy in mid- Victorian England*. David and Charles, Newton Abbot. 1970. p41

infallibility attacked Darwinists as heretics. Gilbert's libretto poked fun in 1870 with;

'Man, however well behaved
At best, is only a monkey shaved.[462]

Bab joined the debate earlier with 'The Monkey in Trouble', 1865.

'Just suppose a great gorilla, came and took the learned beak
Made him fire a gun for siller, beat a tamborine and speak.
Wear a brigand hat and feather, sweep the floor and dance and fight,
play in every kind of weather, don't YOU think he'd want to bite?
Per'aps they're now indictments framing, to be signed and stuck on shelves,
Me, as human fellow claiming, am I then so like themselves?'

JE, p64.[463]

The trochaic octameter of this Ballad recalls Tennyson's *Locksley Hall*, (1842), and there is a curious link with *In Memoriam,* (1850), as it is supposed to be the favourite metre of Arthur Henry Hallam's father. Famously, *In Memoriam* offered an earlier challenge to Genesis with Canto 56.

'Who trusted God was love indeed
And Love, Creation's final law
Tho' Nature, red in tooth and claw
With ravine, shrieked against his creed.'

Interestingly, this is one of the rare ballads which Gilbert never illustrated: unlike Lear or Carroll, he did not appear to enjoy drawing animals and concentrated almost entirely on the human form. (Yet Gilbert loved his own animals and visitors to Grims Dyke were often startled to find themselves staring at the two ring-tailed lemurs who lived on his shoulder).

In the topsy-turvy world of Bab, survival of the fittest meant competition along some unlikely lines and winners with unwelcome genetic traits. Old Paul and Old Tim both court young Emily who promises to marry whichever might bring, good proofs of his doing the pluckiest thing. But Emily chooses the cowardly Paul for boxing little boys' ears instead of brave Tim who thrashes French pacifists for not defending their shores.

Bernard Powles, a hideous humbug, courts Ellen, a rustic belle.

'No kind of virtue decked this priest
He'd nothing to allure
He wasn't handsome in the least
He wasn't even poor'.

---

[462] Lady Psyche's song in *Princess Ida*. G & S, p500/501
[463] James Ellis believes this ballad referred to an actual event as indeed it may, but I also believe that Darwin is involved.

But when the suitably poverty-struck curate Aaron Woods appears as a rival with matchless skills on the harmonium and serenades Ellen with the virtues of bees and ants, she unaccountably continues to prefer the wealthy and landed Bernard. Max Keith Sutton describes how Bab's plots 'bristle with keen rivalry: a sexual rivalry in particular accounts for much of their brutality'.[464] John, a life guard, battles with James, a policeman, for the hand of Emily during the Epsom Races. John scurrilously contrives James to be arrested and locked up for life when he strays upon the course. Nastier still is Bab's tale of MacPhairson Clonglocketty Angus MacLan who was cut in half by jealous rival Pattison Corbay Torbay – but Torbay's venom was only partly on account of Ellen McJones Aberdeen. Some responsibility must lie with Clonglocketty's bagpipes. Bab is aware that fortune, aka Darwin, favours the handsome.

> 'Men, absolute iniquity, with bandiness assess
> And physical obliquity with moral twistiness
> There, natural deformity, or curvature of bone
> Is viewed as an enormity, no penance can atone'.

And so when the charitable but misshapen Baker Coote realises his suit for the 'sensible and dutiful and kind and well-to-do Marian' is hopeless against well-made James, he shoots him. Marian refuses to be grateful.

Professional rivalries are demonstrated in 'Damon and Pythias'[465] a neat contradiction of the Greek myth of eternal male friendship and loyalty which inspired Dionysius to reprieve Damon from death. Bab tells the grim tale of an amity torn asunder by a legal battle which becomes an actual physical struggle and kills both men as they topple over a cliff. Their rivalry also serves to symbolise the nonsense inherent in adversarial law: Gilbert's early training for the Bar only served to reinforce his passionate sense of justice and never succeeded in convincing him that the answer to human dilemmas lay in the courtroom. In 'The Ghost, the Gallant, the Gael and the Goblin' English phlegm and Scottish stoicism combine to defeat those curious rivals,

---

[464] Sutton, p39
[465] JE, p282

'an elderly ghost of easy ways
And an influential goblin.
And as they exercised their joints, promoting quick digestion
They talked, on several curious points, and raised this pregnant question.
Which of us is No. One: the Ghostie or the Goblin?'

JE, p150.

Ultimately, neither Ghostie or Goblin wins as neither succeed in frightening away their targets. Gilbert occasionally borrowed the supernatural for plot effects, notably with an 'influential Fairy' in *Iolanthe*. Victorian fairies were whimsical, fantastical or nonsensical: today, they have assumed a new and wholly peculiar modern meaning.

The word 'professional' began to assume a new significance in the 1850s and a new relationship to competition. One reform to the Civil Service proposed by the Northcote-Trevelyan Report (1853), was recruitment via competitive examination. We have seen how Gilbert himself entered the Education Department by this novel route and how the idea that it could be extended to the peerage features in *Iolanthe*. Previous advancement in the Civil Service, and to a certain extent, the army, the law and the Church depended upon patronage, money or a combination of both.[466] Competitive examinations continued to tickle Bab's fancy: even Georgie in 'The Fairy Curate' passes examinations to become a clergyman.

Competition for social advancement, otherwise known as English snobbery, delighted Bab. England, unlike France, Germany or Italy, retained a flexible system of caste, entry into which was always possible through money or good looks. Despite the growing power of the bourgeoisie, and the occasionally influential intellectual élite, an English Milord was generally regarded as a pretty fine fellow, however inbred, brainless or plain. Top of the tree in 1869 was the Prince of Wales. In 'Prince II Baleine', (a reference to the

---

[466] The position of the Bishop's Examining Chaplain, a clergyman appointed to interview and examine prospective clerical ordinands, predates the 1850s.

generously built Edward as *baleine* is French for whales) sycophantic crowds and

'the British Snob, besieged that Prince in plenty
The snob adores a Nob, and follows him to rob, his dolce far niente'

Politely evading the fan club, the Prince suggests that his valet Brown might become an acceptable substitute.

'I am his special care, he brushes, combs and laves me
He parts my chestnut hair, he folds the clothes I wear
And strops the blade that shaves me'.

It works.

'The snobs with joy insane, kotoo'd to Brown unseemly
While good Prince II Baleine, enjoys his rest extremely,[467]

JE p 260.

Writers other than Bab single out Edward as the pinnacle of social advancement. In *The Young Visiters*[468] Daisy Ashford describes how her hero Alfred Salteena, (who is not quite a gentleman but you would hardly notice it) pays to be introduced to 'various members of the Aristokracy and the Prince of Wales who wears a lovely ermine cloak and a small but costly crown as he laps up strawberry ice cream and complains that all he wants is peace and quiet and a little fun'.

Dukes and Earls strut through the ballads, alternating between hero and villain. In 'Gregory Parable, LL.D,' 'the Earl, a very wicked man, whose face bore Vice's blackest ban' rebuffs a worthy cleric's daughter. She is obliged to marry her father's poor pupil who turns out to be the Duke of Gretna Green. In 'The Policeman's Story', a toadying magistrate gives a drunken Duke a lesser fine, even if admitting,

'because the prisoner's a Duke would not be worth his salt
That you're the Duke of A. is your misfortune, not your fault
And I don't see why I should be severe,
because you're not a peasant but a first class peer'.

JE, p307.

The Duke weds the beak's daughter and 'as he had to choose a crest, the whole affair to clench it was a flunkey rampart on a magisterial bench'. But it is a mere Baronet whose bumps contain Bab's sharpest barbs. When tackled by a burglar, Sir Herbert White explains he has studied phrenology and would find a criminal's head interesting. But the burglar is full of shining Christian virtue in contrast to Sir Herbert whose head 'teems with inhumanity.'

---

[467] How Gilbert would have enjoyed the antics of Paul Burrell.

[468] Discovered in a desk drawer in 1919 by J.M. Barrie.

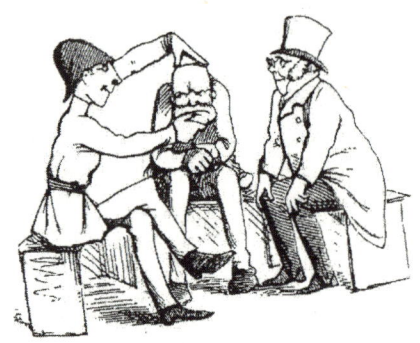

'Here's Murder, Envy Strife, propensity to kill any
And lies as large as life, and heaps of social villainy;
Here's love of Bran New Clothes, embezzling, arson, Deism,
A taste for slang and oaths, and fraudulent Trusteeism.
Here's love of Groundless Charge, here's malice too, and trickery
Unusually large, your bump of pocket-pickery'.

JE, p290.

Phrenology, or the study of character from external features, particularly bumps on the head, was an absorbing fascination for the Victorians and one which was practised by professional anthropologists as well as amateurs such as Charles Dickens and William Powell Frith. Faces and heads existed to be 'read' in the most literal sense and a London crowd supplied the greatest variety of raw material.

Gilbert did not attend one of the new boarding public schools. His education at the private establishment of Great Ealing School would have lacked those components deemed essential for the formation of a 'gentleman', a concept so readily recognised and so difficult to define but so highly prized in Victorian social advancement. Public schools, newly invigorated by the 'godliness and good learning' of Thomas Arnold at Rugby offered a seductive package of manly virtues, team-spirit duty and confidence –inspiring leadership.[469] Their end product became instantly recognisable and universally prized, if only minimally educated; cheerful Philistines' toiled at games and played with books'.[470] The obsession with team sports in public schools was a useful channel for competitive energy, distracting boys from sex and moulding compliant conformity but offering little encouragement for intellectual development. J.A. Mangan has described 'the deep-rooted Anglo-Saxon suspicion of brilliance' and argues that non-conformist free-thinkers were troublesome to authoritative schoolmasters and the power structure of public schools. Originally founded as institutions for poorer boys from non-

---

[469] Quarterly Review of Education 4(1979)467

[470] J.A. Mangan, p111.

aristocratic backgrounds who could not afford tutors, dozens of new Public Boarding Schools became breeding grounds for an aspiring éelite in the 1850s and 1860s. It is possible that Gilbert resented their effortless superiority: it is possible that some of his competitive energy came from a small, but influential chip.

In 'Etiquette' two shipwrecked 'gentlemen', despite their occupation in trade, find themselves the only survivors on a desert island. They cannot share the oysters and the turtles together because they have not been introduced. Finally, Gray overhears Somers reminisce about a school friend at Charterhouse. They are overjoyed: they may shake hands and become friends. But the Carthusian friend Robinson appears on the horizon, rowing a boat from a convict ship.

> 'an unattractive fellow, pulling stroke
> Condemned to seven years for misappropriating stock
> They laughed no more, for Somers thought he had been rather rash
> in knowing one whose friend had misappropriated cash,
> and Peter thought a foolish tack he must have gone upon,
> in making the acquaintance of a friend of Robinson'.

JE, p274.

Robinson's fall from grace alienates his former school friends and they retire to opposite sides of the island in solitary state.

> 'To allocate the island, they agreed by word of mouth
> And Peter takes the North again, and Somers takes the South
> And Peter has the oysters which he hates with horror grim
> And Somers has the turtle: turtle disagrees with him.'

JE, p274.

Neither Bab or Gilbert were interested in the obvious competition implicit in horseracing (although Gilbert is suspected of trying to improve his income with an occasional bet) but The Derby was the major national holiday of the year when even Parliament closed and joined the exodus to Epsom Downs. *The Illustrated London News* described the Derby as 'the most astonishing, the most varied...and the most glorious spectacle that ever was, or ever can be visible to mortal eyes,[471] The bacchanalian occasion on which respectable Victorians, even ladies, got drunk and misbehaved, famously attracted William Powell Frith in 1858. His huge canvas with its jostling, meandering crowd of almost ninety figures organised in groups, each with its own dramatic focus, has become an iconic symbol of Victorian realist painting. 'Realism' could equal a moral fidelity which subconsciously enhanced the popular appeal of Frith's work even if the 'realism' lay close to caricature. Bab's doggerel version of Frith's narrative Derby painting came six years later in a Ballad entitled 'Down to the Derby', for *Fun* on 28th May 1864. Bab, like Frith before him, barely notices the horses.

---

[471] *Illustrated London News*, 23 May, 1863. p566

'Wagon and cart, ready to start
Early in morning at six, six,
Gallons of beer, stowed away here, twiggery, swiggery, quick sticks
Empty before, fill'em once more, women look trim in their caps, caps.
Screaming in fun, never say done, joking and poking the chaps, chaps.
Sweeps in a truck, swells out of luck
Laughery, chaffery, grin, grin.
Travelling show, dwarf hid below, eye on his giantess' gin, gin.'

JE, p51.

Twelve stanzas of rollicking verse follow whose Nonsense lies, for once, in Bab's invented words rather than in character or plot. 'Flunkeydom, monkeydom, whinery, shivery, fowlery, growlery' race along with 'drinkery, winkerly, palery, alery, laughery, chaffery' meeting 'bobbery, watchery, smokery, jokery' along the way.

INTRODUCTION – LEWIS CARROLL AND
THE HUNTING OF THE SNARK

Lewis Carroll is the third subject of this thesis and the final writer in my Victorian Nonsense triumvirate. Theologian, mathematician, inventor, photographer and poet, his literary output included dozens of comical verses, two volumes of the prose drama *Sylvie and Bruno*, a fantasy poem *Phantasmagoria*, and the epic Nonsense of *The Hunting of the Snark*, (1874).[472] *Alice in Wonderland*, (1865), and *Alice in the Looking Glass,* (1872), stories for 'child friends' were instantly successful, translated into every known language and remain permanently in print. Yet, although the language, character and incident of the two Alice books have become part of the national psyche, anecdotally quoted more than the Bible and Shakespeare and continually mined by scholars and critics, they are not the point of this chapter.[473]

No writer on Victorian Nonsense can ignore Alice completely, and so I will acknowledge her superiority in <u>prose</u> and note that her creator was nurtured and inspired by a similar context to *The Hunting of the Snark* a decade later on.[474] But it is not merely my focus on Nonsense <u>poetry</u> which obliges such a detailed examination; the 'Agony in Eight Fits' of the Snark has been described as 'the greatest of all epic Nonsense poems'[475] with an enduring reputation as 'immaculate fiction', or a structure that resists all efforts at allegory, a 'system equitable with already existing systems in a non-fictive world'.[476] Carroll's fabulous poem has attracted a certain amount of critical interest and admiration, but never to the same extent as the Alice books, something that this study aims to redress. In the view of a contemporary critic, 'the possible meanings and its autobiographical significances have

---

[472] Carroll wrote a certain amount of serious poetry but it never reached the inspiration of either his Nonsense verses or his fantasy prose and is generally considered best forgotten.

[473] Nabokov produced the Russian *Anja v Strane Chudes* in 1923 and its influence on *Lolita* has been noted; over 30 French versions reflect that country's belief in Alice as proto-surrealism. Modern writers who owe a debt to Alice include James Joyce, T.S. Eliot, Luis Borges and Samuel Beckett. Alice has inspired artists Salvador Dali and Arthur Rackham together with filmmakers Lou Bunin (1949) Johnathan Miller (1966) William Sterling (1992) and Tim Burton in 2010 with Johnny Depp.

[474] The Nonsensical *poems* in the Alice books would require a separate investigation: I have not space to do them justice here.

[475] Selwyn Goodacre, *All The Snarks: An Exploration for the Illustrated Edition of The Hunting of the Snark.* Oxford, Inky Parrot Press, 2007.

[476] Michael Holquist, 'What Is A Boojum? – Nonsense and Moderation'. *French Studies*, 43, (1969)145–164

attracted almost no literary analysis. Its power, its essential and acute adultness have been lost, perhaps as Dodgson himself half wanted them to be 'lost behind a single image'.[477] The role of Nonsense as a 'bridge' between the adult world and the innocence of children will be discussed in the conclusion to this thesis. Related to it is the fact that the books we most recall reading are those books we read in childhood – nothing ever makes the same impact in adult life as the first fairy tales, adventure stories – or Nonsense rhymes.

Carroll scholar Edward Guiliano believes that *The Hunting of the Snark* is 'in the Nonsense tradition of Thomas Hood[478] and William Schwenck Gilbert...indeed Dodgson may well have been influenced when writing The Snark by Gilbert's Bab Ballads'.[479] We know that Carroll was familiar with Gilbert's work, both on paper and on the stage and that both men shared a passion for the London theatre (Although they were contemporaries and writers with more in common than might at first seem likely, they were never friends). We know, too, that Carroll was an accomplished parodist with a carefully observed repertoire from celebrated poets and writers and that, like Gilbert, he tried to enter the hallowed portals of *Punch* as well as a legion of contemporary comic journals for his own Nonsense writing.

Guiliano extracts themes of death, life-as-a-dream and time as central to the poem, focussing particularly on the character of the bellman whose bell is so regularly and significantly struck. He comments on 'the tension that exists between the comic tone and the underlying terror that characterises the poem for readers today' noting that comedy enables a degree of mastery over fears or threats by removing them from a conscious and immediate world and setting them apart.

Michael Holquist believes that The Snark is one of the first significant and enduring texts of literary modernism – a text that is what it is. Despite Alice and Humpty Dumpty's celebrated dialogue over whether words mean what they say, or what you want them to say. Words in *The Hunting of the Snark*, mean the words themselves. Jean Gattegno quotes Carroll himself as saying that 'no word has a meaning inseparably attached to it: a word means what the speaker intends by it, and what the hearer understand by it, and that is all – I meet a friend and say 'Good morning!' Harmless words enough, one would think. Yet in some language he and I have never heard, these words may convey utterly horrid and loathsome ideas... the thought may serve to lessen the horror of some of the language used by the lower classes...often a collection of unmeaning sounds'.[480] (Carroll's upper middle class consciousness is echoed by his Alice, extremely anxious not to be Mabel, who

[477] Karoline Leach, *In The Shadow of the Dreamchild*. London, Peter Owen, 1999. p225

[478] 1799–1845. Writer and humourist, creator of the Comic Annual in 1830 which reduced every contemporary issue to a sympathetic caricature, and best known for 'Song of the Shirt'.

[479] Edward Guiliano, 'A Time for Humour'. *Essays on the 150th Anniversary of the birth of Charles Dodgson*, New York, Clarkson Potter. 1982. p124

[480] Jean Gattegno *Lewis Carroll, Fragments of a Looking Glass*. New York, Crowell, 1976. p273

lives in the 'poky little house and has next to no toys to play with'.[481] Jackie Wullschläger argues that this reflects 'a national self-confidence, an assumption that the status quo would continue, the belief in the future which made the child a natural icon, all are in the background').[482]

The Hunting of the Snark is the purest Nonsense language imaginable and interpretations, allegories and meanings reflect our imagination, our contexts and our ingenuity: they may have no connection with Carroll's consciousness, or indeed his unconsciousness at all. Yet, as we have established, nothing comes from nothing and where *The Hunting of the Snark* comes from, what it might mean and how it relates to Carroll in particular and Victorian society in general are questions that this chapter attempts to answer. T.S. Eliot, when asked for the meaning of *The Waste Land*, is reported to have said that he couldn't tell you that, he was only the poet who wrote it, in similar vein to Carroll who apologised for the mystery of the Snark: 'I'm afraid I didn't mean anything but Nonsense, still, if words mean more than we mean to express when we use them, and if there are some good meanings in the book, I'm very glad to accept them'.[483]

The Hunting of the Snark tells a tale of a handful of strange adults and one animal: a Butcher, Baker, Barrister, Bonnet maker, Broker, Boots, Billiard marker and the Beaver who set off on a journey on a ship that only sails backwards. They are captained by a wise and admirable Bellman who is guided by blank maps. The purpose of their journey is to find the Snark, a mythical monster, known to all, but seen by none. They encounter the Snark, but cannot succeed in capturing it. Various trials and tribulations attend their quest and some of the crew do not survive the expedition. The tale does not have an obviously happy ending – for the Snark was a Boojum, you see.

This section follows the pattern set by Edward Lear and William Gilbert. The Introduction will be followed by a short biography of Carroll, a resumé of earlier studies on both the author and *The Hunting of the Snark*, a discussion on the art and illustration of the Snark, Fit by Fit analysis and annotation of The Snark itself, some alternative versions of the Snark and conclusion.

[481] Lewis Carroll *Alice in Wonderland* . Penguin Classic Edition, 1999. p19

[482] Jackie Wullschläger *Inventing Wonderland*. London, Methuen. 1996. p16

[483] Lewis Carroll Diaries, March 29th 1876, p351

CHARLES DODGSON, BIOGRAPHICAL

Charles Dodgson was born at Daresby, Cheshire, on January 27th 1832 into a solidly respectable family with clerical connections.[484] He was the eldest boy in the family of ten children and, by all accounts, was fortunate in a happy and secure childhood, only suffering when attempts were made to 'correct' his lefthandedness. Left-handed children are particularly quick to realise that a mirror (looking glass) reverses images and are able to write backwards. (Carroll even considered mirror-writing part of Alice, but changed his mind). He was an inventive and imaginative child, writing and illustrating stories for his own magazine *The Rectory Umbrella* which his siblings read with great amusement: he also established a miniature railway in the garden and built toy theatres for puppet shows at home.[485] Initially educated by his mother, preserved reading lists attest to a precocious intellect – he read *The Pilgrim's Progress* at the age of seven and continued his early love of literature with a study of Shakespeare, Charles Dickens, George Eliot and Alfred Tennyson. We know from a letter to his sister Elizabeth that, aged sixteen, he read *David Copperfield*, Macaulay's *History of England, Laneton Parsonage* and *Diversions of Hollycott*. (*Laneton Parsonage*, (1846), by the Rev. W. Sewell featured 'the practical use of a Portion of the Catechism' in three volumes.[486])

After a happy period at Richmond School, Carroll was sent to Rugby, Warwickshire until 1849. Academic success came easily and helped to compensate for the discomforts and bullying of a public school: Arnold's belief in the liberty allowed to all and the power exercised by senior boys over juniors could have unpleasant consequences and it seems very likely that the attractive young scholar was subject to homosexual abuse. Carroll disliked his senior school intensely and survived by retreating into a private world of his own imagination.[487]

Rugby was succeeded by Christ Church, Oxford, his father's old College and Lewis Carroll went up in January, 1851 under the guidance of his father's friend, Dr Edward Bouverie Pusey. Despite the precedence of Canon Dodgson

---

[484] 'Dares' was the young author's first choice for a nom de plume, and suggested by him to Edmund Yates, editor of *The Train*, a contemporary journal for railway reading. Yates did not approve and so Carroll suggested four alternatives: Edgar Cuthwellis, Edgar U.C. Westhall, Louis Carroll and Lewis Carroll. To avoid confusion, this thesis will follow where Dodgson led and continue to describe him as 'Lewis Carroll'.

[485] Walter de la Mare, *Lewis Carroll*. Faber and Faber, London. 1932. p20

[486] 24th May 1848. Quoted in *The Letters of Lewis Carroll*. Editor, Morton Cohen. Macmillan. 1979. p8

[487] Thomas Arnold, 1795–1842. Reformer and educator. Succeeded as Head Master of Rugby by Archibald Tait in 1842.

and Edward Pusey, Christ Church, 'dominated by wealth, by privilege...beset by unfathomable rituals' was an odd choice for an intellectual.[488] Scions of the aristocracy went up to 'The House' to hunt with their own pack of beagles, play cards and mess about on the river.[489] There could be scant chance of finding a kindred spirit even if Carroll had felt so inclined. Christ Church had included intellectual giants – former graduates included Wellington, Peel, Gladstone, Ruskin, Henry Liddell and A.P. Stanley[490] – but the particular dreaming spires of The House were not notable for encouraging academic distinction in the 1850s, a situation exacerbated by the arrival of Edward VII, then Prince of Wales, in 1859.

Alone in his rooms, Carroll developed a range of games, hobbies and interests which fascinated his child friends, but which were rarely shared with equals and contemporaries. Essentially, he became a solitary recluse, grudgingly admitting that college life was 'by no means unmixed misery though married life has no doubt many charms to which I am a stranger.'[491] Mechanical gadgetry of all description was of absorbing interest: today, he would be skilful and progressive with computers and internet technology. He was introduced to photography by his mother's brother, Skeffington Lutwige, and quickly became proficient at the new science which seemed to combine chemistry, optics and art. In 1856, Carroll bought a fine rosewood camera, thus embarking on a voyage of aesthetic expression which would develop into a rival career to academe and would, moreover, act as an introduction to the higher levels of society. It seems that Lewis Carroll was a snob.

He was clever, almost brilliant: he took a B.A., and M.A., a Boulter Scholarship, a Bostock Scholarship, first class Honours in mathematics, Second in Greats, third class in history and philosophy: he was made a student of Christ Church, sub-librarian, full member of the teaching staff, Deacon of the Church of England and Curator of the Common Room. Literature remained central in his life, manifesting itself in a stream of articles, poems, parodies and satire, principally for his home journals *Mish Masch* and *The Rectory Umbrella,* but occasionally for professional publication in *The Whitby Gazette, The Oxonian Advertiser* and *Comic Times.*[492] Most biographies tend to make Lewis Carroll sound almost unbearably priggish but Morton Cohen presents a livelier portrait of an attractively humorous young don with a particular sense of the ridiculous – certainly more than a few of his Oxford colleagues were the target of squibs and pamphlets in a stream of comic verses, satire and parody. It seems that Carroll's scattergun sense of humour operated as a defensive shield against helpless anxieties and inborn depressions.

---

[488] Karoline Leach*, In The Shadow of The Dreamchild.* London, Peter Owen, 1999. p83

[489] Sebastian Flyte is a perfect example: Evelyn Waugh's *Brideshead Revisited*, 1945, sets him in Meadow Buildings, Christ Church, along with his teddy bear and plovers' egg luncheons.

[490] Arthur Penrhyn Stanley, later Dean of Westminster, had accompanied Edward Lear on a walking tour to Ireland in 1834: he became an intimate friend of Henry Liddell, Dean of Christ Church and father of Alice.

[491] de la Mare, p. 36

[492] Cohen, p71

Carroll was constantly inventing tales to amuse young children and he was, in his own quiet way, a performer. His camera acted as introduction to the Liddell family whose father was promoted to Dean of Christ Church in 1855, but his interest in Ina, Alice and Edith lay far beyond their posing for photographs. There is considerable evidence to suggest that he never stopped telling stories in ways that children themselves later describe as both magical and personal – and always new and different. Jenny Woolf argues that Carroll was 'primarily a verbal storyteller…that is why so many of his comic poems are still popular today. They sound good when spoken…they are rhythmic, subtle, enticing and they demand to be said aloud'.[493] Reciting his poems or telling stories to children has a theatrical element and we need to remember Carroll's interest in the stage. Despite a certain priggish and clerical anxiety about 'unsuitable' productions, he remained an ardent theatre-goer all his life with actresses Isa Bowman and Ellen Terry among his closest friends. When he recited his own compositions, (he had worked up a few stories into parlour performance, 'The Pixies', 'The Little Foxes' and 'Bruno's Picnic') he didn't stammer.

Virginia Woolf believed him to be 'a man with no life'[494] and certainly he had none of the external stimuli which characterised the lives of Edward Lear and William Gilbert. He never travelled (save for one unlikely visit to Russia) and remained a Fellow of Christ Church, Oxford, for forty-seven years, venturing out for regular holidays in an Eastbourne boarding house. In 1862 he moved to the rooms in Tom Quad which he kept until he died in 1898. He is known to have spent the occasional summer holiday with a Rev. H.A. Barclay who kept a Gentleman's Boarding School at No.ll, Lewes Crescent, Brighton, between 1874–887;[495] inaccurate, if optimistic, local guide books suggest that it was the tunnel through the private gardens of Lewes Crescent to the sea which inspired the rabbit hole in Chapter One of *Alice in Wonderland*, (1865). There were trips to Wales, the Lake District and the Isle of Wight. He ate plainly, dressed almost entirely in black with high wing collars and enjoyed attending serious drama at the London theatres. Luncheon was invariably a biscuit and a glass of wine.

What did matter to Lewis Carroll, throughout his life, were his family. He was a model brother and beloved uncle who took upon himself to succour and maintain his siblings after the death of their parents. Friendships at Albury, near Guildford, led him to The Chestnuts, a handsome redbrick house near the castle in which he installed his six unmarried sisters and various family members including his brother Edwin who came and went from missionary work in Zanzibar and Tristan da Cunha, and his old Aunt Lucy Ludwige. Although Carroll took Holy Orders himself, he never held clerical office nor willingly preached: the combination of stammer, slight deafness and premonition of epileptic seizures may have been responsible. Carroll was a

[493] Internet Site www.lookingforlewiscarroll.com/ Accessed 25/02/008

[494] Virginia Woolf, *The Moment and Other Essays*. London, Hogarth Press. 1947.

[495] Page's Brighton Directory for 1876 and 1877 list this curious institution. Perhaps it was a clerical and therefore wholly honourable and respectable seaside lodging house for gentlemen – only?

frequent visitor to The Chestnuts, voted in the Guildford Parliamentary elections and was listed as the householder in the rate books. It was during one such visit to help nurse his godson, through what was ultimately a mortal illness, that Carroll conceived *The Hunting of the Snark* in 1874. Twenty-three years later, he himself lay dying of pneumonia in the same house. He is buried in Trinity Churchyard, Guildford.

Genius lies in the continuing relevance of creativity to an audience of any period, age or fashion. The Nonsense of Alice, the *Hunting of the Snark*, the 'Dong with the Luminous Nose' the 'Jabberwocky' and the 'Owl and the Pussy Cat' remain on Waterstone's bookshelves today. Alice transcended the earnest moralising of most Victorian children's literature and holds her own against Narnia and Hogwarts. (Shared themes include David versus Goliath, time backwards and magical worlds reached through cupboards, railway station platforms and rabbit holes.) *The Hunting of the Snark* continues to inspire new readings, annotated editions[496]and a loyal following of Snark Clubs[497] which meet for 'sailings' in London Clubs today and whose members 'tingle bells' and 'slip softly and suddenly vanish away'.[498] A new species of tree has been named 'The Boojum,' and Elspeth Huxley entitled her African Memoir[499] *Forks and Hope*, a reference to the Hunting Chorus of the Snark. Both Lear's Nonsense creatures and Alice's adventures are the trials of a child battling against authority: echoes of the 'they' in Lear's limericks and the joke bureaucrats in Bab. What *The Hunting of the Snark* is all about, where it came from and what it tells us about Carroll and his contemporary existence, the following chapters are designed to explain.

There is neither space nor obligation in this study to discuss at any length Carroll's predilection for immaculately dressed, perfectly behaved and beautifully well-bred girls aged between ten and twelve. Prurient examinations by biographers and literary psychologists have been concerned with what remains a mystery: the precise nature of Carroll's relationship with any of the Liddell women, or indeed with his many 'child friends' and adult actresses. Voluminous diaries and letters are confusing, crucial pages razored out. We know that the Victorian images of childhood were different to our own, and that Carroll's were different yet again: not for Carroll the idealised, wing-sprouting fairy creatures surrounded by smiling putti and trailing clouds of glory, but real, barefoot rascals wearing very little clothing – or none at all. Carroll's images were at odds with the Victorian idealised fantasy of childhood as innocence and purity: they demonstrated the reality of underage and unwoken sexuality. Adult sexuality in an era of virgin marriage as social control and class breeding was repressed and stifled, and the child privileged as a being for whom sex had no meaning. Carroll may have subconsciously longed to 'develop' the innocence of a naked child: or he might have wished to return himself to a state unsullied by his own experiences at Rugby. Victorian

---

[496] Martin Gardner, *The Annotated Snark*. London, Penguin Classic Edition. 1995.

[497] One Snark Club, founded in Cambridge, 1934, met for a sailing in 2005 at the RAC, Woodcote Park, Surrey, posting 10 Club Rules including a blank No. 8.

[498] Hunting of the Snark, Fit 8.

[499] Elspeth Huxley, *With Forks and Hope*. London, Chatto & Windus, 1964.

tableaux of sentimental children include Dickens' Little Nell and the clichéd *Bubbles* in black velvet, Millais' idealised portrait of his grandson. Ruskin, famously repelled by the adult nudity of his wife, focussed his erotic attention on the nine year old Rose de la Touche. All this may relate to Lewis Carroll, Alice, Wonderland and Mirrors – but it does not have any bearing on *The Hunting of the Snark*. The Hunt, a wholesome, manly occupation, features an entirely masculine cast (the beaver's sex is indeterminate) engaged in sailing, exploring and the law, none notable for feminine participation. There is no young lady in sight.

THAT WHICH WENT BEFORE:
EARLIER STUDIES OF LEWIS CARROLL AND
THE HUNTING OF THE SNARK

B iographies of Lewis Carroll follow what has begun to seem a familiar pattern – initial hagiography, followed by critical reaction and the sound of toppling statues. In Carroll's case, there was serious scope for re-assessment following the first study by his nephew, Stuart Dodgson Collingwood, son of Carroll's sister Mary and the Rev. Henry Collingwood, in 1898.[500] As a trusted intimate and family member, Collingwood was given unique access to papers and diaries and produced a 400-page idealised portrait. It is likely that Collingwood, himself an undergraduate at Christ Church, knew his uncle to be selfish, moody and famous for getting up late – very different from the near-saint he described. Collingwood could not have missed the gossip about 'an artistic life that touched the edge of respectability and one which featured some unorthodox friendships' but there seems little doubt that Carroll's family strove to conceal some uncomfortable truths.[501] They needed to sustain the myth that the creator of 'Alice' was a stammering, reclusive Oxford mathematician whose unworldly genius flourished by the inspiration of his innocent friendships with very young girls. Victorian society pretended to believe that, as no sexual element could exist in relationships with girls under twelve, Carroll's 'child friends' were entirely acceptable. Several women later claimed to be among their number when proof exists that they were aged between sixteen and twenty-five.[502] Isa Bowman, in particular, blurred fact and fiction in her portrayal of the little girl and the grave Professor: when she shared his lodgings for a seaside holiday in Eastbourne, she was nearly twenty.

The centenary of Carroll's birth in 1932 prompted the second full biography by the American purveyor of Nonsense, Herbert Langford Reed. Both the Liddell and Dodgson families remained tightlipped and suspicious, but Reed's account is charming, anecdotal and fictionalised: the oft-related tale of Queen Victoria being unamused when presented with a Euclid textbook after requesting the next work from the creator of Alice is untrue – sadly. Despite any lack of stringent or thorough new analysis, Langford Reed's reputation from *The Complete Limerick Book*, (1925), and his film *She Snoops to Conquer,*[503] lent authority to his study and helped place Carroll as an

---

[500] Stuart Dodgson Collingwood, *Life and Letters of Lewis Carroll*. London, Fisher Unwin. 1898.

[501] Karoline Leach, *In The Shadow of the Dreamchild*. London, Peter Owen, 1999, p24

[502] Most notably Ruth Gamlen and Isa Bowman.

[503] 1944. George Formby starred in the comic tale of a council oddjob man who accidentally uncovers corruption.

important contributor to the contemporary comic and satiric scene.

The centenary of Carroll's birth in 1932 inspired the poet Walter de la Mare to enlarge his 1930 essay into a short biography, notable for the insight of one story teller about another.[504] Jo Elwyn Jones and Francis Gladstone[505] claim that de la Mare was the first major critic to place the Alice books in the top rank of world literature. It is de la Mare's preface that has inspired the title of this book.

'The Victorian age was rich in exotics. It amuses us moderns, having cut and discoloured them, to make little herbariums of them. We forget to remind ourselves that many of our own prize blossoms are of the hothouse and will suffer a similar desiccation. But there is one Victorian wild flower which makes any such condescension absurd – and it is   called Nonsense'.[506]

Florence Becker Lennon was the first to address the quirks in Carroll's character and provides a certain psychological insight, particularly since sufficient time had passed for Carroll's mythic status to be addressed[507] Becker Lennon, a talented writer and insightful critic, also considered Carroll's works beyond Alice and *The Hunting of the Snark*, placing Carroll in a scholarly context of children's literature.

Derek Hudson's straightforward biography[508] remains a study of an earnest mathematician who never reached emotional maturity, the gentle pre-Freudian of Reed and Collingwood. Hudson ridiculed any psychoanalytical approach and believed it was dangerous to read too many allusions and hidden meanings into Carroll's characters, for Carroll did not construct them from observation, except in the most general sense: his ideas were 'wont to come of themselves'.

Ann Clark continued what begins to seem an American obsession with Carrolliana and tackled a full length biography in 1979.[509] Devotees of Carroll praised the book as clear and thorough, the ideal primer for a new student of Alice, but Karoline Leach criticised the continuous presentation of baseless supposition and yet another idealised portrait of a saint. We shall briefly examine the work of Leach whose *In The Shadow of the Dream Child* is an important contemporary corrective to the Carroll mythology.[510]

Morton Cohen has become the doyen of Anglo-American Carroll scholarship. His research into Victorian literary bibliography and letters is responsible for a stream of annotated discoveries, diaries and publications,

[504] Walter de la Mare, *Lewis Carroll*. London, Faber & Faber, 1932.

[505] Jo Elwyn Jones & Francis Gladstone, *The Alice Companion*. New York University Press, 1998.

[506] de la Mare, p7

[507] Florence Becker Lennon, *Lewis Carroll* London, Cassell & Co, 1947.

[508] Derek Hudson ,*Lewis Carroll* London, Constable. 1954, Revised & reissued , 1976.

[509] Ann Clark, *Lewis Carroll*. New York, Schocken Books,1979.

[510] Karoline Leach, *In The Shadow of the Dream Child*. London, Peter Owen, 1999.

culminating in a 500-page *Lewis Carroll* in 1995[511] – a passion ignited in 1960 by the work of Roger Lancelyn Green.[512] Cohen presents Carroll as a thoroughly mature and responsible adult with a highly developed intellect and free-flowing imagination. The portrait which emerges is that of an attractive, rounded, even if austere and controlled personality, frequently capable of acts of great kindness, especially towards his family. Jones and Gladstone comment that Cohen's work 'will be hard to displace as the standard biography' although they note that it discounts the importance of contemporary Oxford controversies concerning either religion or the curriculum. Yet the depth of Cohen's research validates a portrait of a far more normal Carroll than usually portrayed and this, to my mind, makes the Alice books and *The Hunting of the Snark*, far more extraordinary.

Notwithstanding Cohen's pre-eminence, biographers and researchers still write books, papers and theses on Carroll and the subject shows no sign of exhaustion. Michael Bakewell and Donald Thomas published biographies in 1996 and Graham Darien Smith produced 'Contextualising Alice' as a Ph.D. thesis for Bangor University in 2005. Countless articles, reviews and studies continue to appear, most particularly in the specialist journal *The Carrollian* (formerly the Jabberwocky) published by the Lewis Carroll Society.[513]

Karoline Leach's controversial book was designed to scrape back the accretion of myth and legend that surrounds Carroll. She argues that accident and confusion, occasional deceit and wild imagination have conjured up an image based on what the public wanted to believe. As the readers of the Alice books became obsessed with Alice, so they imagined that Carroll was obsessed by her – and indeed with little girls in general. Leach painstakingly examines the evidence and her scholarly and well-documented study cannot be ignored, even if certain particular assertions can be challenged, most particularly that Carroll's main emotional and sexual interest lay in adult women.

The extraordinary nature of Carroll's imagination, as exercised in the creation of Alice and *The Hunting of the Snark*, has attracted almost as many literary and psychological theorists as general readers. Neither Lear nor Gilbert have suffered the same faintly perverted magnifying glass, nor the plethora of often ludicrous explanations. Freudian theories concerning the unconscious have become such a familiar tool in literary criticism today that we forget how startling and even shocking they once seemed. One reaction to anything new and unfamiliar is to laugh at it, and both Leach and Hudson consider that *Wonderland Pyschoanalysed*[514] by Balliol undergraduate Anthony Goldschmidt was a very clever joke indeed. Goldschmidt argued that Alice was a cryptic message from Carroll's subconscious describing symbols that modern psychology could decode: the fall down the rabbit hole equals sexual penetration, the doors in the hall represent female genitalia...and so on and

[511] Morton Cohen, *Lewis Carroll*. London, Macmillan, 1995.

[512] 1918–1987: Merton College, Oxford; academic, student of C.S. Lewis, member of the Inklings Discussion Group, biographer and children's writer.

[513] Editor, Mark Richards. 50, Lauderdale Mansions, Lauderdale Road, London. W9 1NE.

[514] Anthony Goldschmidt , *The New Oxford Outlook*. 1933.

such forth.

Even if Goldschmidt himself never really believed this, others did, a fate dreaded by Alexander Woollcott. 'At least the new psychologists have not explored this dream book, nor pawed over the gentle, shrinking celibate who wrote it'.[515] Not yet, Mr Woollcott, not yet, but soon enough they did, often with hilarious results. Esmé Wingfield Stratford wrote an anti-Freudian book containing a burlesque psycho-analytical interpretation of Jabberwocky, purporting to reveal Carroll's Oedipus complex.[516] William Empson thought it all came down to wombs.[517]

Generally, biographers of Carroll have not devoted more than polite attention to *The Hunting of the Snark* – with the exception of Morton Cohen. For Cohen, the Snark 'soars as least as high as the Alice books in its invention. It is taut and measured, like a symphony or a mass. Its musical quality is important…it is through the music of the words that Charles gets to his readers, not through the transmission of thought'.[518] Cohen describes the genesis of The Snark in some detail and bravely includes a selection of the negative contemporary press comment. He argues that the subterranean meaning of The Snark did not relate to any fear of death or annihilation as 'underscoring everything he (Carroll) wrote and did and said was his conviction of a moral universe and life after death'[519] Cohen, like Graham Darien Smith, underlines Carroll's absolute faith in God and His world beyond human comprehension.

Karoline Leach's contemporary and controversial new study of Carroll considers that the *The Hunting of the Snark* may be 'his greatest work of genius…ruthlessly adult in its humour and its satire, and, like the far inferior *Sylvie and Bruno*, a jumble of personal and political references'.[520] Her view is at odds with that of Jackie Wullschläger who, a mere six years later, considered that *The Hunting of the Snark* is 'forced and studied by comparison (with the Alice books) although it contains magnificent characters such as the earnest and despairing Bellman whose job is endlessly to toll the bell'.[521] Perhaps it is the 'adult' quality of the Snark that Wullschläger resists: her admirable study is primarily to site Nonsense or 'wonderland' in the broad context of Victorian and Edwardian children's literature, out of which The Snark somehow escapes. It is to Leach that I owe a connection with the leitmotif of 'The Mistletoe Bough', one of the most popular songs of the 1860s whose haunting refrain ' they sought her that night, they sought her next day, they sought her in vain when a week passed away' seems to bear more than a

[515] Alexander Woollcott, Preface, *The Complete Carroll*. New York, Random House, 1939.

[516] Esmé Stratford-Wingfield, 'New Minds for Old'. Quoted in Becker Lennon, p323

[517] William Empson, *Seven Types of Ambiguity*, 1930. Empson devotes the last chapter in his English *Pastoral Poetry, 1938,* to a study of the Alice books.

[518] Morton Cohen, *Lewis Carroll* London, Macmillan , 1995. p411

[519] Ibid. p410

[520] Karoline Leach, *In the Shadow of the Dreamchild*. London, Peter Owen, 1999. p225

[521] Jackie Wullschläger, *Inventing Wonderland*. London, Methuen, 2005. p62

coincidental resemblance to the Snark chorus.[522]

Florence Becker Lennon supports what she believes to be Carroll's own assertion that *Jabberwocky* and *The Hunting of the Snark* are the same poem. Carroll claimed that the Snark 'lives on an island frequented by the Bandersnatch and the Jubjub – no doubt the very island in which the Jabberwock was slain.'[523] She argues that 'Carroll's stifled impulses towards self-assertion and towards the normal sex life, kept sending him weird messages of which these two poems are about the clearest'.[524]

Martin Gardner, an American mathematician, surveyed most of the earlier reviews of *The Hunting of the Snark* in a Preface to his 1962 edition.[525] He himself believes that the Snark is a 'poem about being and non-being, an existential poem, a poem of existential agony. The Bellman's map is the map that charts the course of humanity: blank because we possess no information about where we are, or whither we drift…the great search motif of the poem, the quest for an ultimate good'.[526] Ominously, Gardner sees in the Snark, the possibility of unintentional prophecy: that the letter B, so significant and consistent in The Snark, could actually relate to the atomic bomb. Gardner reveals that the US Air Force has an intercontinental guided missile with a thermo-nuclear warhead which it has christened The Snark…. Almost precisely the opposite interpretation was the opportunistic whimsy of Hubert Digby Watson who saw the poem as a paean to peace. As storm clouds gathered over Europe during 1936, Watson believed that 'thimbles' alluded to the Women's Peace Crusade, the Baker was a mild-mannered pacifist, the Butcher was a truculent war monger, the Beaver, an isolationist and the Bellman, the pacific Stanley Baldwin, whose name began, yet again, with a B.[527]

A focus on the 'hunting' provided one far-fetched theory which linked the Bellman to John Peel's dog, the Beaver to Belvoir and the title as an echo of 'The Hunting of the Cheviot' an alternative title to 'Chevy Chase' from the Allingham Ballad Book of 1865, which also contained 'A Lyttel Geste of Robyn Hode in 8 Fittes, no less. 'The notion of hunting began with thimbles and slippers and brought with it the lore of the field'.[528] Etymological explanations of the Snark might be on firmer ground. Ellis Hillman[529] believes that Carroll's knowledge of Latin, Greek, Anglo-Saxon and possibly Hebrew[530], as demonstrated in his parodies, inspires the choice of the anti-hero. In the Anglo-Saxon dictionary, the word closest to Boojum is 'bugan' –

---

[522] Ballad by Samuel Rogers from *Ginevra,* 1823, music by Henry Bishop - the story will be told in the relevant `Chapter for this section.

[523] Becker Lennon, p177.

[524] Ibid.

[525] Revised, 1974

[526] Martin Gardner, Preface, to Lewis Carroll *The Hunting of the Snark.* London, Penguin Classics. 1995. p28

[527] Gardner, p99

[528] Denis Crutch, 'Hunting the Snark', *Jabberwocky,* Autumn, 5 (1976) No. 4

[529] Ellis Hillman, 'Hunting the Boojum', *The Carrollian,* 8 (2001) 125

[530] Dr. Pusey, Carroll's mentor in Oxford, was Professor of Hebrew.

to flee. 'Boo' in Latin means to roar and 'iumentum' is beast. Another dictionary of early English includes the echoic words 'snirt' which means to laugh in a suppressed fashion and 'sniff, snort and snurr'. (It is just possible that Carroll's downland walk between Guildford and Farnham in July 1874 when 'for the Snark was a Boojum' first occurred was subconsciously prompted by the vernacular name for the path 'Hogs Back' (Boar) which lies above the village of Compton, pronounced Cumptum.)

We shall meet Henry Holiday, as Carroll's illustrator for the Snark, later in this thesis in a chapter dealing with the Snark pictures. Holiday knew Carroll well and, unusually among Carroll's artists, became a friend as well as a colleague. Describing his reaction to *The Hunting of the Snark,* he believed that 'when the Nonsense seems most exuberant, we find an underlying order, a method in the madness…whether the humour consists chiefly in the conscious defiance of logic by a logical mind, or in the half conscious control of its lovely and grotesque fancies: in either case, the charm arises from the author's well ordered mind'.[531] This view of the Snark, and indeed of Nonsense in the most general sense, as pertaining to logic and order is shared by Michael Holquist who describes how Carroll's inventions and innovative language represent his search for the utmost precision of meaning and expression. 'The portmanteau word is a combination of two systems, language and logic…it is also the third element in a three part progression…like the rule of three, it results in a new truth and like the rule of three, it is a unique kind of syllogism. In order to get a logical conclusion to the syllogism, it must grow out of a divergence between two prior parallel statements'.[532]

Henry Holiday's contemporary, known only by his initials M.H.T., believed that the one possible explanation for The Snark was a representation of material wealth, with railway shares and soap newly existing to underline this thesis. (Sadly for M.H.T., the huge wealth generation of soap by Lever Bros. at Port Sunlight took place in 1880, five years after the Snark appeared). More theories connecting the Snark with rampant consumerism were proposed in 1911 when Devereux Court believed the poem to satirize a risky business venture with the ship representing a 'floated' company, full of speculators fond of ' quotations' and a Snark as a landshark who eats the company.[533]

Adherents of the Snark as a metaphor for commerce arrived during the Depression in the 1930s and set about with considerable ingenuity to connect members of the crew with stockbrokers, skilled workers and speculators. Boots represents unskilled labour, the Baker is a small businessman in luxury goods and the Billiard Marker is a speculator. Dean Donham of the Harvard School of Business Administration advanced an updated version of this idea in 1929, reinforced by Arthur Ruhl in a remarkable article entitled 'The Finding of the Snark' in which a complete *dramatis personae* for the poem is assembled: the Jubjub is Disraeli and the Bandersnatch who grabs the banker in Fit Seven is

---

[531] Henry Holiday 'The Snark's Significance.' *The Academy*, January 29th, 1898.
[532] Michael Holquist, 'What Is A Boojum? Nonsense and Moderation.' Yale French Studies, 43 (1969). 145-164
[533] Martin Gardner, Preface, *The Annotated Snark*. London, Penguin. 1962. p24

the Bank of England, repeatedly raising interest rates preceding the panic in 1875.

One of the most creative earlier interpretations was that penned in 1901 by 'Snarkophilus Snobbs', more realistically christened F.C. Schiller, in a hilarious spoof critique for *Mind,* a parody issue of the *British Philosophical Journal* in which he defined The Snark in terms of a Hegelian discourse on the Absolute.

'It is well known that Hegel thought the wrong kind of Absolute (that of other Professors) was like the night in which all cows are black…the pursuit of the Absolute was a form of Intellectual *thimble-rigging* which only the *forktunate* can hope to obtain'..etc, etc.

Finally, I salute the unknown scholar who versified his interpretation for 'The Wykehamist' in May, 1876, hiding his identity under the pseudonym 'frumious

'You ask me, Mr. Editor, to state
Views on a problem, mooted much of late.
What is the Bellman? Why he rings the bell?
And what the Butcher? And, oh, save the mark
Who, or what, or which, the mischief is, the Snark?

Brothers! A moment, leave the ice half done
Forsake the jamless tart, the sanded bun.
And listen, while I struggle to expound
The sense that Nonsense hideth underground!'[534]

---

[534] Edward Guiliano 'Lewis Carroll Observed' Unpublished Miscellany for the Carroll Society of North America. 1976.

GENESIS AND DEDICATION OF THE SNARK

Carroll was composing the Snark when he first met Gertrude Chataway on holiday in the Isle of Wight, September, 1875. In later years, Mrs Gertrude Atkinson (nee Chataway) remembered the occasion. 'Imagine the sea-side at Sandown…where lodgings stretched along the front each with its balcony on the upper floor and standing in a little garden with steps down to the shore. Imagine a little girl about eight and a half absolutely entranced with the lodger next door. To her, he seemed quite an old gentleman. In the morning, he came out onto his balcony breathing in sea air as if he could not get enough: whenever she heard him coming, she would rush out to see him. After a few days, he spoke to her. 'Little girl, why do you come out onto the balcony whenever I come out?' 'To see you sniff' she said, 'it is lovely to see you sniff like this' and she threw up her head and drew in the air. Thus began a long friendship which ended only with his death'.[535]

Mrs Atkinson's memoir described how Carroll 'told the most lovely tales that could possibly be imagined, often illustrating the exciting situations with a pencil as he went along What made his stories particularly charming to a child was that he often took his cue from her remarks – a question would set him off on quite a new trail of ideas so that one felt one had somehow helped to make the story and it seemed a personal possession. It was the most lovely nonsense imaginable and I naturally revelled in it. His vivid imagination would fly from one subject to another and was never tied down in any way by the probabilities of life'.[536]

We need to remember Carroll's fondness for the theatre and a latent skill and interest in performance. Inventing and relating stories for children was his preferred method of self-expression – this should have made him a marvellous teacher but the ability to communicate seems to have been limited only to fantasies of his own invention.

Carroll was forty two years old when he met Gertrude, a number of immense significance in the Snark.[537] The Baker leaves forty two items of luggage on the beach. John Vernon Lord established that the digits in the years 1874–1876 when Carroll was writing Snark add up to forty two. The Preface

---

[535] A.G.Atkinson, 'Memories of Lewis Carroll' *Hampshire Chronicle*, March 13, 1948 p3. Quoted in Morton Cohen, *The Letters of Lewis Carroll*. 1979 p230

[536] Ibid, quoted in John Vernon Lord Foreward to *Illustrating The Hunting of the Snark* .Artists Choice Edition. 2006. pvii

[537] In Douglas Adam's *Hitchhiker's Guide to the Galaxy,* 42 is the number that represents the meaning of life, the Universe and Everything Else. Quoted in John Vernon Lord's Introduction to *Illustrating the Snark*. Professor Norman Vance points out that HGG is yet another quest narrative, based on Arthur Dent's *Plain Man's Pathway to Heaven* (1601) known to end in a scene adapted from John Bunyan.

to the Snark refers to Rule 42 of the Naval Code. There are 42 illustrations in the first Alice book, and there would have been 42 in the second, but for a last minute change of plan.[538]

Gertrude became one of his favourite 'child friends' and 'one of the sweetest children it has ever been my happiness to meet'.[539] In this letter, Carroll asked Gertrude's mother if he might dedicate some verses to her as a souvenir of happy holidays. He recorded the event in his diary, commenting that the verses 'might do for a dedication to the book which I think of calling *The Hunting of the Snark'*.[540] The four verses are an ingenious acrostic on his young friend's name.

'Girt with boyish garb for boyish task
Eager she wields her spade – yet loves as well
Rest on a friendly knee, the tale to ask
That he delights to tell.

Rude spirits of the seething outer strife
Unmeet to read her pure and simple sprite
Deem if you wish, such hours a waste of life
Empty of all delight!

Chat on, sweet maid, and rescue from annoy
Hearts that by wiser talk are unbeguiled,
Ah, happy he who owns that tenderest joy
The heart-love of a child!'

Away, fond thoughts, and vex my soul no more
Work claims my wakeful nights, my busy days
Albeit, bright memories of that sunlit shore
Yet haunt my dreaming gaze,

Michael Holquist has pointed out that the initial word in the first line of each of the four quatrains constitutes another acrostic – Girt, Rude, Chat, Away. This is the first indication in the poem that the words in it exist less for what they denote in the system of English than they do for the system that Carroll will erect – the initial meanings of clothed, wild, speak, begone – become secondary to a purely idiosyncratic pattern of Carroll's own choosing.[541] Carroll asked Mrs Chataway for some pictures of Gertrude in bathing dress which he wanted to insert opposite the dedication in a few particular copies of *The Hunting of the Snark*. He continued to write to Gertrude in whimsical fashion, sometimes signing letters 'your ever loving

---

[538] R.B. Shaberman, *Under the Quizzing Glass, a Carroll Miscellany*. London, Magpie Press, 1972. p27

[539] Lewis Carroll letter to Mrs Chataway, Oxford, October 25, 1875. Quoted in Cohen Letters, p.231.

[540] p. 345 of Diary entry, quoted in Cohen Letters, p232.

[541] Michael Holquist 'What Is a Boojum'. *Yale French Studies*, 43. (1969).145–164

friend Lewis Carroll', sometimes 'your ever loving friend, C.L. Dodgson'. Kisses were included, as were the constant admonitions not to grow any older.

THE SNARK IN PICTURES

Lewis Carroll was an artist – but not with a pencil. Unlike Edward Lear or William Gilbert, he was never able to illustrate his fantasies. He knew that his attempts for the original Alice in Wonderland in 1865 were curiously childish: they were to remain as helpful blueprints for John Tenniel. By 1874 when Carroll was composing The Snark, he seems to have abandoned all efforts to sketch his own ideas and relied on constant – and irritating – communication with Henry Holiday. In the 1880s, he joined a life drawing class, but to no apparent practical purpose.

Carroll was able to express visual creativity through his photographs and although these were never Nonsensical, they require some attention in this context. A new study by Douglas Nickel reclaims Carroll as a serious portrait photographer of his age after the unbalanced view inspired by the Liddell hype and the Alice pictures.[542] Carroll's 'charm, grace and naturalness and the feminine light-heartedness of his pictures'[543] was compared to 'the intellectual masculinity of Julia Margaret Cameron'. Nickel cites Carroll's photographs of Arthur Stanley, Dean of Westminster and Frederick, Prince of Denmark as a counterweight to the nude children, describing his art as an essential document of his social world, sanctioned by the agenda of a family memoir.[544]

Lewis Carroll was fortunate in his age and in his world. In 1860, a Conference for the Advancement of Science met in Oxford was attended by, among others, Bishop Samuel Wilberforce and T.H. Huxley. Carroll's camera acted as passport. Sadi Ranson-Polizotti claims that Carroll was almost as interested in the chance to meet Alfred Tennyson, Dante Gabriel Rossetti, Arthur Hughes and even the Royal family as he was in taking their pictures.[545]

Uncle Skeffington's early encouragement was augmented by Reginald Southey, Carroll's friend and fellow mathematician at Christ Church who taught Carroll how to mix the chemicals needed for photographic developing and enlarging. Carroll acquired a studio in London during 1863 and persuaded Christ Church to allow him to make a dark room on the roof at Tom Quad: until the 1870s, his diaries attest more to the expense and difficulty of photography and the sincerity of his ambitions for it than any serious interest in creative writing.

By 1875, the date of his composition of The Hunting of the Snark, Carroll

---

[542] Douglas Nickel, *Dreaming in Pictures*. Yale University Press, 2002.

[543] Helmut Gernsheim, quoted in Nickel.

[544] Collingwood, 1898.

[545] Sadi Ranson-Polizzotti '42 Seconds Underground – the photography of Lewis Carroll'. Internet Sitehttp://tantmieux.squarespace.com accessed 2/3/008

had more or less abandoned photography – but he had begun to catalogue approximately 3,000 prints with his usual obsessive attention to detail, devoting up to ten hours a day and weeks of his life to 'photo-writing'. The albums that survive are often illustrated with other types of art – drawings and sketches – juxtaposing images with poetry. Sometimes the verses were his own, sometimes borrowed from writers whose work he admired, including Edward Lear and Alfred Tennyson.[546]

Critics seem to agree that despite the social and historical value of Carroll's serious portrait studies, the photographs of children possess infinitely greater artistic merit. This is connected to Carroll's ease in the company of children, and his pleasure in their society. Despite his skill in photographing his subjects in costume, he never seems to have considered dressing-up adults to illustrate either the Alice books, or *The Hunting of the Snark*: they are books for children ABOUT adult characters. It is unlikely that he could have persuaded any adult to dress up as The Bellman.

Henry Holiday, who Carroll chose to illustrate the original Snark, was a lesser scion of the Pre-Raphaelite Brotherhood. On arrival at the Royal Academy School in London in 1855 aged sixteen, he was immediately attracted by the work and philosophy of Dante Gabriel Rossetti and Holman Hunt. Holiday joined a circle of painters, artists and writers who met regularly at Burne-Jones' studio, eventually succeeding Burne-Jones as a designer of stained glass for the manufacturing company, Powell & Sons in 1862. It is hard to imagine that he did not met Edward Lear, a close friend and confident of 'Daddy' Hunt during the early 1860s, particularly given their mutual friend and champion, John Ruskin. Although Ruskin later expressed doubts about Holiday, he was even more critical about other artists considered to illustrate *Phantasmagoria;* E & A Fairfield, F.W. Lawson and Hendschel.

Holiday joined the Brotherhood on their journeys to the Lake District where he acquired a small house, 'Betty Fold', Ambleside, now a bed-and-breakfast hotel in the Hawkeshead valley. Unlike Carroll's other illustrators, John Tenniel, Arthur Frost and Harry Furniss, Holiday established a friendly working relationship with his demanding author and they even became friends. (Furniss later described Carroll as a 'bore', 'egoist' and 'spoilt child' and we know that Carroll 'suffocated' all his artists with instructions, sample pictures and fastidious detail.[547])

Although Pre-Raphaelite art has a strong illustrative quality, Holiday was not primarily an interpreter of contemporary literature, much less contemporary Nonsense poetry. His stained glass windows depict scenes dear to the Pre-Raphaelites – stories from the Bible and medieval legends, illustrated with great masses of floating drapery and Italianate classical backgrounds. He toured Italy in 1867 and became inspired by the methods which Renaissance artists chose to break away from the Gothic. In a paper for the R.A. entitled 'Modernism in Art' Holiday asserted 'all great art is modern when it is produced' and 'no art is genuine which is not modern in the sense of

---

[546] Ransom-Polizzotti, p3

[547] John Vernon Lord *Afterward* to *Illustrating The Hunting of the Snark*. Artists Edition, 2006.

expressing the best of which the artist and his age are capable'.[548]   It is tempting to look for versions of familiar faces in Holiday's Snark pictures: certainly the Bellman has a curious resemblance to the midlife images of Alfred Tennyson, and crew members under the deck in Fit One look like Rossetti and Holman Hunt. We see Holiday's work today in the memorial window to Isambard Kingdom Brunel in Westminster Abbey and in the West Window of St Mary Magdalene, Paddington. A curious link with Carroll is Holiday's wife Kate who embroidered work for William Morris and who encouraged Holiday in his support for the Suffragettes. Carroll was a fervent feminist and appears to have believed in equal rights for the education of women and in their ability to practise professional careers as the equals of men.

Holiday's Snark pictures never became as iconic as Tenniel's Alice. But there was no Alice Liddell to inspire the Snark itself as the mythical creature only lives in our imagination. Henry Holiday described how he himself 'not unnaturally invented a Boojum, but Mr Dodgson wrote that although it was a delightful monster it was quite inadmissible. All his descriptions of the Boojum were unimaginable and he wanted the creature to remain so'.[549] Despite initial reservations concerning the scale and substance of the poem which grew from four fits to eight, Holiday eventually declared that he 'found it unquestionably funny throughout and could not wish any part cut out'.[550] Bravely, Holiday adds that although Wagner is supposed to have written 'The Ring of the Nibelung' backwards, with Siegfried's funeral march coming first, 'it is scarcely up to me to maintain that the great German master of musical drama plagiarised in his methods from our distinguished humourist'.[551]

We do not know why Carroll selected this talented, if obscure artist for the Snark. Neither letters or diaries explain his choice. They are believed to have met in July 1870 when Carroll set up his camera and darkroom in Holiday's London house and used Holiday's studio for photography. It seems that the artist was involved in the production of some of Carroll's child nude studies and that his 'graceful and non-objectionable drawings'[552] helped persuade anxious parents to allow their offspring to be thus captured. In January 1874, Carroll suggested that Holiday illustrate his children's book *Sylvie and Bruno* and by the autumn of the same year came the commission to draw 'three pictures for a new poem'.[553] Carroll confided in his diary that 'if only he (Holiday) could draw grotesques, it would be all I should desire – the grace and beauty of the pictures would quite rival Tenniel, I think'.[554] But Ruskin,

---

[548] Internet Site www.visitcumbria.com Henry Holiday. Accessed 12/11/007

[549] Henry Holiday, 'The Snark's Significance'. Quoted in *The Academy,* January 29th 1989

[550] Ibid.

[551] Morton Cohen, *Lewis Carroll and His Illustrators'.* Macmillan, London. 2003. p32

[552] Ibid.

[553] Selwyn Goodacre 'Hunting the Snark – a History of Publication'. *Jabberwocky,* 5(1976), No.4.

[554] Quoted in Morton Cohen *Carroll and his Illustrators,* London Macmillan, 2003. p314

sticking his tusk in, held out no hope that Holiday would be able to illustrate the book satisfactorily.

Holiday's nine illustrations solemnly and perfectly convey the Nonsense of the Snark. His 'Reminiscence'[555] recalls 'that in our correspondence about the illustrations, the coherence and consistency of the Nonsense on its own Nonsensical understanding, became prominent'. All save one include either the Bellman tingling his bell, or the bell tingling itself. We have seen something of Carroll's preoccupation with time, of which the Bellman, a Father Time figure, is a permanent reminder. Alice's White Rabbit always checks his watch but is always late. Holiday made a sketch of a bell buoy on a trip to Land's End in 1873 'picturesque to eye and ear, with the weird irregular tolling of the bell and when Dodgson wanted a motive for the back cover, something that would bear the words, 'It was a Boojum', I bethought me of my bell buoy which exactly met my want.'[556]

(My particular favourite Holiday picture is the lace-making Beaver who shyly watches the Butcher before they have become shipboard mates over the Jubjub bird and a maths lesson: I share the view of some writers that the Beaver is feminine, but Holiday leaves us guessing.)

The injunction not to illustrate the Boojum, combined with a flurry of fantastical interpretations, subversively encouraged a plethora of new pictures. European illustrators used the texts as a surrealist Bible or starting point for some very free explorations of drawing and painting.[557] The Surrealist founder member Max Ernst joined the ranks of artists from France, Germany, Holland, Russia, Poland, Sweden and even The Faroes. Dr Selwyn Goodacre, an acknowledged Snark authority, supports the imaginative interpretations of modern English artists Mervyn Peake and Ralph Steadman as well as Quentin Blake and Helen Oxenbury.

Coincidental with this thesis come the brand new illustrations to *The Hunting of the Snark* by John Vernon Lord. We have already met Lord before in this thesis as an unrivalled modern interpreter of the Nonsense of Edward Lear and so perhaps his Snark intervention should come as no surprise. Despite a certain caution about declaring his intentions too clearly as 'much of the creative impulse is something of a mystery and the results can be the result of either long contemplation or flashes of momentary intuition,' Lord believes utterly in the value of Nonsense. 'There is something that underlies Nonsense that gets to some sort of Truth. Fools and jesters of old were masters of the art'.[558] Lord approached Snark in precisely the same conscientious fashion as Lear's limericks and immersed himself in a study of Lewis Carroll's Nonsense epic. 'The language of rhyme and rhythm plays a crucial role in the direction in which a Nonsense story unfolds. The destiny of the narrative often depends upon a chance connection between rhyming words. The repetition of like sounds links one idea to another. The constraint imposed upon the poet to come up with rhyming words does itself lead a narrative into particular

[555] Quoted in the *Diaries of Lewis Carroll*, 1894. p335.

[556] Holiday, *Reminiscences*. Quoted in the *Carroll Diaries*, 1875. p347.

[557] Selwyn Goodacre, *All The Snarks*. Oxford, Inky Parrot Press, 2006.

[558] John Vernon Lord, 'Afterword' *The Hunting of the Snark*. Artists Edition, 2006.

directions. Rhyme and rhythm have the capacity to hold the interest of the reader and they also aid memory.'[559]

John Vernon Lord's drawings are as detailed and limitless as Dürer's *Melancolia,* (of which this author is reminded). Mathematical symbols, fantastical landscapes, realistic figures, mysterious boxes, Latin inscriptions, books and baggage all repay careful examination. Are the jury in the Kafkaesque trial based on real people, in the manner of medieval gargoyles? Might one expect a Snark to meet the 'Dong with the Luminous Nose'? The Bandersnatch and the Beaver spring straight from the *First Book of Nonsense,* 1846. (We know that Carroll enjoyed Lear's Nonsense Books, but no mention of Lear himself can be found in the available transcripts of Carroll's adult letters or diaries and of his own childhood, we know tantalisingly little.)

---

[559] Vernon Lord, ibid.

SNARK PICTURES BY HOLIDAY AND VERNON LORD

U nlike either Edward Lear or William Gilbert, Lewis Carroll could not draw well enough to illustrate his Nonsense poems. He was obliged to rely upon a series of artists whom he drove nearly insane with his perfectionist demands but the results are interpretations as close to Carroll's personal vision as possible. In order to consider Holiday's Snark pictures, I have compared them to John Vernon Lord's new drawings.

FIT ONE – The Landing

'Just the place for a Snark'
The Bellman replied, as he landed his crew with care,
Supporting each man on the top of the tide,
By a finger entwined in his hair'.

Holiday and John Vernon Lord have chosen different verses for Fit One. Holiday illustrates an entirely literal version of the Bellman holding the Banker up by his hair in an unforgettable image of sensible representation in a Nonsensical context.

'The crew was complete, it included a Boots
A maker of Bonnets and Hoods.
A Barrister brought to arrange their disputes,
And a Broker to value their goods'.

By contrast, Lord's crew seem quite conventionally disposed and appear to be going about the business of running a ship. Both Holiday and Lord feature the Beaver: Lord's Beaver sits on the capstan, ignoring the Butcher who ominously sharpens his knife…Holiday's Beaver makes lace and tries not to watch the Butcher who is painfully adjacent.

FIT TWO – The Bellman's Speech

'He had brought a large map representing the sea
Without the least vestige of land;
And the crew were much pleased when they found it to be
A map they could all understand'.

Despite this Fit's detailed description of Snark hallmarks (its meagre, hollow but crisp taste, habit of late rising, fondness for bathing machines and inability to laugh at jokes) as well as the Bellman's grandiose quotations, both artists have chosen to illustrate the blank map. Holiday's picture is completely blank save for an outer rim of vaguely geographical indication whilst John Vernon Lord depicts a Nelsonian barrister peering at the white space with a telescope. Lord does include separate drawings of a bathing machine and has a valiant effort at illustrating later rising and 'crisp'.

FIT THE THIRD – The Baker's Tale

'You may seek it with thimbles - and seek it with care:
You may hunt it with forks and hope,
You may threaten its life with a railway share
You may charm it with smiles and soap'.

We hear the Snark chorus for the first time in this Fit, in a pattern of words echoed by the first verse;

'they roused him with muffins - they roused him with ice
They roused him with mustard and cress.
They roused him with jam and judicious advice,
They set him conundrums to guess'.

The Baker is the focus for both artists. Holiday's pixilated version sits up in bed and warns his 'beamish nephew' of the perils of Snark hunting. Through a mullioned window can be seen the sailing vessel, Carroll's symbolic forty-two piece baggage and the Bellman constantly tolling his bell. Lord illustrates a more literal version of the Baker being roused with muffins to tell his doleful story to a very participative crew. All Carroll's elements can be found in this delightful puzzle picture which repays very careful examination.

FIT THE FOURTH – The Hunting

'for the Snark's a peculiar creature, that won't
Be caught in a commonplace way.
Do all that you know, and try all that you don't
Not a chance must be wasted today'.

The focus for this Fit is the preparation by crew members for the assault. Each individual requires to hone his particular skill: the bonnet maker planned ferocious bows, the Boots and the Broker sharpened spades, the Banker changed his silver into notes, the Baker combed his whiskers and the Butcher felt too nervous to do anything but dress for dinner in yellow kid gloves and a ruff. The Beaver continued to make lace.

Martin Gardner thinks that Holiday's picture of Hope carrying an anchor is a ship's figurehead, but I believe she is Britannia, ruling the waves. Apart from the possible androgynous figure of the Beaver, Hope, and the sorrowful draped figure behind her, are the only feminine symbols in the poem.

John Vernon Lord's interpretation of this Fit sets the action against piles of luggage and the crew are precisely engaged in a very literal representation of Carroll's verse. One interesting idea is the Pierrot costume demonstrated by the Butcher in this drawing, possibly suggested by the ruff for Holiday's Butcher in Fit Five. But perhaps Holiday's ruff – and the pose for the Fit Five drawing – was inspired by the Elizabethan drama inherent in Millais' *Boyhood of Raleigh*, (1869). We have seen how the Crimean War invoked the glories of the Tudor era during the 1860s: just as our own age looks back for selected inspiration, so Victorians yearned for what seemed to be the simpler and more heroic past of medieval England. Small echoes of this were tangibly present in the philosophy of Auguste Pugin, the craft of William Morris and the architecture of Charles Francis Annesley Voysey.

FIT THE FIFTH – The Beaver's Lesson

'The Beaver brought paper, portfolio, pens,
And ink, in unfailing supplies,
While strange creepy creatures came out of their dens
And watched them with wondering eyes'.

This verse has been chosen by Holiday and Lord to illustrate the Fifth Fit and their images are more alike than usual. In Holiday's faintly surreal picture, pigs not only fly but play brass instruments in a musical ensemble that features nightmarish bats with a musical box and a hurdy gurdy. Both the Butcher and the Beaver are unconsciously besieged by frogs, one of whom is soliciting an income tax demand, the other is busy drilling a hole into the Beaver's tail. Note the reference to Colenso, a celebrated writer of arithmetical textbooks before his controversial appointment as Bishop of Natal in 1846, and a missionary to the Zulu states in Cape Province. Lord seems to have left the Bellman out of his picture - unless it has become the weird tongue of an unknown serpent to the left of the desk.

Martin Gardner believes Holiday's flying pigs demonstrate the Scottish proverb 'pigs may fly, but it's not likely' and recalls various riddles concerning pigs with wings in the Alice books.

'taking three as the subject to reason about
A convenient number to state
We add Seven and Ten. And then multiply out
By One Thousand diminished by Eight'.

Lord draws a mathematical equation based on 'taking three' but this writer cannot tell you if either Carroll's sum or Lord's illustration work out.

FIT THE SIXTH – The Barrister's Dream

'He dreamed that he stood in a shadowy court
Where the Snark with a glass in its eye
Dressed in a gown, band and wig, was defending a pig
On the charge of deserting its sty'.

Both Holiday and Vernon Lord draw the Judge/Snark from the back but
Vernon Lord concentrates on the jury in contrast to Holiday whose focus is
with the barristers and the defendant. Is the burly figure to the right in
Holiday's drawing the Tichborne claimant? Apparently, Counsel for the
Defence bears the features of the later disgraced Keneally.

Holiday illustrates the 'dream' by a rolled blanket under which a bell
tingles in the Barrister's ear. There is no feeling of dream in Vernon Lord's
sharp and angular interpretation, but the Judge/Snark is particularly menacing.
Yet again, Vernon Lord proves the most literal ally to Carroll's verse as his
Prosecuting Counsel is clearly reading from 'The Case of a Pig Who Deserted
His Sty' in English and in Latin whereas Holiday's lawyer seems to be
confused with a brief for Trespass, Libel and Contempt of Court.

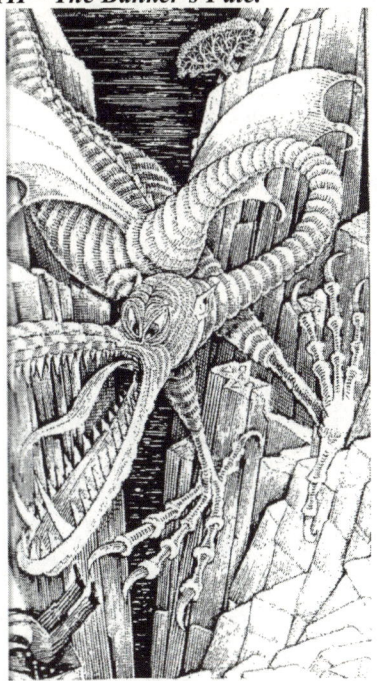

'To the horror of all who were present that day
He uprose in full evening dress,
And with senseless grimaces, endeavoured to say
What his tongue could no longer express'.

The sheet music that Holiday has drawn at the Banker's feet is marked 'con imbecillita' showing that the Banker has clearly gone out of his head. Madness lay close to the imagination of Victorian artists and writers: or are Carroll and Holiday demonstrating the lunacy of railway shares?

'But while he was seeking with thimbles and care
A Bandersnatch swiftly drew night
And grabbed at the Banker who shrieked in despair
For he knew it was useless to fly'.

This verse is Fit Seven's inspiration for Vernon Lord who bravely draws the Bandersnatch, a liberty that Carroll would almost certainly not have allowed his contemporary artist.

FIT THE EIGHTH – *The Vanishing*

'they shuddered to think that the chase might fail
And the Beaver, excited at last
Went bounding along on the tip of its tail

For the daylight was nearly past'.

Vernon Lord draws a bouncing beaver in contrast to Holiday whose image seems to show silence. In fact, closer examination of Holiday's drawing shows the huge, almost transparent image of the Baker in stark terror as a gigantic claw drags him off, like Mozart's Don Giovanni, down to the Unknown. The Bell is being tolled by an unseen Bellman.

WORD PLAY, VOCABULARY AND STRUCTURE IN THE HUNTING OF THE SNARK

The epic Nonsense poem is subtitled an 'Agony in Eight Fits' derived from 'agon' a Greek term for struggle, and 'fit' a medieval term for a section of song or poem.[560] It consists of one hundred and forty one quatrains whose rhythms are not the standard iambics of narrative verse but comical, balladic structures which recall parlour song or nursery rhymes. W.S. Gilbert's Bab Ballad *The Baron Klopfzetterheim* (1864) was divided into 'fyttes' as were Richard Barham's *Ingoldsby Legends* (1840–43) – the latter incidentally illustrated by John Tenniel. Inner rhymes occur in the first and third lines of irregular stanzas, a device effective enough to have been pursued but obvious logic in any sense, is not a feature of the Snark. The versification is melodious and compact, demonstrating Carroll's sense of rhythm and proportion, yet none of his poetry ever quite matches the magic and emotion of his dream stories; ' the intense perception of the eternal lying behind the accidental, reaches the core of every reader, whether with laughter, tears or exaltation. That is poetry – but not necessarily verse'.[561]

'Snark' itself is a portmanteau word made up of 'snail' and 'shark', the snail passive and harmless, the shark active and destructive, a construction which R.B.Shaberman illustrates the 'essence of Carroll's dualism'.[562] Although 'portmanteau' is itself a French construction, Gilles Deleuze has charmingly described it as 'mots valises' in his *Logique du Sens*, a comprehensive study in French of Carroll's significance for language.[563] Readers familiar with Carroll's poem 'Jabberwocky' will recognise the 'mots valises' – frumiousish, galumphing, outgrabe, mimsy (in Snark, appearing as 'mimsiest') and some Nonsense livestock, the Jubjub Bird and the Bandersnatch.

Carroll himself explains 'frumious':

'Make your mind up that you will say both words, 'furious' and 'fuming' but have it unsettled which you will say first. If your thoughts incline ever so little towards 'fuming', you will say fuming-furious, if they turn, even by a

---

[560] Professor Vance points out that the juxtaposition is a terrible pun or 'sick joke'.

[561] Florence Becker Lennon, *Lewis Carroll*. London, Cassell & Co, 1947. p241

[562] R.B. Shaberman & D.Crutch, *Under the Quizzing Glass, a Carroll Miscellany.* London, Magpie Press, 1971

[563] Holquist, 'What is a Boojum'.p159

hair's breadth towards furious, you will have furious-fuming, but if you have that rarest of gifts, a perfectly balanced mind, you will say – frumious,[564]

Carroll defined 'uffish thought' as a state of mind when the voice is gruffish, the manner roughish and the temper huffish. 'Burble' comes from bleat, murmer and warble. Humpty Dumpty, that celebrated literary critic, himself explains that ' mimsy' in *Alice Through the Looking Glass* is 'flimsy and miserable' and 'outgrabe' is etymologically linked to 'outgribing', something between bellowing and whistling and something with which, once Alice has heard it in the wood, she will be quite content.

The alliteration of the crew, whose names all begin with 'B' has been described as having some possible relation to a stammer, but the exploitation of a particular letter appears elsewhere in Carroll.

'...and they drew all manner of things – everything that begins with an 'M'.

'Why with an M?' said Alice.

'Why not?' said the March Hare – 'that begins with an M such as mousetraps, and the moon, and memory and muchness – did you ever see such a thing as the drawing of a muchness?'[565]

The alliteration allows a free association of totally incompatible elements. Nonsense is produced by what might seem random ideas, linked by letters of the alphabet. In *Through the Looking Glass*, Carroll plays a similar game with the letter 'H'.

'I love my love with an H', Alice couldn't help beginning,' because he Is Happy. I hate him with an H because he is Hideous. I feed him Ham sandwiches and Hay. His name is Haigha and he lives on the Hill'.[566]

'This use of a simple letter assumes an autonomy of its own and eventually demands obedience from the author'.[567]

Vocabulary in *The Hunting of the Snark* other than the 'portmanteau' words is accessible to adults and to children alike. 'Antediluvian,' 'symmetrical' and 'parenthesis' are chosen for reasons of rhyme rather than sense – which is, in any case, not the point in Nonsense poetry.

---

[564] Lewis Carroll, Preface to *The Hunting of the Snark*. London, Penguin Classic Edition, 1995, p42

[565] *Alice in Wonderland*, Penguin Classic Edition. 1998. p66

[566] *Through the Looking Glass*. Penguin Edition, 1998. p196

[567] Jacqueline Flescher, 'The Language of Nonsense in Alice'. Yale French Studies, No. 43(1969)128-144.

THE HUNTING OF THE SNARK – FIT BY FIT ANALYSIS.

E ven the most imaginative of writers cannot create something from nothing. However nonsensically autonomous the origins of a poem, painting or book may appear to be, there will have been some basis for the creative impulse. This could be tangible, such as owning a dog, intangible, such as dreaming about the dog (hypnagogic) or secondarily, such as reading about the dog. Samuel Taylor Coleridge had never even crossed the Channel when he wrote *The Ancient Mariner* but 'because his memory was stored with the spoils of omnivorous reading, we find in this poem the authentic splendours and terrors of the polar ice'.[568] Incubation or gestation of the original impulse may take days, months or even years and this process is beyond our control.[569] A degree of insight into the various components of thought process is relative to the creativity of the individual concerned. Carroll was engaged in forging skilful links between the familiar and the fantastic, between the real and the product of his imagination. He set store by his dreams, aware that they enabled him to live a life of the absurd and to have an existence in another world, undreamt of in reality.

> 'Alice! A childish story take
> And, with a gentle hand
> Lay it where Childhood's dreams are twined
> In memory's mystic band'.[570]

Despite Carroll's own assertion that *The Hunting of the Snark* was nothing but Nonsense, he knew that most of his creative work bore currents of hidden meaning and, mischievously, he encouraged his readers to guess what these might be. He wrote to a child friend, Florence Balfour on April 6th, 1876.

'My dear Birdie. When you have read 'The Snark' I hope you will write me a little note and tell me how you like it, and if you can quite understand it. Some children are puzzled by it. Of course you know what a Snark is. If you do, please tell me for I haven't got an idea what it is like. And tell me which of

---

[568] Peter McKellar, *Imagination and Thinking*. London. Cohen and West, 1957. p77

[569] Lenin's comment that listening to Beethoven's *Appassionata* would make revolution impossible was the acknowledged spark – the original creative impulse – for Florian Henckel von Donnersmarck's award winning film about the East German Stasi, *The Lives of Others*, 2007.

[570] Lewis Carroll, *Alice's Adventures in Wonderland*. Preface. London, Macmillan, 1898.

the pictures you like best.

Yours affectionate friend, Lewis Carroll.'[571]

When another young man inquired what the Snark really was, Carroll laughed and said 'when you find out, please tell me'.[572] Carroll's favourite explanation was that the Snark was an allegory on the search for happiness.

FIT ONE. The Landing

What Happens…

The Bellman lands on the site he believed the Snark would be found. Significantly, he told his crew three times that they were in the right place: life holds to a rule of three. His complete crew comprised a Boots, a maker of Bonnets, a Barrister, a Broker, a Billiard Marker, a Banker, a Baker, a Butcher and the sole animal, a Beaver who made lace and who had previously saved the crew from shipwreck. The Baker forgot his name and all his luggage. He could only bake wedding cake for which there were no ingredients. The Butcher felt obliged to explain that the sole animal he could kill was a beaver which made the Beaver cry. (Even a dagger proof coat and life insurance could not prevent the Beaver from feeling shy around the Butcher).

'Just the place for a Snark, the Bellman cried,
As he landed his crew with care
Supporting each man on the top of the tide
By a finger entwined in his hair'.

The Bellman is the Captain of the expedition and perhaps Lewis Carroll himself. Carroll spent forty-seven years summoned by the bells of Christ Church, an Oxford College founded in 1524 by Cardinal Wolsey. Although all the Oxford colleges depended upon bells, Christ Church alone devolved the peculiar tradition of tolling the great bell in Tom Tower one hundred and one times every day at nine pm, local time. This represented the original hundred students, plus the one extra, admitted in 1663. In 1847, Greenwich Mean Time was introduced to standardise national railway timetables but Great Tom, a few minutes off the meridian, continued to be struck at nine o'clock Oxford time. (Five minutes past nine, GMT!.) The seven ton bell is seven feet in diameter and was recast from Oseney Abbey. Carroll, always much concerned with matters concerning his College and meticulous about time, waded into the controversy surrounding alterations to the bell tower in 1874 with a Shakespearean parody for a pamphlet entitled 'The New Belfry'.

'Five fathom square the Belfry frowns
All its sides of timber made
Painted all in greys and browns

---

[571] Morton Cohen, ed, *The Letters of Lewis Carroll*. London, Macmillan, 1979, p246
[572] Morton Cohen, *Lewis Carroll*, London, Macmillan, 2003. p408

Nothing of it that will fade.
Christ Church may admire the change
Oxford thinks it sad and strange
Beauty's dead! Let's ring her knell.
Hark! Now I hear them, ding dong bell.'

Carroll fulminated about the ugly temporary wooden belfry and the expensive new stone bell tower in his diary (October 29th, 1874) and in a plethora of letters to Christ Church students, tutors and lecturers, but to no avail.

'Bellman' is the ancient word for a town crier whose bell marked the passage of time. Bells in Snark are tingled, not tinkled, possibly on account of 'tingle' having weightier associations with 'spine tingling' and thus foreshadowing the terror to come. The regularity of their 'tingling' is a reminder both real and symbolic of the passing of time, the pulsating rhythm of life and its inevitable end.

Why do all the characters in the Snark begin with the letter B? Why not, Carroll is believed to have replied, but Francis Huxley claims that a stutter is responsible in this poem which was, as were most of Carroll's Nonsense poems, designed to be read out loud.[573] Sufferers who struggle with hard consonants find B, T, and Q particularly difficult and one solution is to make the inevitable repetition useful: shining a very fierce light on the problem may change its character. The stammer itself may have been the result of changing Carroll from left to right handedness in childhood, something we shall look at later in this chapter.

But alliterations abound. If incidents in *The Hunting of the Snark* seem to echo some of the Arctic voyages of the 1850s, we can recall that one of Edward Belcher's boats was trapped through the Bering Straits at Banks Island and one of Franklin's boats was beached at Beechey Island, named after Frederick Beechey who discovered Point Barrow in 1825. We need to remember Darwin's voyage on the *H.M.S. Beagle* in 1836 and we can usefully consider the nautical alliterations of boat, bow, board, bowsprit, bottom, belay and batten. Henry Holiday hoped that Darwin's future trips in the Beagle to collect new species would 'find the Boojum – or its remains' and could confirm Holiday's rejected illustration.[574]

FIT TWO. The Bellman's Speech.

What happens…

The Bellman proudly demonstrated his navigation skills by sailing with a blank map and tingling his bell. He admits the bowsprit got mixed up with a

---

[573] Francis Huxley, *The Raven and the Writing Desk*. London, Thames and Hudson, 1976, p30

[574] Henry Holiday, 'The Snark's Significance'. *The Academy*, 29th January 1898, pp128-130

rudder sometimes,[575] but his main anxiety lay in hoping his ship would follow the wind and not take the opposite direction.

> 'He had bought a large map representing the sea
> Without the least vestige of land
> And the crew were much pleased when they found it to be
> A map they could all understand'.

Sailing with a 'blank map' in search of gold or the Holy Grail, the ancient notion of voyage as a quest into the unknown for adventure or pilgrimage is one of the earliest narratives known to man. The Irish St Brendan sailed on an 'immram,' voyage of discovery in a legend that inspired Charles Kingsley's *Water Babies*, (1862).

Tennyson's *Ulysses* (written 1836 but not published until 1842) was a Victorian version of a Greek Odyseus, as developed by Dante, who sailed forever to the West with his crew. The seventy lines of blank verse in iambic pentameters glow with heroic vision in a hymn to the questing spirit of youth and a battle cry for courage, death and glory. Tennyson's poem is usually regarded as a heroic response to the death of Arthur Hallam in 1833.

Carroll knew and admired Tennyson and although he never claimed intimate acquaintance, he was allowed to photograph the poet and his sons at Trent Lodge in the Lake District. In 1857, Carroll visited Tennyson hoping to be allowed to read 'The Idylls of the King' but Tennyson refused: his grandson Charles Tennyson speculates that the reason was Carroll's spiky parody of Tennysonian verse in 'The Three Voices' written for *The Train* in 1856. However, they discussed dreams together and Tennyson related to Carroll his 'enormous poem about fairies which began with very long lines that gradually got shorter and ended with fifty or sixty lines of two syllables. This reminiscence probably gave his guest the idea for the 'Mouse's Tail' in *Alice in Wonderland*.'[576]

The boy Carroll learned Greek myths and legends at school. The bookish young student would have read James Anthony Froude's essay on 'England's Forgotten Worthies'[577] which celebrated the voyages and explorers of Elizabethan England and Gloriana, Queen Elizabeth I herself. Froude's dramatic histories, together with an upsurge of patriotism which followed the Crimean War, may well have lain behind the inspiration for Charles Kingsley's *Westward Ho!*, (1855), an Elizabethan sea story featuring a Devon adventurer who wages war against the Spanish Armada.

Contemporary maritime adventures were chronicled by stirring accounts in the English press of the struggle to find the North West Passage. This was a fabled route which would enable the wealth of the Orient to be accessed by

---

[575] Carroll declared that if ever a charge of writing Nonsense were to be brought against him, it would be based, he was certain, on this line. Preface, *The Hunting of the Snark*. London, Penguin Classics. 1995, p41
[576] Charles Tennyson, *Alfred Tennyson*. London, Macmillan & Co., 1950, p316
[577] Westminster Review, 1852.

sailing ships through the Canadian North Western territories on the fringes of the Arctic ocean: a commercial sea route between the Atlantic and the Pacific north of the North American mainland. In the first half of the nineteenth century, a number of expeditions explored parts of the route but the most celebrated attempt was that made by Sir John Franklin in 1845. His well-equipped two ships, *The Erebus* and *The Terror* failed to return, despite several relief expeditions and only traces have ever been found (*Illustrated London News*, 28 October, 1854). Early in 1848, the Admiralty organised a three-fold search with a £10,000 reward for news of the expedition. In August, 1851, Franklin's quarters on Beechey Island was discovered, along with graves of three crew members and masses of tinned supplies, fatally polluted by lead poisoning. The reward was claimed by explorer Dr John Rae who learned of the expedition from Inuit hunters.

Grisly tales of ships slowly strangling in the ice, of starvation and even possible cannibalism of crew members along with their desperate, doomed efforts to reach help overland, made headlines. The fate of Franklin and his crew gripped the imagination of the country: it preyed upon the mind of Charles Dickens who debated aspects of the tragedy with John Rae in *Household Words*. In 1856, Dickens collaborated with his friend Wilkie Collins to write a stage melodrama based on Franklin's ill-fated journey, *The Frozen Deep*. A Prologue specifically sets the main action, 'Where Parry Conquered, Franklin Died'. The semi-professional theatrical was performed before Queen Victoria and Prince Albert at Tavistock House and subsequent performances were given as a charity benefit for Franklin's widow and children. *The Frozen Deep*[578] attracted capacity audiences (including Hans Christian Andersen and Thackeray) and required staging in larger theatres with a new professional cast. Dickens was gratified to learn that his play reduced over two thousand people to tears.

We know that Lewis Carroll read Charles Dickens and Wilkie Collins: he said that the White Queen in *Alice Through the Looking Glass* reminded him of Mrs. Wragge in Collins' *No Name*, 91862).[579] Did he see Dickens and Collins' melodrama? Given his taste for dramatic theatre with no possibility of a sexually salacious element, it seems highly likely.

Although there is clearly a deeper symbolism in the questing narrative of the Bellman's journey in search of the Snark, I believe that the actual facts of Franklin's expedition supplied an outline idea. The Bellman's 'blank' map was actually a picture of snow. The courage of the crew setting out in uncharted waters, the Admiralty's three-fold search, the ultimate failure of the expedition despite a glimpse of the goal, all fit the poem – but we must be aware of the strange prescience of Carroll's magical tales and how they can 'fit' so many situations, personal or abstract, past or present. The old maxim that each reader finds the Snark they want, holds true to some certain extent.

---

[578] An adaptation of *The Frozen Deep* was performed at the 2005 Edinburgh Festival. Reviews described it as 'dark and moody'.

[579] Mrs Wragge, a 'constitutionally torpid' towering giantess suffering from tinnitus and mad as a march hare, is unfortunately married to Captain Wragge, a manipulative schemer after Magdalen Vanstone's fortune in Collins' sensational story.

Landing on a rocky shore, the Bellman cheers up his disconsolate crew with rum and jokes saved for the purpose. He explained that the Snark may be recognised by its taste (meagre and hollow but crisp), its habit of getting up so late that it dines the evening after, its ambition and its fondness for bathing machines. Snarks are divided into those with feathers that bite and those that have whiskers and scratch. The Bellman continues…

'For, although common Snarks do no manner of harm
Yet I feel it my duty to say
Some are Boojums -' the Bellman broke off in alarm
For the Baker had fainted away'.

FIT THE THIRD. The Baker's Tale.

What happens…

The Baker required reviving with mustard, cress, jam and advice before adding some Snark wisdom inherited from an uncle who memorably commented that Snarks can be served with greens and are handy for striking a light. The Baker bewails his dark dreams in which he engages with the Boojum. He knows that his survival depends upon not meeting it in daylight. We hear the Snark chorus for the first time in this Fit.

'You may seek it with thimbles – and seek it with care
You may hunt it with forks and hope
You may threaten its life with a railway share
You may charm it with smiles and soap'.

As earlier indicated, the pattern of the words bears more than a coincidental similarity with a popular folk ballad, 'The Mistletoe Bough' c.1830, a grim tale of the newly married bride playing hide and seek in a castle who locks herself accidentally in a wooden chest and who is never found… 'they sought her that day and they sought her that night/they sought her in vain when a week passed away'.

Lewis Carroll's first home was the parsonage at Daresbury, Cheshire, where his father was Perpetual Curate of a church in the gift of Christ Church, Oxford, since the dissolution of the monasteries. (It is thought possible that the Cheshire Cat grin comes from a gargoyle on one of the pillars, still to be seen.) When he was eleven, the family moved to a living at Croft, on the River Tees, North Yorkshire. Carroll wrote an early poem about it.[580]

'Fair stands the ancient Rectory,
The Rectory of Croft
The sun shines bright upon it
The breezes whisper soft.

---

[580] Walter de la Mare, *Lewis Carroll*, London. Faber & Faber, 1932. p22

From all the house and garden
Its inhabitants pour forth
And muster in the road without
And pace in twos and threes about
The children of the North'.

In the 1840s and 50s, almost more important for Croft than the sun which shone upon it, were the railways. Strategically placed on the new east coast route from Edinburgh to London, Croft was served by three companies – the North British Railway, the North East Railway and the Great North Railway – before they agreed a Joint stock company called the East Coast Mainline in 1860. Croft station, known as Croft Spa, disappeared under Dr Beeching's axe in 1963 but the railway still runs close to the town.

Young Charles' fascination with trains may be compared to the mania for computer games which absorb the creativity and attention of many young boys today. Our dot. com.bust explosion, fired by dramatically innovative technology, has many parallels to the railway fever which swept through the country in the 1840s. In both cases, the promise of investing in an enterprise that would not only produce vast individual returns but also transform society as a whole was irresistible. New lines were planned to transport coal and fuel to city centres with the aim of reducing costs for poorer classes, demonstrating that material gain could combine with social responsibility and Christian duty. But enthusiasm for connecting the country with rapid travel led to the creation of stations or even entire lines for which there was no need and the cost of construction usually outweighed the social benefits. Little thought was given to the question of where railways were to go, which parts of the country deserved to be opened up first and which could wait. 'Military and strategic considerations which operated to influence Continental railway building, were absent in England.[581] Commercial considerations were all-powerful, according to the anarchical gospel of laissez-faire, and qualified by the fear of letting a monopoly grow up by accident'. [582]

Happily unaware of mainline railway perils, young Charles constructed a branch railway in the Croft rectory garden. He made a train from a wheelbarrow, a truck and a barrel, appointed himself Station Master, sold tickets and wrote the Rules.

'All passengers when upset, are required to lie still until picked up, as it is requisite that at least 3 trains shall pass over them to entitle them to the attention of doctors and assistants'.[583]

As a young student at Christ Church, Carroll's interest in railways produced a short spell as a contributor to *The Train*, a monthly publication under the enthusiastic conductorship of Edmund Yates, assisted by Augustus

---

[581] Professor Norman Vance reminds me that Ireland was different and more sensible.

[582] Richard Lambert, *The Railway King*. London. Allen & Unwin, 1934. p19

[583] From Catalogue of the Amory Collection, quoted in Florence Becker Lennon, *Lewis Carroll*, London. Cassell & Co, 1947, p24

Sala and Frank Smedley. The periodical, an eccentric offshoot of *Comic Times,* was founded in 1856 and designed to be read – in trains. Carroll's five poems for *The Train,*

'are not very meritorious, judged by poetic standards, but the author's age – he was only 24 – must be taken into consideration'.[584]

His parody of *Hiawatha* as a photographer's self-help manual is both witty and ingenious and the Tennysonian pastiche is entertaining but the more solemn contributions combine stiffness with sentimentality in equal measure. Contrasts between Carroll playing games and Dodgson the Don are never more striking.

By the time an adult Lewis Carroll went to Guildford to stay with his sisters and walk on the Hogs Back in 1874, the railway network across England was complete. In its wake had come prosperity and good fortune as well as scandal and sensation. Novelists jumped on to the railway wagons, eager to make fictional capital from real life drama. In *The Way We Live Now,* (1873), Trollope invented the archetype City swindler Augustus Melmotte[585] whose peculiar vice was floating a railway company, talking up the stock and selling out before the company made a profit: or even before it produced a railway. Seeking refuge in his heavily accented English, Melmotte

'blurted out his assurance that the floating of this railway company would be one of the greatest and most successful commercial operations ever conducted on   either side of the Atlantic. It was one of the greatest things ever. He was happy to give his Humble assistance to the furtherance of so great a thing'. [586]

As readers discover, there is no such thing and the South Central Pacific Mexican Railway which was supposed to link the 2,000 miles between the Gulf of Mexico and San Francisco remained only a gleam in Melmotte's eye and only a glint of gold for the shareholders. Melmotte bears more than a passing resemblance to George Hudson (1800–1871) a Yorkshire draper whose unlikely inheritance of £30,000 enabled a fantastic career of company promotion, railway building and a lifelong alliance with George Stephenson. Known as the 'Railway King' and celebrated for his lavish hospitality, Hudson, like Melmotte, becomes a Member of Parliament, entertains royalty and lives on the grand scale,until his habit of 'feeding the donkey its own tail' caused scandal and disgrace.

On December 28th, 1869, Carroll's diary records that he attended an

---

[584] Hugh J. Schonfield, *The Train*. London, Denis Archer, 1932. pxviii

[585] Melmotte was portrayed by David Suchet in the BBC production of *The Way We Live Now* in 2006: it is surely no coincidence that the same fine actor portrayed Robert Maxwell in a new film (BBC2, May 4th, 2007.)

[586] Anthony Trollope, *The Way We Live Now*. London, Wordsworth Classic Edition, Chapter 10.

amateur theatrical in Guildford at which 'Mr and Mrs A. Trollope were present' and he felt sufficiently moved by the performance to send an account of the entertainment to the *Guildford Gazette*. (This has never been found.)

Wilkie Collins' horrible Captain Wragge in *No Name* (1873) is ruined by rash railway share deals and Charles Reade in *Hard Cash* (1863) describes the manic speculative fever as 'high and low scrambled for shares even when the projected line was to run from the town of Nought to the village of Nothing across a goose common. The flame spread, fanned by prospectus and advertisement, two mines of glowing fiction, compared with which the legitimate article is a mere tissue of understatements'. *Hard Cash* was serialised in Charles Dickens' *All The Year Round* in 1868: Dickens himself had used the railway stories and scandals as a backdrop to *Dombey and Son* in 1848.

On April 11th, 1860[587], Carroll wrote to his sister Mary, arranging a railway timetable for the visit of his nephew Edwin. It is as detailed as Bradshaw and, I am certain, quite as accurate.

'Croft	9.34. (Richmond train.)
Darlington	9.45. Leave, 9.52.
York	11.30. Leave, 11.45.
Derby	2.40. Leave, 2.25. (or 4.15.)
Rugby	4.00 (or 6.45.)

Now I shall get to Rugby by the 3.50 to meet him at 4. If I miss that, I shall arrive at 6.50 and he will find the station quite as convenient to wait and dine at the hotel. If he does not come at 4, I shall expect him at 6.45'. (Carroll's diary for June 9th, 1872, records that he tried to take the train to Sunderland for the funeral of his Uncle William Wilcox – 'but by an extraordinary accident, a misprint in Bradshaw, I missed my train'.) [588]

Could Canon Dodgson have met George Hudson in North Yorkshire during the 1840s and 1850s? There was almost no municipal enterprise that did not have Hudson on the committee and certainly no commercial undertaking that did not have him on the board. Hudson was obliged to battle in court with the Dean and Chapter of Durham over wayleaves for Stephenson's Newcastle-Darlington route which would have involved Croft Spa Station. Canon Dodgson's[589] living at Croft had been presented to him by Yorkshireman Sir Robert Peel; the same Peel who turned down Hudson's request for £16 million to develop an adequate system of Irish railways in 1847. 'Why should not Irish landlords and gentry subscribe to and institute their own railways without Government assistance; Irish MPs showed themselves lukewarm, or even inclined to question whether Hudson was not wanting to feather his own nest – and the Bill was rejected by a handsome majority'.[590]

---

[587] Morton Cohen, Ed, *Letters of Lewis Carroll*, London. Macmillan, 1979. p41

[588] Roger Lancelyn Green, Ed, *Diaries of Lewis Carroll*, New York, OUP, 1954. Vol 2 p311

[589] Eventually, Dodgson became Archdeacon of Ripon Cathedral.

[590] Richard Lambert, *The Railway King*. London. Allen & Unwin 1934. p206

The first biography, *George Hudson* by Richard S. Lambert, appeared in 1934 and illustrates Chapter One, 'The Enigma' with the Snark Chorus.[591]

'They charmed it with smiles and with soap.'

This last line of the Snark chorus is probably inspired by the need to end the rhyme with 'hope' but it is worth mentioning that Carroll's diary entry for October 19th, 1875, discusses shaving without soap. 'Tried, for the first time, a plan that Uncle Hassard told me, of shaving without soap with such success that I shall probably not use lather again'. Carroll, unlike many of his contemporaries, was clean-shaven, sporting neither sideburns, mustachios or a beard. It gave him a curiously childish appearance, a fact of which he could not have been unaware. (The maxim 'cleanliness is next to Godliness' associated so particularly with the Victorians, came from a sermon by John Wesley in 1791.)

FIT THE FOURTH. The Hunting.

What happens…

The Bellman finds the Baker's susceptibility irritating and complains that he should have been warned. The Baker explains that he did, in Hebrew, in Dutch, in German and Greek, wholly forgetting it's English we speak. The crew prepare for the hunt: the Banker crosses and endorses a blank cheque and changes his silver into notes, Boots and the Baker sharpen spades, the Barrister tries to find precedent, the Bonnet maker arranges bows, the Butcher dresses up with yellow kid gloves and the Beaver makes lace.

'For England Expects – I forebear to proceed
tis a Maxim tremendous but trite;
and you'd best be unpacking the things that you need
to rig yourselves out for the fight'.

'Then the Banker endorsed a blank cheque (which he crossed)
and changed his loose silver for notes.
The Baker with care combed his whiskers and hair
and shook the dust out of his coats'.

(Note the tremendously unheroic, tripping metre.)

The tremendous, if trite, maxim was 'England Expects Every Man To Do His Duty,' a flag signal to the fleet ordered by Horatio Nelson just before he was killed by a musket shot at the Battle of Trafalgar in 1805. It joins another

---

[591] Hudson remains a figure of contemporary interest: the latest biography by A.J. Arnold and S.M. McCartney, *George Hudson, The Rise and Fall of the Railway King*, London, Hambledon Press, appeared in 2004.

famous quotation 'Friends, Romans, Countrymen, lend me your ears' with which the Bellman exhorted his crew to greater courage in Fit Two. 'I come not to praise Caesar, but to bury him' continues Mark Antony's funeral oration from Shakespeare's *Julius Caesar*.[592] Young readers under twelve might have needed an explanation which the pedagogic Carroll would have doubtless enjoyed supplying.

FIT THE FIFTH. The Beaver's Lesson.

What happens…

Despite the Butcher's declared interest in eating the Beaver, coincidentally, the Butcher and the Beaver have invented identical plans to hunt the Snark. The Jubjub bird must sing three times but the Beaver can't count and requires an arithmetic lesson from the Butcher, as well as a Natural History guide to the curious bird. (It never accepts a bribe and is boiled in sawdust and salted with glue.) The Butcher's lessons are received with infinite gratitude by the Beaver and the unlikely pair establish a new and lifelong friendship.

'The Beaver brought paper, portfolio, pens
And ink in unfailing supplies.
While strange creepy creatures came out of their dens
And watched them with wondering eyes'.

Inuit Eskimos hold the Beaver in particular esteem. Their word for it is 'Kigiaq' and although it ceased to roam the Arctic centuries before and only bones and fossils exist to prove its former habitat, tales of its cunning and strength are celebrated in traditional Inuit songs.

Beavers are not found in England, nor do they make much appearance in *The Origin of Species,* 1859. (Darwin limits his discussion on the tree-felling, lodge-living, water-loving animals by a comparison with those species to whom they are related: the musk rat, coypu and capybara).

But there <u>was</u> a Beaver in London in 1871 – in fact, there was a pair of Canadian Beavers, alive and well in the new Zoological Gardens, Regent's Park. A guidebook in the archives of the RZS in 1870 describes the new Beaver pond dug especially for them, commenting that 'the sagacity and social polity of these animals is well known'. According to the present curator Michael Palmer, the London Zoo beavers were well adapted to captivity and bred enthusiastically, finally establishing a colony of between 30–40.

It is possible that Carroll met his Beaver in real life, rather than the newspaper stories of the Arctic expeditions or through the pages of Charles Darwin: perhaps he took a child friend to the zoo. Yet perhaps a more likely introduction lay on the top of his head. Brushed high hats, beloved of the Victorians, were made from beaver fur. Beaver pelts were brushed with a

---

[592] William Shakespeare, *Julius Caesar*, III, ii., 92-93

242

solution of nitrate of mercury which raised the scales on the fur shafts so that they would lock together. If this process, known as 'carrotting' was carried out in crowded and poorly ventilated conditions, brain damage could result, hence the expression 'mad as a hatter'. One symptom of mercury poisoning was an obsession with eating as much bread and butter as possible. Alice's tea time companion is a perfect, if unfortunate, example.

The Butcher's arithmetic lesson for the Beaver proves that two plus one does in fact equal three. His procedure is an example of circular reasoning, one that he is certain to reach whichever number he first thought of.

'Taking three as the subject to reason about
A convenient number to state
We add seven and ten and then multiply out
By one thousand diminished by eight.'

Charles Dodgson taught arithmetic at Christ Church in the tutorial system with one, two or three students gathered together or the occasional lecture to a larger class. Despite his own knowledge and enthusiasm for mathematics, his lessons were considered dry as dust and never attracted popular support.

FIT THE SIXTH. The Barrister's Dream.

What happens…

The Barrister dreamed that the Snark (dressed in a gown with a glass in its eye) was defending a pig who had deserted his sty. The Snark became judge and jury, pronounced the pig guilty and sentenced it to transportation for life, even though the pig had been dead for some years.

'In the matter of Treason, the pig would appear
To have aided but scarcely abetted.
While the charge of insolvency fails, it is clear
If you grant the plea 'never indebted'…

'…but the Judge said he had never summed up before
So the Snark undertook it instead.
And summed up so well that it came to far more
than the witnesses ever had said!'

Martin Gardner believes this Fit was inspired by the Tichborne Trial, one of the longest and silliest cases ever to be tried in an English Court. Gardner's advocacy is given weight by Carroll's diaries which record that he followed the trial with interest, even to recording the final verdict which was delivered on February 28th, 1874. 'Took a walk,and on my return found telegrams about the end of the Tichborne Trial with the verdict of 'guilty' and the sentence of 14 years penal servitude. A more eventful day than usually occurs in an Oxford term'.

The case concerned a wealthy Catholic baronet, Roger Tichborne, who almost certainly perished at sea in a long boat off Rio de Janiero in 1854. His distraught mother refused to believe he was dead, and advertised for news of her son with, amongst others, a Mr Cubitt of Sydney whose missing persons bureau was described in *The Times*. Enter Mr Castro, an overweight, blond, bankrupt butcher from Wagga Wagga who claimed to be the missing slight, wiry, dark Englishman. Castro, carefully coached by accomplices after the substantial reward for news of Tichborne's discovery, explained his worrying lack of education was due to suffering from St. Vitus' dance, and the lack of facial resemblance to Sir Roger due to falling off a horse. He was supported by a Bogle, a black valet to the Tichborne family who now lived in Australia. The trustees of Sir Roger's estate remained unconvinced and brought suit against Castro and his crew. Sir Alexander Cockburn's summary required 20 days after a trial of 188 days and his closing speech spared neither side: 'imputation, accusation and invective' were freely delivered as he passed judgement of fourteen years penal servitude on Castro for perjury and fraud. Barrister Edward Keneally, Counsel for the defence was struck off the legal register and thereafter launched an attack to preserve his reputation in the national press, even standing as Member of Parliament for Stoke-on-Trent in 1875. Castro made friends and lost weight in Dartmoor Prison: he became a touring circus celebrity when he was finally released.[593]

Holiday's Barrister in his Snark illustration is a caricature of Keneally (certainly based on the *Punch* cartoon, Vol. 68, 1875, p91) and I would suggest that the burly, rough figure far right is based on Castro.

The facts of the case are as Nonsensical as anything Lewis Carroll ever dreamt up and there are strong grounds for the popular argument made in *The Annotated Snark*[594] that the entire poem was a satire on the Tichborne Case: elements in common include missing identity, voyages off course, hunting for a mysterious character and the farcical trial.

More farcical law was presented in Gilbert and Sullivan's first collaboration *Trial by Jury* which first appeared as a comic sketch for *Fun* in 1868 and became a forty minute one act opera for D'Oyly Carte in 1875. The suit for breach of promise was effectively dealt with by the judge.

'Put your briefs upon the shelf.
I will marry her myself'.

Carroll saw *H.M.S. Pinafore* but pronounced himself shocked when the good captain swears he never swears. Yet his understanding of Sullivan's 'delicious' music prompted him to ask Sir Arthur Sullivan to write songs for a musical version of *Alice in Wonderland*. Despite a cautious correspondence together, the project stalled: it seems that paying for Sullivan's songs and copywright would have been 'absurdly extravagant'.[595] Carroll might have

---

[593] A considerably abridged version from, 'The Tichborne Case' in J.B. Atlay, *Trials of the Century*, London, Grant Richards. 1897.

[594] Martin Gardner, *The Annotated Snark*, London, Penguin Books, 1967.

[595] *Letters of Lewis Carroll*: to Arthur Sullivan, March 31st, 1877. Editor, Morton Cohen, London, Macmillan, 1979.

seen Gilbert poking fun at the law whilst the Snark was taking shape in his mind: a decade or so back lay two celebrated fictional trials by Charles Dickens.

Carroll's diaries record several trips to see Gilbert's straight plays at the Haymarket; he found the plot of *Dan'l Druce* 'absurdly improbable' (October 10th, 1876.) and didn't like the fairy comedy *Wicked World* (January 8th, 1873.) He did enjoy *Happy Arcadia*, a Gilbertian confection for the German Reeds with music by Frederick Clay to which he took three child friends on January 21st, 1873. With reference to most of Gilbert's serious drama, posterity has agreed with him.

Bleak House appeared in monthly parts between 1852–1853. The multi-faceted detective story is set against the background of Jarndyce v. Jarndyce, a case concerning an inheritance which has endured for many generations and whose monumental and uncountable costs eventually devour the entire estate under dispute. Mr. Pickwick's legal case against his landlady who sues him for breach of promise in *The Pickwick Papers* (1837) is slighter stuff, but there is no mistaking the law's less scrupulous side as represented by Messrs. Dodson and Fogg. Mr Pickwick refuses to pay the damages involved (£750) and goes to the Fleet prison.

The ultimate farcical Trial was Carroll's own. In *Alice in Wonderland*, the Knave of Hearts is in the dock for stealing jam tarts and the whole Court procedure is turned on its head. As usual, Carroll's Nonsense involves something backwards; in this case, 'sentence first, verdict after'.

Transportation, the dead pig's punishment, was formally abolished in 1868. The penalty, first adopted in 1717, was a method of avoiding overcrowded and insanitary English prisons and convicts were sent first to America and subsequently to colonies in Australia. Offences for which transportation was sentenced were often shockingly light: Elizabeth Archer received seven years at Nottingham Crown Court in 1837 for stealing six handkerchiefs and six shawls.

FIT THE SEVENTH. The Banker's Fate.

What happens…

The Banker's enthusiasm for the chase involves an injudicious rush ahead. He is seized by the furious jaws of the Bandersnatch who refuses the bribe of a large cheque to drop him. Even when the crew appear and he is released, the incident has so damaged his psyche that his waistcoat has turned white.

'He was black in the face and they scarcely could trace
the least likeness to what he had been.
While so great was his fright that his waistcoat turned white,
A wonderful thing to be seen!

To the horror of all who were present that day,
He uprose in full evening dress.

And with senseless grimaces endeavoured to say
what his tongue could no longer express'.

Napoleon's jibe that England was a nation of shopkeepers registered as truth. Commerce, most notably in Victorian Britain, counted for more than science, art, literature, language or agriculture: unless any of these could be usefully allied to commercial ends, their growth and development was doomed. New business legislation, allied to the investment boom of the railways in the 1840s, suddenly made financial affairs newsworthy for all classes of society. Our own late twentieth -century flotations of public utilities, dot.com bubbles and the emergence of the private investor after decades of State governance have many parallels with England 1840. Then, for the first time, ordinary individuals could participate in domestic and international commerce through personal investment. The Banker, as a useful crew member on the Snark Expedition, was a very real figure in Victorian consciousness,[596] both in fact and in fiction and sometimes the dividing line is difficult to see. (For them as well as for us.) Dickens began his literary career as a financial journalist, employing the narrative conventions popularised by contemporary fiction for his dramatic accounts of commerce in *Household Words* or *All The Year Round:* in reverse, Victorian writers introduced financial themes in their novels. Mr Tulliver's litigation and subsequent bankruptcy in Eliot's *Mill On The Floss* (1860) has far-reaching effects on Maggie and Tom. Audrey Jaffe has written that Victorian novels 'rely on narratives of romantic love to adjudicate the relationships between feeling and values': that affairs of money are related to affairs of the heart and that the concept of a gentleman is thus necessary as a 'buffer state'.[597]

Allied to the Bank was the Life Insurance business, such as that bought by the Beaver in Fit One.

'…and next to insure
Its life in some Office of Note.
This the Banker suggested, and offered for hire
(on moderate terms), or for sale
Two excellent Policies, one against Fire,
And one against damage from Hail'.

Life Offices occupied the middle ground, socially and economically in the 1850s and their customers, unlike those who purchased marine or fire insurances, demanded a share in interest earned in addition to financial protection against premature death – in the Beaver's case, the strong likelihood of being hung, drawn and quartered by the Butcher. Carroll's diary entry for July 31st, 1857, records that he discussed life insurances with his father.

---

[596] Note Robert Louis Stevenson's 'The Lamplighter' in *A Child's Garden of Verses,* 1885. 'And my papa's a Banker and as rich as he can be'.

[597] Audrey Jaffe 'Trollope in the Stock Market'. Victorian Studies, 45 (2002)121-48

But it is undeniable that the Bankers, real or fictional, who attract attention, are those who live on the margins of financial probity. Villainy on the scale of George Hudson, Dicken's Mr Merdle in *Little Dorrit* (1855), Augustus Melmotte in *The Way We Live Now (*1875), or even Ferdinand Lopez in a Palliser story *The Prime Minister* (1876) give a vicarious thrill to readers past and present. (Our own days can produce rival claimants from Ivan Boesky to Robert Maxwell and Conrad Black.) A striking exception, and one that Lewis Carroll could not have escaped, was the dramatic purchase of a share in the Suez Canal for Queen and country by banker Lionel Rothschild in 1874, the year of the Snark. The coup, illustrated by cartoons in *Punch* and unquestionably in the public domain, was engineered by new Prime Minister Disraeli who borrowed £4m. from his friend Lionel against the security of the British Government. (Rothschild's £100,000 commission was grumbled at by Parliament but it seems cheap at the price)[598].

FIT THE EIGHTH. The Vanishing.

What Happens…

Night dawns and the crew excitedly believe they have found the Snark as the Beaver bounds along on his tail. The Baker is seen poised atop a crag before plunging into an abyss. Then all is silent and the Baker has vanished forever, softly and suddenly away. Despite a desperate search until nightfall, the crew can find no trace of the Baker.

'In the midst of the word he was trying to say
In the midst of his laughter and glee
He had softly and suddenly vanished away
For the Snark was a Boojum – you see'.

The last line of this Fit was the original inspiration for the entire Nonsense poem. Once again, Carroll was operating backwards. On July 14th, 1874, Carroll recorded in his diary that he wrote to his sister Fanny at 'The Chestnuts', their home in Guildford, offering to take a share in nursing Charlie Wilcox. Twenty two year old Charles Hassard Wilcox was Carroll's godson, a cousin and beloved young friend. He was suffering from inflammation of the lungs, a Victorian euphemism for tuberculosis and it seems likely that Charlie was sent south from his home in Whitby for the milder Southern climate possible in Surrey. Morton Cohen describes how Carroll 'immediately began nursing the invalid through the long nights' and 'how the sorrowful task of seeing the young man consumed by pain and fever weighed heavily upon him'.[599]

Carroll's respite from the agonies of Charlie's ultimately fatal illness was a long walk on the Surrey hills and it was high above Guildford that the one solitary Nonsensical line came into his head. 'For the Snark was a Boojum –

---

[598] Virginia Cowles, *The Rothschilds* 1973. London, Weidenfeld & Nicolson. p162

[599] Morton Cohen, *Lewis Carroll*. London, Macmillan. 1995. p403

you see'. Cohen links the death of Charlie with the unhappy ending of the poem. It may play a part – and then again, it may not.

The Nonsense line stayed in Carroll's head and over the next year and a half, he composed the long verse saga of 141 quatrains for which it began the last line. 'I knew not what it meant then: I know not what it means now, but I wrote it down and sometime after, the rest of the stanza occurred to me and so, by degrees, the rest of the poem pieced itself together'. Backwards.

In his Preface to *The Hunting of the Snark*, Carroll describes how the bowsprit needed to be unshipped once or twice a week for revarnishing and when the time came for replacing it, nobody could remember which end of the boat it belonged to, and so it sometimes got mixed up with the rudder. During this confusing period, the ship usually sailed the wrong way round.

Many writers discuss Lewis Carroll in dualistic terms of contrast to his scholarly persona, Charles Dodgson. I believe he should be considered as someone who operated back to front, who appreciated instinctively that mirror reflections are in reverse and that 'evil' is 'live' backwards. In Alice's conversation with the White Knight and the Queen, she picks up a book and realises something is wrong. *The Jabberwocky* is written backwards (which modern computers can't do, but left-handed people like Lewis Carroll and the author of this book can.)[600] Eventually, Alice realises it is a Looking Glass Book and holds it up to a mirror.

We need to remember that Carroll was born left-handed and made to change, a cruel and outmoded Victorian practise with physical and socio-cultural implications and related to neurology: specifically the lateralisation of certain functions in the cerebral hemispheres. Hannah Messkoub, an American researcher into complex symmetrical systems and author of a book on symmetry in brain function writes that 'for the majority of righthanded individuals, language is associated with dominance in the left hemisphere – lefthandedness equals right hemispheric language dominance, left-hemispheric visuo-spatial dominance'.[601] A stammer is known to be one consequence of changing from left to right handedness and Carroll was painfully afflicted by one all his life. His diary for June 5th, 1872 records that

'a day whose consequence may be of the greatest importance to me. I went to Nottingham by the advice of my friend Hine and heard Dr. Lewin lecture on his system for the cure of stammering. Was most hospitably received by Hine and his wife in their little house. The lecture lasted until after midnight, having begun about 9'.

It seems likely that his stammer was one reason for his reluctance to preach before a congregation but I can find no suggestion that it afflicted his private Christ Church tutorials and it was clearly absent from his conversations

---

[600] *Through the Looking Glass*, p131
[601] Hannah Messkoub, 'Theories in Left Handedness and Laterality'. http://serendip.brynmawr.edu/bb/neuroAccessed 26/03/007

with children.[602]

In conclusion to this context and Analysis to *The Hunting of the Snark* must come some mention of the prevailing climate of the Church of England during 1874, although there is no overt reference to Christianity in the poem. The secession of John Henry Newman to the Catholic faith in 1845 had struck deep at the general unquestioning assumption of the early Victorians that Protestantism was the best of all religions and that England was the best of all countries. Newman's ideas were shared by his contemporaries at Oriel and Christ Church in the 1830s – John Keble and Edward Bouverie Pusey. Dr Pusey became Regius Professor of Hebrew, attached to a Canonry of Christ Church, Oxford, and a friend of Canon Dodgson, Lewis Carroll's father. Less dramatic than Newman, and never taking the final step to Rome, Pusey's sermons nevertheless became acknowledged for reviving the practice of confession: high sacramental doctrine was complemented by his advocacy of a medieval penitential system. Despite his beliefs in the pre-Reformation Church and his meticulous investigations of primitive theology, Pusey worked towards reconciliation and a smooth passage between Roman Catholics and English Protestants, echoing the views of High Churchmen, William Ewart Gladstone and the liberal Archibald Campbell Tait, Archbishop of Canterbury in 1874, and Carroll's old Rugby Headmaster. Florence Becker Lennon makes it clear that Dr Pusey, buried in gloom and visions of eternal damnation, represented the worst aspects of a joyless Victorian religiosity: a terrible model for a sensitive and emotional young man[603].

Disraeli, elected Prime Minister in 1874, was confronted with raging ecclesiastical debate from a Parliament which included a substantial proportion of Nonconformists as well as a smattering of Jews and which brought on to the Statute Books, the Public Worship Regulation Act in 1874. This forbade certain ritual acts – mixing wine and water in the chalice and wearing Eucharistic vestments – valuable in provoking much underlined support from Queen Victoria who had an instinctive feeling that the Church of England was becoming too High for her and that Roman Catholics were ' dreadfully aggressive people who must be Put Down – just as our Ritualists'. [604]

Despite a family friendship with Edward Pusey and his own clerical collar, Lewis Carroll kept his head down in national Church politics. He was mildly curious – but did not intervene. A diary entry for April 3rd, 1868 records that 'Ward Hunt, lately of Christ Church took us in (to the House). The debate was most interesting and included a two-and-a- half hour speech from Disraeli and one-and-a-half hour from Gladstone.[605] It was on Lord Stanley's amendment on Gladstone's Resolution that the Irish Church must be disestablished, the amendment being that the question ought to be left to the Reformed Parliament

---

[602] Florence Becker Lennon quotes a cruel trick played on Carroll by fellow undergraduates who manoeuvred him into reading the Biblical lesson where S...saul changes his name to P...paul. (Becker Lennon, p103)

[603] Becker Lennon, p.57

[604] A.N. Wilson, *The Victorians* London. Hutchinson 2002. p368

[605] Modern parliamentarians, note.

of next year'. Through all the storms of religious controversy, Carroll's diary confirms his clear tenets of the Christian faith which he supported without any doubt or deviation – or Dr Pusey. Carroll writes in his diary...

'A year of great blessings and a few trials, of much weakness and sin, yet I trust I have learned to know myself better and to have striven – yet how feebly and ineffectively – to live nearer God'.[606]

Could *The Hunting of the Snark* represent a Pilgrim's Progress? Bunyan's celebrated allegory on the Christian faith was delivered 'under the similitude of a dream', like much of Lewis Carroll (and a handful of Gilbert's *Bab Ballads*). Are the crew of the Bellman engaged upon a voyage to discover the Eternal? Surely their astonishing and inconsequential variety tallies with the general lot of mankind. In *Endgame,* Brian Sibley[607] supports this idea of the Snark as a religious quest.

'A metaphor of Man's search for God – the Infinite, the Supreme Unknown, the Ultimate Being, Elohim, the No-Thing, ill-equipped with second hand hearsay evidence and the awful fear of the presence of God that it engenders.
Had He not told Moses – 'Thou can'st not see my face for there shall be no man see My face and live?'[608]
The idea that the Snark does not necessarily represent a Being, but simply being, in the existentalist sense, has been entertaining for philosophers but I support Sibley's theory of Christian allegory and there can be no doubt that it carries weight from a writer steeped in Victorian religious certainty and an unshakeable personal faith in God. Morton Cohen agrees that the quest narrative of *The Hunting of the Snark* has a religious mainspring because 'underscoring everything Carroll wrote and did was his conviction of a moral universe and a life after death. His faith in God was absolute. The voyage in Snark must in some way represent the voyage of life, just as the Alice books do, but the message is not one of despair. The voyage is a grand adventure, like life, and each of the crew represents some strain of society, perhaps even some personal quality in Charles himself.'[609]
In the most recent example of Alice scholarship, Darien Graham-Smith confirms Carroll's Christian faith by contrasting it with Darwinian science and current social mores. 'While he (Carroll) considered social intercourse merely a system of arbitrary rules reinforced and referenced by his peers, morality for Carroll proceeded from a Higher Authority'.[610] Graham Smith continues to argue that Carroll's 'humble prayers and matter of fact statements of religious intent occur frequently with no special fanfare: they appear an every day part

---

[606] December 31st, 1867.

[607] *Jabberwocky*, Autumn 1976. Vol.5, No. 4.

[608] Ibid.

[609] Cohen, p410

[610] Darien Graham-Smith, 'Contextualising Carroll'. Ph.D. thesis, University of Wales, Bangor, 2005, p47

of Carroll's life'.

And surely the failure of the obvious commercial approaches to the voyage and the pursuit of the Snark by the Banker has a Biblical feeling to it? Rich men, camels and the eyes of needles come unbidden to mind. Learning lessons, such as that from the Butcher to the Beaver in Fit Five bring friendship and new love as the primary outcome: arithmetic and natural history do not seem to count for much. 'Colenso', the name on Holiday's Fit Five illustration refers to the then colonial Bishop of Natal whose earlier claim to fame was as the author of a mathematics primer. Synonymously with the publication of *The Snark*, Colenso was in trouble with the English clerical establishment for some flexible interpretations of the scriptures for Zulu tribesmen.

The trial scene, so familiar in Carroll's Nonsense, has obvious connections with Christ before Pilate, but contains a deeper symbolism of truth in opposition to venality and perhaps a Gilbertian sense that no man-made laws can ever provide answers to a non-earthly problem. Was the Baker's sudden disappearance into the abyss, a plunge into hell: could his missing luggage and confused earlier identity represent a denial of Truth? Did the Baker's shocking end inspire Sherlock Holmes and Professor Moriarty's final moments at the Reichenbach Falls in 1891? : could Conan Doyle have borrowed the solution for an unwanted hero from Carroll? We shall never know, but William Stuart Baring-Gould invents a curious friendship between Lewis Carroll and Sherlock Holmes who were both residents at Christ Church[611] – Holmes guesses Carroll's interest in photography by the acid-stains and flash powder burns on the don's right hand.[612] Or has he silently slipped into a world as yet unknown? Yet Hope springs eternal, an idea illustrated by Holiday for Fit Four by a magnificent woman holding a (sheet) anchor,[613] the traditional image for a 'mainstay'. There is no easy path to the Everlasting, however many thimbles and forks you use, and however many railway shares and how much charm and soap. It eludes the obvious: it lies where none of us ever looks.

---

[611] William Stuart Baring-Gould, *Sherlock Holmes, The Biography,* London, Rupert Hart Davis, 1962.

[612] Ibid. p23

[613] Professor Vance has given me the Biblical reference: Hebrews 6:19 for the Christian analogy of God as hope and <u>anchor</u> for our soul 'as sure as it is firm and reaching right through beyond the veil.' Jerusalem Bible, Popular Edition, 1974.

THE SNARK LIVES ON...

The physical absence of Carroll's Snark continues to act as an inspiration. Because the Snark is nothing, it becomes everything. Jean Paul Sartre's ideas make *The Hunting of The Snark* an existentialist possibility; his theories on a philosophical existence which precedes human essence postulate that we simply exist into a world not of our choosing and must define our own identity or characteristics in the course of our own lives. The poem's real meaning is anti-meaning. It is about existence, not function: listening, not seeing: feeling, not thinking. The blank canvas, just as the blank maps, mean that we can adapt *The Snark* to our own situation and it becomes ourself.

Critics find different symbolism in the Snark. Dante Gabriel Rossetti, fast sinking into the grip of chloral, considered it a veiled attack upon his work,[614] Morton Cohen believed that perhaps *The Snark* spoke of the hallowed relationship of person to person, of Charles to his child friends, about a sacredness that must never be violated',[615] and Graham Darien Smith analysed *The Snark* in 'an imagery of dreams and sleep to existential purpose'.[616] Edward Guiliano 'agrees that the Boojum can be viewed as an existential horror…an expression of Dodgson's dread, his nightmare, his anxiety about facing the end of his being',[617] but ultimately this writer shares the view that 'the moral of the Snark is that it has no moral. It is a fiction, a thing which does not seek to be real or true'.[618] Carroll himself declared that *The Snark* was an allegory on the search for happiness.

If existentialist possibilities are one reason for the continuing life and vitality of the Snark, what Leach calls the 'acute adultness' of this 'infinitely strange and wonderful *Hunting of the Snark'* is another.[619] Alternative versions and new illustrations have been attempted since the poem was first written, all aimed at adult audiences but, interestingly, none have quite succeeded. The wild flower of Victorian Nonsense is not easily grafted on to a twenty-first century stem: the original is sufficiently hardy to have survived climate change without requiring variation. Moreover, part of the genius of *The Hunting of the Snark,* despite Leach's adherence to its 'grown-up' character, lies in its appeal to audiences of any age, in any time. Unlike more conventional texts, Nonsense rhymes, untethered to period posts, move freely between the

---

[614] *Letters*, 1876, p351

[615] Cohen, p411

[616] Darien Smith, p127

[617] Guiliano, p128

[618] Holquist, p164

[619] Leach, p225

generations and indeed often serve as a bridge between them.

It seems likely that Sergei Prokofiev's *Peter and the Wolf*, (1936), lay behind the inspiration for a handful of narrated versions of *The Hunting of the Snark* accompanied by orchestral tone poems. Just as Prokofiev's music lifted the children's fairy tale into an adult spectrum, complete with Wagnerian 'leitmotifs', so a variety of contemporary composers attempted a similar trick with Carroll's nursery Nonsense. Kevin Scott (b. 1956) and Douglas Young (b. 1947) both produced versions written for chamber orchestra, piano, soprano and narrator. Ezra Laderman, distinguished American Professor of Composition at Yale University, whose combination of lyrical style and contemporary concepts allied to a preference for unusual formal structures make him an ideal candidate for Snark composition, produced an operatic *Hunting of the Snark,* an Entertainment in One Act and Eight Fits, in 1958. James Earl Jones was the unmistakable voice in Caleb Simpson's 1989 composition for an animated film of the Snark. In 1957, the BBC produced Max Saunder's musical *Hunting of the Snark*, 'a work which combined a gay irresponsibility with passages of becoming seriousness and gravity'.[620]

The most ambitious reinterpretation has probably been the Australian musical *Boojum!* written in 1979 by Martin and Peter Wesley-Smith. The authors believed that *Boojum!*'s book and lyrics would reflect the opposites in Carroll: dream versus reality, sense versus nonsense, emotional versus rational, conventional versus radical and religious faith versus existentialist despair. *Boojum!* would use a range of Carroll's own writing to ask questions about the author himself 'in a manner designed to evoke his world, his hopes and fears, his loves, wit and whimsy, his intellectual vision and the human characteristics that are reflected in the charm and creative intelligence of his Nonsense'.[621] Musical inspiration came from Carroll's music boxes and from Victorian nursery rhymes, played in Carrollian style, back to front or upside down. *Opera* was enthusiastic: 'the music employs many devices that would have tickled Dodgson's fancy mightily - inverted and crab versions of nursery rhymes for example – and always sounds fresh, lively and richly expressive'.[622]

The Wesley-Smiths portrayed Carroll as the Baker in a Snark hunt which linked biography and fantasy, much as Aldous Huxley had attempted to do with the Alice books for Walt Disney in the 1940s.[623] 'I think something nice might be made of this...the unutterably odd, repressed and ridiculous Oxford lecturer in mathematics and logic seeking refuge in the company of little girls

---

[620] Hudson, p18

[621] Peter and Martin Wesley-Smith 1988. Notes on 'Boojum!' Internet Site. accessed 19/4/2007.

[622] 'Opera'.Vol.37, No. 7, July 1986.

[623] The eventual film flop always rankled. Julian claimed Aldous only took the Disney shilling on the advice of his friend Anita Loos who knew that wartime English families were short of everything. The Huxley connection with Carroll and *The Snark* continued when Elspeth Huxley entitled her African adventure *With Forks and Hope.* (London, Chatto & Windus, 1964).

and his own fantasy',[624] but Disney found Huxley's treatment too literary and his 1951 Alice film does not list Huxley's name in the credits. The Wesley-Smiths used childhood material to develop the Jubjub, invented new portmanteau words ('thaunt' means taunt and haunt) and reinvented Alice's caterpillar as a yuppie vegetarian aerobics freak. Despite the Sydney Philharmonic Motet Choir, conductor John Grundy, and a full cast of soloists, singers, actors, production specialists and recording engineers, *Boojum!* did not last long. Reviewers were kind about 'absurdity theatre dealing with existential nihilism – Beckett with bells on'[625] and 'a delightful result with much potent popular appeal'[626] but *Boojum!* went the way of the Baker. (A recording is believed to exist: I haven't found it.) Carroll, unlike Lear or indeed Gilbert, was not inherently musical. He attended concerts and doubtless sang hymns but his collection of musical boxes was to entertain his child friends in Tom Quad. (He enjoyed running the rolls of punched paper backwards.) Becker Lennon claims that he was 'never a supremely musical poet…yet Carroll uses a versification often melodious and unusually compact…except when rhyme or reason seduce him into a little padding'.[627] A diary entry records that Carroll,

'tried to compose a piece of verse imitating the effects of music, but had not had much success. Some of what I intended as an Explanatory Note to it, I have today set down to form a portion of an Essay on 'Word Music'[628]. (This has not survived)

Undeterred by the failure of the Australian *Boojum!* Mike Batt wrote a musical *Hunting of the Snark* in 1994. This began life as a 'concept album' featuring Art Garfunkel, John Hurt, John Gielgud, Roger Daltrey, Julian Lennon and Cliff Richard with the London Symphony Orchestra. It was performed at the Barbican, followed by a costumed concert at the Royal Albert Hall with Billy Connolly as the Bellman and performers recreating their roles from the original album. On October 24th, 1991, *The Hunting of the Snark* opened at the Prince Edward Theatre in London with striking scenery and costume designs – 12,000 slides from 152 computer linked projectors beamed images around the theatre. Yet again, reviewers praised aspects of the production and the visual concept – but savaged the show. It closed seven weeks later.

A purely musical 'tone poem' Snark with no words, was composed in 1903. American composer T.H. Rollinson wrote what he described as an 'epic parody of a quaint and fanciful theme in verse published many years ago'. Rollinson's manuscript for Six Cantos for Brass Ensemble with Solo Brass Instruments exists in the British Library, together with the composer's

---

[624] Aldous Huxley, letter to Violet Ocampo. From *The Letters of Aldous Huxley*, ed. Grover Smith, New York, 1969/70 p535
[625] Brian Hoad, *The Bulletin*. Sydney. March 25, 1986.
[626] Ibid.
[627] Becker Lennon, p
[628] March 12th, 1857

programme notes for each movement.

Canto One: Andante Pastorale, a peaceful hamlet.
Canto Two: Moderato Pomposo, sees the Bellman, an ancient mariner, relating the terrible tale of the Snark
Canto Three: Maestoso, a fearful hunting, danger is near
Canto Four: Mysterioso, danger is near.
Canto Five: Allegro Vivace, a general stampede, leaving the Baker to his Fate.
Canto Six. Marziale, a rousing Finale when the Hunters congratulate themselves, but the Baker has met with the Snark.

This was recorded on a vintage classic entitled 'A Trip to Coney Island', from *Brass Band Ensembles from America's Golden Age of wind music.*

In 1934, Percival Robert Brinton, Rector of Hambleden, Buckinghamshire produced a version of *The Hunting of the Snark* in Vergilian hexameters. In his Introduction, Brinton explains that he has found 'a certain affinity in character as well as experience between the hero of the Aeneid and the hero of the Snark. Both the Bellman and the pious Aeneas were leaders of an adventurous expedition by sea and by land: both pursued their quest with simplicity and single mindedness. Each had devoted followers: each found himself threatened by a hostile and mysterious power: each has survived to interest later generations in the story'.[629] (This could apply to Ulysses, the Jumblies, Christ and the Apostles, and C.S. Lewis' *The Voyage of the Dawn Treader.)*

'Spe simul ac furcis, cura et digitalibus usi
Quaerebant praedam socii: via ferrea monstro
Letum intendebat: risus sapoque trahebant.'

Note that this completely obliterates any sense of English Nonsense and produces an epic solemnity which Carroll's ballad metre deliberately eschews. Parodic Latin is occasionally used to produce Nonsense of another order altogether…

'In fir tar is
In oak none is;
In mud eels are,
In clay none are'.

Almost inevitably undergraduate Snark Clubs sprang up at Oxford and Cambridge. The Oxford Snark Society was founded in 1879 at New College and met regularly, during the 1880s and 1890s but for obvious reasons the last official meeting took place in 1914. In 1952, the Club address book surfaced and thirty five guests including John Galsworthy and A.P.Herbert attended a London dinner. *The Observer* in a colour supplement for January 8th 1967 carried an 1888 photograph of the Oxford Snarks with a young John Galsworthy sporting a monocle.

---

[629] Martin Gardner, *The Annotated Snark*, Penguin Classics, London. 1995. p99

The Cambridge Snarks were founded in 1934 by a group of medical students and continues to meet once a year for a formal dinner and a reading of *The Agony in Eight Fits*. It has exactly ten members, each of them corresponding to a member of the Snark hunting crew. Cambridge Snarks obey eleven rules including the injunction that members shall be replaced as they 'softly and silently vanish away' and that the Bellman be responsible for the upkeep of the bell and it may be his peculiar privilege to tingle it.[630] Current internet sites reveal the Cambridge Snarks to be alive and well; colour photographs show members celebrating regular 'sailings' and tingling the bell during dinners at the Royal Agricultural College, Cirencester (2004) the Travellers Club, Pall Mall (2003) and Christ Church, Oxford (2001).

The Hunting of the Snark has been read on BBC radio by Alec Guinness and again by Alan Bennett, and recorded on disc by Boris Karloff. Caedmon (now part of HarperCollins) who specialise in recording literature and whose lists include Cyril Cusack reading Hopkins, Joyce and Yeats, produced an audio book of Karloff's Snark.

Carroll never wrote another epic Nonsense poem. *The Hunting of The Snark*, written nearly twenty five years before his death, remained unique. *Phantasmagoria,* (1881), is a long comic fantasy which concerns a trainee sprite who haunts the wrong house but once we have accepted that the ghost talks, likes roast duck with gravy and drinks beer, everything else is merely an extension of the joke. *Phantasmagoria* reflects something of Carroll's skill and interest in photography, new techniques of which allowed a superimposition of images, of shadowy forms merging one into another and fading in half-developed bromide prints. It also serves to demonstrate Carroll's own growing interest in spiritualism and the paranormal. Carroll visited a certain Mr Heaphy, an artist who claimed to have painted a ghost: other varieties of spirit 'appeared' to stage illusionists, mountebanks and hypnotists as well as featuring regularly in Carroll's dream world. Carroll joined the Society for Psychical Research in 1882. *Phantasmagoria* illustrates a commercial acumen not often associated with Lewis Carroll. New middle class monthly magazines of the 1860s and 1870s almost always featured a ghost story, designed to be read around the fireside on a winter's night, an idea which became compulsory for Christmas editions. George MacDonald published 'Uncle Cornelius, His Story' a sombre tale of a domesticated, miserly female ghost for *St. Paul's Magazine*, December, 1869 and Mrs Gaskell contributed 'The Old Nurses' Story', a tale of the supernatural for *Household Words*, Christmas edition, 1852.

Phantasmagoria has a simple rhyming pattern, some witty lines and some

---

[630] Snark Societies information quoted in the Preface to Martin Gardner *Annotated Snark*. Penguin Classics, London, 1995, p12. and from internet sites, accessed 19/4/2007.

excruciating puns[631] – but it survives mainly on account of its author. (This author thinks it belongs in a school magazine.) As far as I am aware, no critic or writer has attempted an investigation or allegorical analysis of it, unlike, for example, Carroll's *Walrus and the Carpenter*[632] which has attracted the theory that the Walrus represents Buddha, (Eastern religion) and the Carpenter represents Jesus, (Western religion). The two characters exploit all the oysters (young people) and demonstrate the hypocrisy and corruption of religious organisations.

---

[631] There is an Inns Spectre and a Night Mayor......

[632] *Alice Through the Looking Glass*. Penguin Classic Edition, 1998, p159

CONCLUSION

This study has established contexts for selected Nonsense poetry by Edward Lear Lewis Carroll and W.S. Gilbert. Academic research has uncovered at least some of the roots of Walter de la Mare's wild flowers, establishing their credentials as a proper species worth cultivation, growth and analysis, thus underlining their value in generating a lateral view of social history.

Lear, Carroll and Gilbert were natural born, full-blooded Englishmen whose Nonsense derives in large part from this shared inheritance. No Celtic magic leavened the Anglo-Saxon heritage of all three men: none could claim Irish tale tellers, Welsh singers or Scottish poets as forebears. Lear liked to pretend his grandfather was a Danish Mr Lør which is picturesque and untrue. Gilbert attended a boyhood school in Boulogne yet he remained as English as any man who ever lived and Dodgson's ancestors, north country gentry since the eighteenth century, included the Bishop of Elphin, 1722–1795.[633] They were mid-Victorian and middle to-upper-class, from successful, hardworking and prosperous families who nodded upwards to the aristocracy and left a careful gap between them and the working poor below. They were educated in the best manner of their class and their age although perhaps only Carroll approached the world through the channels of his formal schooling. Their ability to translate Greek odes or parse Latin verbs would make them scholars today but in the 1840s such learning amongst their milieu was standard.[634]

The character of a nation may be defined as 'a mental organisation connecting the minds of all the members of a national community by ties and connections as firm as silk and as strong as steel'.[635] The English mind is believed to be 'conspicuous for modesty, pugnacity, sensibility to the blessings of his government, straightforward and of good sense, though inclined to excess and bereft of delicacy of taste and artistic sensibility'.[636] The 'ties and connections' were particularly strong in the nineteenth century when England had the peculiar confidence which came from victories in overseas wars, colonial conquests on a massive scale and great national wealth from prosperous trade and industry.

In 1850 and 1860, it would have been difficult not to accept the idea that England was an elite nation, the envy of half the world and conqueror of the

---

[633] Dodgson's grandfather succeeded Edward Synge, a member of that remarkable Irish clerical dynasty, in the Irish Bishopric of Elphin, Roscommon.

[634] Even if Greek and Latin syntax, grammar and prosody were the ONLY valued aspects of education for proper young men of the day.

[635] Ernest Barker, quoted in Roberto Romani, *National Character and Public Spirit in England and France, 1750-1914*. CUP, 2001,p1

[636] Ibid. p167

rest. It was precisely this powerful, confident, collective identity which made Nonsense possible in symbiosis. Where there is no acknowledged national consciousness, no moral consensus as reflected in law and only the relativity of personal taste or prevailing fashionable ethics, Nonsense has nowhere to go. Professor Alan Fischler[637] argues that the comedy of Gilbert's Savoy libretti upheld and supported bourgeois values, a claim which might allow them a designation of Nonsense, yet a certain daft logic prevails in the libretti, crucially absent in the anarchical Nonsense of the *Bab Ballads*. It is Bab who offers a frisson on a comfort blanket: a momentary and pleasurable dislocation possible from the security and safety of a profoundly well-ordered nation state.

English library shelves bulge with theories on nationalism, almost inevitably written by foreigners,[638] but defining the English character was most memorably achieved by Pont in a series of cartoons for *Punch* in the years between the two world wars.[639]

The British Character; Love of Fair Play. Punch cartoon by Graham Laidler.

Certain clichés are accepted as true, even though they offer Gilbertian contradictions. The English live in a republic with a monarch. The secular state contains an established church. Conservatives are radical. Sports-mad schools have produced great scholars. Pugnaciously strong opinions, tempered by

[637] Alan Fischler, *Modified Rapture*, Charlottesville, University of Virginia Press, 1991.
[638] I include Hume and Carlyle.
[639] Pseudonym for Graham Laidler, 1908-1940, and derived from his family nickname of Pontus Maximus. See cartoon on p179

innate sense of fair play, are schooled to perfection on the games pitch to allow another point of view. The English set enormous store by manners and protocol especially concerning meals which remain badly cooked. A love of gardening never seems to produce fresh food for the table, neither does a tradition of embroidery enable fashionable clothing. An insular mentality, conditioned to some extent by the weather, makes both mind and body impregnable. ''E's a blinking foreigner, 'eave 'alf a brick at im,' still probably remains the popular view, even if cited more than seventy years ago. [640]

The Englishness of Lear, Carroll and Gilbert is related to their gender. Up to around 1914, assertions of nationality were assumed to be masculine.[641] Men remained absolutely prevalent in all evaluations of collective mentality. (Some positive comfort for feminists exists in the notion that sisterhood transcends nationality, but only some.) It is notable that Lear, Carroll and Gilbert came from families with particularly dominant fathers. Canon Dodgson was an austere and challenging figure who appears to have dominated his more sensitive son, Dr William Gilbert's opinionated crusades would have crushed a lesser boy than WSG, and the financial enterprise of Jeremiah Lear kept the family uncomfortably poised between fortune and famine. Wives, mothers and sisters seem to have played subordinate roles in the Lear, Carroll and Gilbert households, (Ann Lear's loving care for her younger brother Edward is the exception) a state of affairs which may have contributed to the bachelor status of both Lear and Carroll. Neither Lear, nor Carroll nor Gilbert had children of their own.

Yet despite their inheritance and the intensely masculine worlds in which they moved professionally, Lear, Gilbert and Carroll developed particularly close and rewarding friendships with women, carried on by correspondence in Lear's case, theatre visits in Carroll's and on the stage by Gilbert. None could ever be described as misogynist. (It appears that Carroll's friendships with very young girls has been exaggerated at the expense of Isa Bowman and Ellen Terry.) Lear came close to replacing the love of his absent mother with Gussie Bethel and never ceased to regard Emily Tennyson as his dearest confidante. The childless WSG and his wife Kitty all but adopted Nancy MacIntosh, a young American singer who created the role of Princess Zara in *Utopia, Ltd*.

Nonsense is masculine. It exemplifies the utmost brilliance, creativity and imagination. It represents the exact opposite of anything feminine: it is neither useful, nor practical, nor sympathetic: it is abstract, useless and life-enhancing. An all-male crew hunt the Snark (Henry Holiday's illustration of a female 'Hope' in Fit Four is artistic licence as Carroll does not mention her) in a series of lunatic Boys' Own adventures involving intrepid Victorian explorers and an all-male courtroom drama. Lear's Nonsense heroes in his longer verses include a romantically-inspired Dong, a Scroobious Pip, a Quangle Wangle and a Pobble who has No Toes. Old Women and Young Girls appear in the limericks

---

[640] Raymond Postgate & Aylmer Vallance, *Those Foreigners*. London, George Harrap, 1937, p88
[641] Although 'nations' were often feminine: Germania, La Belle France, Britannia, Helvetia... Professor Vance argues that feminised nations and masculine standard bearers are reciprocal concepts.

significantly less often than Old Men or Young Persons. Gilbert is occasionally attacked for his gallery of female grotesques (critics never take note of equally caricatured dukes, dustmen, soldiers, sailors and peers of the realm) yet a more salient rationale for the inherent masculine ethos surely lies in the wholly masculine preserve of the institutions that he came from, and sent up. Gilbert's life in the theatre belongs to a later period than the *Bab Ballads* although women do not fare noticeably better in the Savoy Operas than the Ballads: Katisha and Little Buttercup are pantomimic dame figures and the Fairy Queen in *Iolanthe* is Victoria. England's Queen had passed from domestic icon through reclusive widowhood to become the nanny-figure of She Who Must Be Obeyed.[642] (The English wholly reverential approach to the monarchy was ever only possible with a touch of irreverence, then as now.) Ian Bradley believes that 'Gilbert and Sullivan is very much a male taste' citing not only the 'gross caricaturing of middle aged women' but perhaps the echoes of the parade ground and school chapel in Sullivan's music.[643]

Nonsense is original. G.K. Chesterton described Edward Lear's *Dong with the Luminous Nose* as 'original in the way that the first ship and the first plough were original'[644] but we need to define 'original'. It does not necessarily mean new as, in one sense, nothing is new: it is claimed that the seven basic storyline plots in fiction which have been recycled since Greek mythology, account for nine tenths of all tales, from *Beowulf* to *Jane Eyre*.[645] Gilbert recycled both his own material and that of J.R. Planché in particular but his entirely original mind created a fresh approach, even within an accepted orthodoxy. Carroll's fabulous Snark is an original invention, despite the images and incident from Carroll's own experience which accompany its entirely futile hunt and its antecedents in quest-literature and voyage-narrative. It is the originality of Nonsense which has guaranted its survival – and which helps separate it from the contemporary mores of parody and satire. Over reliance on puns and pastiche lent Victorian comic versifiers C.S. Calverley, Thomas Hood and Richard Harris Barham a short shelf life and none is much read today.[646] (It was the parodic element in Sullivan which renders his music ineligible for immortality, despite its eternal tunefulness and skilful orchestration. Handel, Verdi and Wagner are shamelessly borrowed, to great

---

[642] A reference to Ayeesha, Arabic heroine of a tribe enslaved by a woman, an idea borrowed seriously by Rider Haggard and comically by John Mortimer for Hilda Rumpole.

[643] Ian Bradley, *The Complete Annotated Gilbert and Sullivan,* OUP Paperback edition, 2001. pxi

[644] G.K. Chesterton, *In Defence of Nonsense.* London, R.Brinsley Sheridan, 1902, but taken from a Nonsense.org. Internet site. Accessed 14/2/2008.

[645] These are: overcoming the monster/rags to riches/quest/voyage and return/comedy/tragedy/rebirth. Although 'plot series' lists exist in every publisher's office, Christopher Booker's *The Seven Basic Plots,* London, Continuum, 2004, a massive work which took the author 35 years to write, sets out the stall more plainly than many.

[646] Thomas Hood's *Song of the Shirt,* 1843, may be an exception; this polemic designed to bring the struggles of the working class to more general attention was beyond the average remit of a comic verse.

comic effect.) Nonsense is not a discovery: it has not lain in wait for a Madame Curie to render radium from pitchblende, nor an Einstein to formulate relativity from existing science. Nonsense is an original invention.

Nonsense represents freedom and freedom is represented by England. ' The national spirit of the English is a consequence of one of the freest governments ever to appear on the face of the earth and Britain is the guardian of the general liberties of Europe and patron of mankind'.[647] It was an era of very settled peace and prosperity which enabled the Nonsense writing of Lear, Carroll and Gilbert.[648] Revolutions which grumbled around Europe in 1848 did not reach English shores, although anxieties concerning precisely which ambitions had been inherited by Napoleon's nephew kept some statesmen on keen alert. Such wars as took place in the period 'were either brief operations decided by technological and organisational means like most European campaigns overseas, and the rapid and decisive wars by means of which the German Empire was established between 1864 and 1871: or mismanaged massacres on which even the patriotism of the belligerent countries refused to dwell with pleasure, such as the Crimean War of 1854–1865.'[649] Hobsbawm's *Age of Capital* precisely replicates the heyday of Lear, Carroll and Gilbert. It was an age marked by the drama of progress: 'that key word of the age, massive, enlightened, sure of itself but inevitable',[650] an age when economic and technological concerns dominated the political scene. There were battles over railway routes or the site of a new coal mine, but it was during this period of immense prosperity and peaceful political freedoms at home that the brightest and best Nonsense flowers were both enabled and encouraged to bloom.

Nonsense belongs to no movement in particular, but it resonates with both romance and romanticism: literally, both the preposterous narrative and the cultural celebration of personal imagination. Edward Lear was the most personally romantic of my three heroes and the one closest both in time and spirit to the Romantic poets of the early nineteenth century. The romantic movement was the major consequence of the 1789 revolution and one which, for better or for worse, first endowed modern man with the confidence of an independent, individual existence – in imagination, if not always in practice. 'It aimed at liberating human personality from the fetters of social convention and social morality',[651] or, in the vernacular – to be romantic meant to be free. English romantic poets from Byron to Tennyson celebrated sometimes escapist freedoms for man and nature with new, personal 'romantic' expression, in immediate and direct reaction to the classical constraints of the eighteenth century. Their emphasis on travel, alienated individualism and a romantic aesthetic of suffering and melancholy make Byron and Tennyson particularly

---

[647] Romani, p169

[648] W.L.Burns, *The Age of Equipoise*, London, Allen & Unwin, 1964.

[649] Eric Hobsbawn, *The Age of Capital,* London, Weidenfeld & Nicolson, 1975.p4

[650] ibid

[651] Bertrand Russell, *A History of Western Philosophy*. London, Unwin Hyman. 1979. p658

significant inspiration for my three Nonsense writers; their ultimate romantic dream of liberty requires a subtle subversion from classical conventions just as the liberties taken by Nonsense subverts both the real and the romantic.

Contemporary Victorian readers of Nonsense would be familiar with Byron, Shelley, Keats, Wordsworth and Coleridge and their reaction to Nonsense could only benefit from the mutual acquaintance: they would have appreciated and understood the frequent references better than we can today. Lear and Carroll wrote both serious and Nonsense verses in romantic vein and even Gilbert was not immune from romance in metre, form or sentiment. Like the actor he wished to be, WSG disguised the romantic aspects of his character by barking loudly and presenting an alarming truculence in opposition – but posterity is not fooled. All creativity involves 'aesthetic sensibility, emotional resonance and gift for expression'[652] no matter how heavy the watchchain, nor strangle-tight the knot of the old school tie.

We have noted that there is never nonsense in music. The heights of 'emotional resonance, aesthetic sensibility' and power of expression in music must rely upon formal principles and physical instruments which remain immutable even in the most extreme inspiration of the Darmstadt School.[653] But there is music in Nonsense. There is an actual music in the rhythm of the verse and an emotional music in the undercurrents of feelings expressed. Music exists in the lilting echoes of Tennyson which haunt Lear's longer verses: in the rollicking metre of Bab's Ballads even before Sullivan borrowed tunes for them from Handel and Verdi – or made up his own with martial memories from a Sandhurst childhood. The Snark has inspired musical tone poems, narrated orchestral versions and a variety of modern musicals. The Nonsense limericks of Lear prompted that most serious composer Charles Villiers Stanford[654] to long-lost flights of fancy under the pseudonym of Carel Drofnatski. Stanford, (1852–1924) Irish born, but English domiciled, wrote operas, symphonies and chamber music whilst occupying academic posts at Cambridge University and the Royal College of Music. Ralph Vaughan Williams was a pupil. As his *alter ego* Drofnatski, Stanford seems to have forgotten his notoriously tetchy manner and the combination of Edward Lear and an Irish inheritance inspired the wondrously clever, silly settings with their equally daft Notes. Adrian Welles Beecham's settings of Bab are interesting, if lesser creations from the pen of a composer who never quite came out from

---

[652] Edward de Bono, *Lateral Thinking*, London, Ward Lock,1970, p11

[653] Influential European music school c. 1950- 1960, whose major figures were Karlheinz Stockhausen, Pierre Boulez and Luciano Berio.

[654] Henry Wood recalls a conversation with Edward Vlll as Prince of Wales when they discussed a new portrait of Stanford (by Orpen) in the Royal College of Music, February, 1924. 'Of course I know Stanford' declared the Prince, 'he wrote the Hallelujah Chorus!' Wood was obliged to point out the error. 'What a bloomer' said Edward, magnanimously. (Henry Wood *My Life of Music*, London, Victor Gollancz, 1938, p403

under the shadow of Sir Thomas.[655]

Nonsense has been claimed as Surrealism, an art form which believed in the power of the unconscious to liberate the imagination. In its written form, surrealism disdained the literal meaning and focussed on hidden undertones and poetic currents beneath the surface which is why *Alice in Wonderland* became known as the first surrealist text. The movement proper was born in Paris during the 1920s, fathered by André Breton, a doctor who had studied Freud and who worked to heal shell-shocked survivors of WW1. Just as the conflict and terror of the 1790s gave birth to the Romantic, so the brutality and insanity of 1914–1918 inspired the surrealists. Max Ernst, René Magritte, Georges Chirico and Paul Eluard believed that realism was propping up ancient edifices in forms of chaos and contradiction. Their new art defined realism as a positive expression of the reunion between the conscious and unconscious realm of experience: it sought to explain how dreams and fantasy become a familiar part of everyday life. Surrealists believed that a spontaneous execution of art without censorship or canonic anxiety was a revolution that would transform prevailing societal values. Ordinary and depictive expressions were vital, but the sense of their arrangement should be open to the full range of personal imagination, conscious or unconscious, dreamt or awake, spoken or silent. It is the importance of dreams in both Carroll's Alice books and *The Hunting of the Snark* which uphold their right to be considered 'surreal', long before the term officially existed. Some of Lear's drawings are as surreal as anything by Chirico or Dalí. They combine disparate elements linked only by an alliteration or rhyme of the accompanying verse. But there is always a sense of fun in Lear's surrealism, in contrast to the vaguely ominous dread which accompanies the images of Max Ernst or Yves Tanguey.

Gilbert is the least surreal of my heroes. Perhaps his feet were more firmly on the ground: he was the most 'regular chap' of the three, the least romantic and the most practical. His uncomplicated negotiation with society did not require a violent reaction against it, at least not one that dripped watches over mantelpieces or steamed trains out of the fireplace. But Bab finds himself in some surreal situations requiring surreal solutions and both Gilbert and Bab retire frequently to a sharply visualised dream world of the topsy-turvy. In Gilbert's unconscious, where the imagination reigns supreme, contemporary mores are reversed.

'for that which we call folly here,
Is wisdom in that favoured sphere.
The wisdom which we highly prize
Is blatant folly in their eyes'.

JE, p280.

---

[655] Difficult...even though Beecham's two sons by his separated wife Utica lived a distant life from their celebrated father. ' His sons no longer regarded him as a close member of the family but rather as a kind of Uncle figure who was on the edge of the household, yet did not properly belong'. Alan Jefferson, *Sir Thomas Beecham*. London, MacDonald and Jane's, 1979, p38

It is interesting to learn that ***veedyech voh snye,*** the Russian word for 'dream', literally translates as ' to see in your sleep'.

There is an abstract quality to Nonsense poetry, but it is not Abstract. Most non-referential artistic abstractions continue to employ an assembly of referential language, whether in paint, in piano keys or in words: the often bizarre, sometimes fantastic and always unfamiliar results still rely upon conventional constituents. In any case, abstract remains a misleading term for artistic endeavour. More properly employed, the word means a digest of existing information. 'Non representational' or 'non objective' would be more appropriate but Abstract has stuck and so 'abstract' must remain to describe those non-representational aspects of Nonsense poetry. Some of these have been hijacked by poetry purists as 'ultimate poetry' which requires only sound and rhythm to make its effects and whose words mean nothing at all. Some are claimed by linguists who develop a new vocabulary from the Nonsense words: some exist to avoid being reasonable and thus incapable of producing art. There is an implicit invitation to the audience to join in the game of thinking that because reason and logic do not produce art, the unreasonable and illogical just might.

Nonsense does not subvert authority: it underpins it. Social codes, political regimes, religious beliefs and aesthetical standards are demonstrated by imaginative variation. Nonsense upholds the rules whilst turning them upside down. The values of the existing order are implicitly acknowledged, in the strangest of circumstances: Gilbert's petty criminals have the utmost respect for all the conventions which their profession does not require them to violate. The Butcher teaches the Beaver in a classroom lesson that the Jubjub bird should be boiled in sawdust and salted in glue,[656] and the formal marriage ceremony of the Owl and the Pussy Cat is conducted by a turkey with a pig's ring. Once again, we are obliged to recognise a certain English quality in our three Nonsense writers, if, by English, we mean a natural respect for the institutions concerning law and order. Neither Lear, nor Carroll nor Gilbert set out to challenge any social code directly, but chose to break away from conformity by their singular imagination and personal individuality. Nonsense was their spontaneous and particular expression of freedom, a concept dear to the English heart and one which gives rise to the soubriquet 'eccentric'. None of them adopted bohemian dress or Tennysonian hairstyles: none behaved in ways other than that of perfect Victorian gentlemen. The extreme seriousness and solemnity which characterised their more formal endeavours of art, mathematics or drama belongs to the age – the Nonsense, which escaped, is timeless.

Although Nonsense is never directly <u>about</u> anything in particular, this book has demonstrated that, unwittingly, it illustrates aspects of mid-Victorian

---

[656] *Hunting of the Snark*, Fit Five.

life in a unique and fascinating fashion. This is not only valuable to posterity: contemporary readers and listeners would have enjoyed the harmless anarchy offered by a nonsensical reversal of traditional values. Gilbert's topsy-turvydom offered delightful challenges to a world in which all felt safe, comfortable and prosperous. The voyage of Carroll's Snark, forever searching for it knew not what, it knew not where, by means of familiar references to railways and current courtroom dramas, and Lear's melancholic wanderings through Nonsense landscapes, leavened by improbable plants and animals, seem to demonstrate the existence of another world altogether. Both adults and children could explore this strange other-world in the security of a return ticket in their back pocket. The references and contexts researched for this study offer a certain truth to Nonsense inspiration, and even if they cannot provide the whole truth, they remain within a decent boundary of chance, unlike, for example, the recent attempt to claim C.S.Lewis' *Narnia Chronicles* as 'the seven spheres of Ptolemaic cosmology'.[657]

Each Nonsense writer is characterised by certain motifs which relate to, and explore in, his own particular personality and experience. Moreover, the unconscious element in Nonsense allowed an escape for those aspects of a human pysche that are less easily expressed and acknowledged. Edward Lear's Nonsense demonstrates his love for the natural world, synonymous with the early nineteenth century romantic conception of nature and the dawning of environmental conservation and the protection of wildlife. In it, we hear his musical gifts of rhythm and sound, illustrated by lively poetic metre and constant references to Tennyson. We note the momentum of constantly dancing people and flying animals and birds as well as a certain preoccupation with eating, food and drink. Lear's Nonsense drawings are informed by his skill as a botanical illustrator and later studies in topography, with glimpses of a relationship with the Pre-Raphaelite Brethren and his teacher, Holman Hunt. Through all the nonsense can be glimpsed the desperate sadness of incurable ill health, only mitigated by constant travel, slightly obsessive friendships and Marsala.

There are occasional descriptions of Lewis Carroll as not one person but two: the Mr. Hyde of dry-as-dust books on Symbolic Logic and Dr. Jekyll, creator of a mystical fairyland. Prescient application of the philosophy of William Blake enables an understanding of the disparate, contrary elements within us, of which Carroll constitutes a perfect example. Yet the struggle to accommodate contrary characteristics leads to certain tensions which modern psychologists may decide offer clues to creative genius. Carroll's Snark demonstrates a pedagogic teacher of entirely unnecessary information, and yet capable of the purest flights of fancy.

The Snark chorus allows us to share Carroll's fascination for railways which is always linked to an obsession with time and timetables. An endless series of bizarre experiments, facts and statistics point to a man obsessed with gadgets, games and detail – a limitless quest suggests both a romantic longing

---

[657] Michael Ward, *Planet Narnia*, OUP, 2008; a scholarly thesis with wide-ranging philosophical, theological and scientific theories whose conclusions would, perhaps, surprise Professor Lewis as much as this writer.

and an ambitious character never entirely at peace. The Baker's engagement with the Snark every night, after dark, unconsciously reveals not only Carroll's insomnia, but his reliance on a dream world, familiar to readers of Alice and prominent in Victorian mythology.[658] The Barrister's Dream in Fit 6 offers a similar courtroom nightmare to that of Gilbert's Lord Chancellor in *Iolanthe*. More material substance in *The Snark* allows us to share in the opening up of new continents and Victorian dramas of exploration and endurance. We make a more powerful connection between Carroll's left-handedness and his portrayals of life backwards or through a looking glass. Again, we consider Nonsense as an unfamiliar arrangement of familiar form and language – this time, back to front.

Gilbert's *Bab Ballads* allow the closest portrayal of his own experience. Barristers, soldiers, journalists and actors are grounded in reality despite their nonsensical goings-on, and Gilbert's knowledge of the clubroom, the courtroom, Fleet Street and the racecourse are easily glimpsed, as is his personal feud with the clergy. Less tangible is his self-portrait as a sensitive yet highly competitive alpha male, driven to succeed in the strange new world of a mass media. Gilbert's small, razor-sharp sketches add to the impact of the Ballads, making an effective contrast to the Victorian craze for the immense, the voluminous and the realist. Despite a tetchy perfectionism, he was a shameless plagiarist, borrowing themes from past writers and current newspaper stories: it would require several theses to track down all the sources of Gilbert's inspiration.[659] Ballad nonsense mocks the rituals of arranged marriage, sneers at cowards, laughs at foreigners and upholds a keen sense of national pride.

We have seen that our three Nonsense heroes are quintessentially English, masculine and middle class. They share, and eccentrically apply, a privileged education, an ability for concentrated and prolonged endeavour and a driving ambition. All three were perfectionists. Carroll's mania for collecting trivia and his obsessive concern to record minutiae would probably lead to a diagnosis of addictive/compulsive disorder today. Gilbert's endless, exhausting rehearsals and his insistence that actors took his Nonsense entirely seriously, drove them to the brink of despair. Lear's feverish financial insecurity obliged him to work day and night, thence to hassle friends ceaselessly for subscriptions to his books and paintings. Several studies have concluded that there is a relationship between creativity and psychosis and Hans Eysenck has drawn a parallel between the divergent, lateral thinking of artists and the

---

[658] Questions have been raised concerning Carroll's possible use of laudanum to enhance a dream-state but there is no proof, nor mention in any document that appears to exist. It appears extraordinarily unlikely.

[659] Gilbert's gentle and wholly inadequate policemen may well have been borrowed from 'Les Deux Gendarmes' in *Genevieve de Brabant* (1859) a comic opera by Offenbach, translated into English by H.B.Fernie. All WSG's bobbies in the Ballads and in the *Pirates of Penzance* appear a decade or so later.

tendency to overinclusive behaviour in psychotics.[660] Lear certainly suffered from severe epilepsy and there is some evidence to suggest that Carroll had occasional bouts of TLE (temporal frontal lobe epilepsy). The physical endurance required for Lear's travels or Carroll's twenty mile walks may be related to their desire to escape their demons and sleep. Only Gilbert <u>appears</u> to have been entirely mentally and physically robust.[661]

All three saw Nonsense in words, sound, pictures and music: Lear and Gilbert were artists – Carroll was a photographer. Lear actually wrote Nonsense songs and Gilbert translated the *Bab Ballads* into libretti for Sullivan's tunes. Carroll collected musical boxes and sang hymns. How much they knew of each other's work must remain largely conjecture, but we do know that Lewis Carroll owned a first edition (1869) of the *Bab Ballads*[662] and he decorated his own copy of Lear's Nonsense: we know also that Chichester Fortescue wrote to Edward Lear in 1869 asking if he had read *Alice in Wonderland*.[663] All three began writing Nonsense in their twenties reaching a peak in their mid-forties but only Lear continued to invent Nonsense in his old age. Carroll, dying aged sixty-six, did not have an old age, and Gilbert became a magistrate. None of them ever grew up.

The Introduction asked several questions to which I hope this Conclusion attends.

Nonsense was not a reaction to the solemn seriousness of much Victorian endeavour: it was part of it. Each depended upon the other in an utterly symbiotic relationship. Nonsense cannot exist without a solid set of impregnable values linked to a tradition of national consciousness. In reverse, revered and accepted traditions inspire a mildly anarchical thumbs-up. Don Quixote cannot tilt at windmills, giants or otherwise, if there are no windmills to be tilted at. It is the very facts of Victorian existence; the combination of

---

[660] Hans J.Eysenck 'The Measurement of Creativity' in Margaret Boden, Editor, *Dimensons of Creativity*, MIT Press, 1994, p211

[661] Rather tactlessly, WSG celebrated his enjoyment of this in himself and others. In *Utopia, Ltd*, Mr Goldbury sings a ballad of which John Betjeman would be proud. 'A wonderful joy our eyes to bless/in her magnificent comeliness/is an English girl of eleven stone two/and five foot ten in her dancing shoe'.

[662] Derek Hudson, *Lewis Carroll*, London, Constable. 1954, p229. It appears that Carroll possessed a comprehensive collection of light verses by Calverley, Hood, Leigh Hunt, and Praed.

[663] Noakes, p242

secure and established institutions combined with a spirit of independent free enterprise in mid-nineteenth century England which made Nonsense possible. The issue of freedom, so crucial in our study, relates to nationalism and the English character and goes some way to explain the absence of Nonsense in France, Italy or Spain, countries with a patchy tradition of democracy and uncertain civic liberties[664]/[665].

Where did Nonsense come from? I hope I have answered that question in the body of the thesis, but in essence, it came from a multi-layered context of contemporary social mores which included religion, music, literature, art, drama, poetry, natural history, science, travel and law. There was no one moment when certain fashions became certain facts. Factors which transformed what might have remained euphemeral phenomena into the coinage of our cultural capital are complex and various.[666] We have forgotten, for example, the songs of Henry Bishop and the furniture of Napoleon's Empire: we no longer buy upright pianos with giraffe necks or swim from bathing machines. We cannot forget the Victorian Nonsense poetry of Edward Lear, Lewis Carroll and William Gilbert because the impact it made on us as children guides us into bookshops today, in the tradition established by parents, grandparents and great-grandparents. Our own childish pleasure in Nonsense is reinforced by the tacit support of earlier generations. The first books we read are the books that we most remember, just as our school years remain imbedded in the memory even when they occupy an ever-smaller fraction of adult life.

Could Nonsense become part of a literary canon? I believe the answer to my own inquiry is no, despite a tentative appropriation of *Alice* by the surrealists. Nonsense remains as fresh and startling today as when it was first written and any academic belief in the possibility of canonisation adheres more to the sheer survival of Nonsense than to cultural mores which have enshrined the more generally acceptable artefacts. Nonsense is the fish which cleans the shark's teeth: it is the small bird who flies without fear in the mouth of the hippopotamus: it is the one, wild flower of Victorian literature.

Author's Note.

My initial reaction to the dependence of my family on Nonsense writing for communication was childish and harsh. With the research for this study, I now understand that Nonsense was always more than a device for the powerfully inarticulate: it offered some comfortable certainties in the immediate postwar years. Ballads, limericks and Nonsense verses remained when much of London

---

[664] Only perhaps the inspired silliness of opera bouffeé librettists Meilhac or Halevy come close.

[665] The Americans can claim Oliver Wendell Holmes and Wetmore Carryll as Victorian counterparts to Lear, Carroll & Gilbert; Ogden Nash is their contemporary Nonsense poet who ranks as an immortal.

[666] Concept of 'cultural capital' borrowed, with grateful thanks, to Pierre Bourdieu.

did not. Custom neither withered them, nor staled their infinite variety and their gentle mockery of foreigners in particular was soothing balm.

THE END

BIBLIOGRAPHY

Unpublished Theses.

Blake, Peter 'The Paradox of a Periodical', M.A. Dissertation, Sussex University, 2006.

Crowther, A.J. 'Dramatic Works of W.S.Gilbert', M.Phil. Thesis, Bradford University, 1988.

Graham-Smith, Darien 'Contextualising Carroll'. Ph.D. Thesis, Bangor University of Wales, 2005.

Lodge, S 'Parodies, Puns and Pence in the works of Thomas Hood', Thesis, Oxford 1999.

Philip, N .A. 'Aspects of Myth & Folklore in Children's Folklore', Ph.D. Thesis, London University, 1979.

Reynolds, K G 'Girls Only: Development of Juvenile Fiction in the Late Victorian period', D.Phil. Thesis, Sussex University, 1989.

Rossiter, E 'A Theory of Nonsense', Ph.D. Thesis, London, Westminster, 1997.

Seabrook-Hendry, Therie 'Unpacking Punch', D.Phil. Thesis, Sussex University, 2004.

Wolfreys. J. 'The Performance of National Identity. Narratives and Idioms of Englishness from Coleridge to Trollope', D.Phil. Thesis, Sussex University, 1993.

Published Material.

Abraham, Gerald *The Concise Oxford History of Music,* Oxford University Press, 1979.

Allen, Reginald *First Night G & S,* London, Chappell & Co, 1958.

Ashford, Daisy *The Young Visiters*.(sic) London, Chatto & Windus, 1919.

Atlay, Beresford J. *Victorian Chancellors,* London, Smith Elder, 1909.

Atlay, Beresford J. *Trials of the Century,* London, Grant Richards, 1897.

Ayer, A. J. *Language, Truth & Logic.* London, Penguin, 1946.

Baker, Gordon & Hacker, P.M.S. *Critical Investigation into Modern Theories of Language,* Oxford, Blackwell Press, 1984.

Baker, Michael *The Rise of the Victorian Actor,* London, Croom Helm, 1978.

Baily, Leslie *The Gilbert and Sullivan Book,* London, Cassell & Co., Revised and reprinted, 1956 & 66.

Bailey, Peter *'A Mingled Mass of Perfectly Legitimate Pleasures: The Victorian Middle Class and the problem of leisure',* VPR 21(1977-88)7-28

Baring-Gould, William *Sherlock Holmes - The Biography,* London, Rupert Hart Davis, 1962.

Barker, Emma *The Changing Status of the Artist,* New Haven and London, Yale University Press in association with the Open University, 1999.

Barreca, Regina *Untamed & Unabashed; Essays on Women and Humour in British Literature,* Detroit, Wayne State University, 1994.

Barzun, Jacques *Classic, Romantic and Modern,* London, Seeker & Warburg, 1943, reprinted 1969.

Bashford, Christopher and Langley Leanne, (Editors) *Music and British Culture: Essays in Honour of Cyril Ehrlich,* Oxford University Press, 2000.

Baugh, Albert C. *A Literary History of England,* New York, Appleton Century Crofts, 1948.

Becker Lennon, Florence *Lewis Carroll,* London, Cassell & Co, 1947.

Beecham, Adrian Welles, *Introduction to The Collected Bab Ballads,* London, Hutchinson, 1930.

Belloc, Hilaire *Cautionary Tales,* London, Duckworth & Co, 1923.

Bertelsen, Lance *The Nonsense Club: Literature and Popular Culture* 1749–1764 Oxford University Press, 1986.

Bishop, A.S. 'Ralph Lingen, Secretary to the Education Department, 1849–1870', BJES Vol.16 No.2 (1968)128-163

Booth, Michael R. *Victorian Spectacular Theatre,* London, Routledge, (Editor)

Booth, Michael R. *The Revels History of Drama in England,* Vol. VI, London, Methuen, 1975.

Bowen, Desmond *The Idea of the Victorian Church,* Montreal, McGill University Press, 1968.

Bradley, Ian (Editor) *The Complete Annotated Gilbert and Sullivan,* Paperback 2 Vols, Oxford University Press, 2001.

Bratton, J. S. (Editor) *Music Hall Performance and Style,* Milton Keynes, Open University Press, 1986.

Bratton, J. S. (Editor) *The Victorian Popular Ballad,* London, Macmillan, 1975.

Brown, Penny 'The Captured World of Victorian Childhood'.
YWES 74 (1993)371-451

Browne, Edith *W.S.G.,* London and New York, John Lane, 1907.

Briggs, Asa *Victorian Cities,* London, Pelican Books, 1968. (with Susan Briggs)

Briggs, Asa *Cap and Bells,* London, MacDonald, 1972.

Byrom, Thomas *Nonsense and Wonder: the poems and cartoons of Edward Lear.* New York, Penguin Books, 1977.

Calverley, C.S. *Fly Leaves,* First published in London, Deighton Bell, 1884.

Cammaerts, Emile *The Poetry of Nonsense.* London, Routledge, 1925.

Campbell, G.A. *The Civil Service in Britain,* London, Duckworth, 1955.

(Carroll, Lewis, see under Dodgson, Charles)

Cazamian, Louis *The Development of English Humour,* AMS Press, Part 1, 1930. Part 1, 1952, reprint New York, 1965.

Chadwick, Owen *The Victorian Church,* London, Adam and Charles Black, 1966.

Chesterton, G.K. *In Defence of Nonsense,* R.Brimley Johnson, London,1901, now available on Internet 'Project Gutenberg' .

Chesterton, G.K. *The Man Who Was Thursday*, The Essential Chesterton, Oxford University Press, 1987.

Chitty, Susan *That Singular Person Called Lear: A Biography of Edward Lear, Artist, Traveller and Prince of Nonsense*, New York, Atheneum, 1988.

Clark, Anne *Lewis Carroll,* New York, Schocken Books, 1979.

Cockshut, A.O.J. *Anglican Attitudes: A Study of Victorian Religious Controversies,* London, Collins, 1959.

Cohen, Morton, *Lewis Carroll,* London, Macmillan, 1995.

Cohen, Morton, *Letters of Lewis Carroll,* (Editor) London, Macmillan, 1979.

Cohen, Morton, *Lewis Carroll and His illustrators,* (With Edward Wakeling), London, Macmillan, 2003.

Colley, Ann 'Edward Lear's Limericks and the Reversals of Nonsense', VP 26 (1988)285-299

Collingwood, Stuart *The Life and Letters of Lewis Carroll,* London, T. Fisher Unwin, 1898.

Cowles, Virginia *The Rothschilds: a family of fortune,* London, Weidenfeld & Nicolson, 1973.

Crowther, M.A. *Church Embattled: Religious Controversy in mid- Victorian England,* Newton Abbot, David & Charles,1970.

Cruse, Amy *The Victorians and Their Books,* London, George Allen, 1935.

Daiches, David *Critical History of English Literature.* New York, Ronald Press, 1970.

Dale, Jacquette *Schopenhauer and a Philosophy of the Arts,*Cambridge University Press, 1996.

Davidson, Angus *Edward Lear: Landscape Painter and Nonsense Poet,* London, John Murray,1938, revised, 1968.

Davis, Tracy & Donkin, Ellen, 'Women and Playwriting in 19th century Britain.' YWES 80(2001)529-604

Dark, Sidney and Grey, Roland *W.S.Gilbert: His Life and Letters,*London, Methuen, 1923.

De la Mare, Walter *Lewis Carroll.* London, Faber and Faber, 1932.

Dellamora, Richard *Masculine Desire and Sexual Politics of Victorian Aestheticism,* University of North Carolina Press, 1990.

Dickens, Charles, *Hard Times*, first published 1854.

Dickens, Charles, *Little Dorrit*, first published 1855-57.

Dilworth, Thomas, 'Society and Self in the Limericks of Lear', Review of English Studies 45(1994) 42-64

Dodgson, Charles, *Alice's Adventures In Wonderland,* together with *Alice Through the Looking Glass:* London, Penguin Classic Centenary Edition, 1988, Introduction and Notes by Hugh Haughton.

Dodgson, Charles, *The Hunting of the Snark.* London, Penguin Classic Edition, 1995. Introduction and Notes by Martin Gardner.

Dollimore, Jonathan *Sexual Dissidence,* Oxford, Clarendon Press, 1991.

Drabble, Margaret, Editor, *The Oxford Companion to English Literature*, Oxford University Press, 2000.

Drotner, Kirsten *English Children and their Magazines, 1751–1954.* Yale University Press, 1988.

Dyhouse, Carol 'The Role of Women', *The Victorians*, Editor, Laurence Lerner, London, Methuen, 1978.

Eden, D.J. *Gilbert and Sullivan – The Creative Conflict.* New Jersey, Farleigh Dickenson University Press, 1986.

Eden, D.J. *W.S. Gilbert, Appearance and Reality.* Saffron Walden, The Arthur Sullivan Society, 2003.

Edinger, George (with E.J.C.Neep) *Pons Asinorum.* London, Kegan Paul, 1929.

Ehrlich, Cyril *The Piano - A History,* Clarendon Press, Oxford, 1999.

Ellegaard, Alvar *Readership of the Periodical Press in Mid Victorian Britain,* Goteborg, 1957.

Elwyn Jones, Jo & Gladstone, Francis *The Alice Companion,* London, Macmillan, 1998.

Empson, William *Seven Types of Ambiguity. 1930.*
London, New Directions Publishing Company, 1966.

Feiling, Keith *History of England,* London, Book Club Associates, 1974.

Fischler, Alan *Modified Rapture: Comedy in WSG's Savoy Operas,*
Charlottesville, University Press of Virginia, 1991.

Flescher, Jacqueline, 'The Language of Nonsense in Alice', Yale French
Studies 43 (1969)128-144

Flint, Kate 'The Woman Reader, 1837-1914', YWES 74 (1993)371-451

Foucault, Michel, *Madness and Civilisation,* London, Routledge, 1971.

Foucault, Michael, *Social Theory andTransgression,* New York, Columbia
University Press, 1982.

Galbraith, Gretchen 'Reading Lives - Reconstructing Childhood, Books and
Schools', YWES 78 (1997)574

Gale, Maggie & Viv Gardner, (Editors) *Women, Theatre and Performance,
New Histories*, Manchester, Manchester University Press, 2000.

Gardner, Helen, (Editor) *The New Oxford Book of English Verse,* Oxford
University Press, 1984.

Gardner, Martin *The Annotated Alice: The Definitive Edition,* (Lewis Carroll),
Penguin, London 2001. Originally published by Allen Lane 1970.

Gardner, Martin, (Editor) *The Hunting of the Snark*, (Lewis Carroll) London,
Penguin Classics, 1995.

Gattegno, Jean *Lewis Carroll, Fragments of a Looking Class,* New York,
Crowell, 1976.

Gilbert, W.S. *The Bab Ballads.* Edited by James Ellis, The Belknap Press of
Harvard University Press, Cambridge, Massachusetts, 1970.

Gilbert, Dr. William *Memoirs of a Cynic,* London, Tinsley Bros,1880.

Goldberg, Isaac *The Story of Gilbert and Sullivan, or The Compleat Savoyard,*
New York, Crown Publishers, 1929

Gombrich, RH. *The Story of Art,* London, Phaidon, 1974.

Goodacre, Dr.Selwyn *All The Snarks: An Exploration for the Illustrated
Edition of the Hunting of the Snark.* Oxford, Inky Parrot Press, 2007.

Gopal, S. *British Policy in India, 1858-1905.* Cambridge University Press, 1965.

Gray, Donald 'Snakes in Greenland', Victorian Poetry 26(1988)211-230

Gray, Thomas 'Elegy Written In A Country Churchyard', as consulted in the Oxford Book of Collected Verse, Oxford, Clarendon Press, 1931.

Grayling, A. C. *The Quarrel of the Age: the Life and Times of William Hazlitt,* London, Weidenfeld & Nicolson, 2000.

Grayling, A. C. *The Meaning of Things,* London, Weidenfeld & Nicolson, 2001.

Guiliano, Edward *A Time for Humour: Essays on the 150th Anniversary of the Birthday of Charles Dodgson,* New York, Clarkson Potter.

Hall, James *Jungian Dream Interpretation*, www.psycheu.com Assessed 17.6.2008

Hardy, Thomas *A Pair of Blue Eyes.* London, 1873.

Hark, Ina Rae 'Edward Lear: Eccentricity and Victorian Angst'. Victorian Poetry 16 (1978)112-122

Harper, George McLean 'Coleridge's Conversational Poems', Essays in Modern Criticism, Oxford University Press, 1960.

Haughton, Hugh (Editor) *The Chatto Book of Nonsense Poetry,* London, Chatto & Windus, 1988.

Haughton, Hugh (Editor) Introduction to the Penguin Classic Centenary Edition of *Alice's Adventures in Wonderland* and *Alice Through the Looking Glass*, London, 1998.

Hibbert, Christopher *A Social History of England,* London, Grafton Books, 1978.

Hill, Rosemary *Pugin – God's Architect*, London, Allen Lane, 2007.

Hobhouse, Hermione (Editor) *Survey of London.* London, Athlone Press, for the Greater London Council, 1986.

Hobsbawn, Eric, *The Age of Capital*, London, Weidenfeld & Nicholson, 1975

Hofer, Philip *Edward Lear as Landscape Draughtsman,* Oxford University

Press, 1967.

Holms, Dr. Mark *Health Report and Dreaming* www.pyschoanalysis.org.uk/solms2.htm, Accessed 17/6/2008

Holquist, Michael 'What Is A Boojum?; Nonsense and Moderation', French Studies 43 (1969)145-164

Honour, Hugh & Fleming, John *A World History of Art,* London, Macmillan, 1982.

Hopkinson, Amanda *Julia Margaret Cameron,* London,Virago, 1986

Hudson, Derek *Lewis Carroll,* London, Constable, 1954.

Huizinga, J. *Homo Ludens: A Study of the Play Element in Culture,* London, Routledge, 1949.

Humble, Nicola   (with Kimberley Reynolds) *Victorian Heroines,* New York, Harvester Press, 1993.

Huxley, Aldous *Selected Letters.* Editor, Grover Smith. London, Chatto & Windus, 1969.

Huxley, Elspeth *With Forks and Hope,* London, Chatto & Windus, 1964.

Huxley, Francis *The Raven and The Writing Desk,* London, Thames & Hudson, 1976.

Ince, Richard B. *Calverley and Some Cambridge Wits of the 19th Century,* London, Grant Richards, 1929.

Jackson, Patrick *Education Act Forster: a political biography of WEF, 1818–1886*, London, Associated University Presses, 1997.

Jackson, Russell *Victorian Theatre in Its Time,* Franklin, New Amsterdam Books, (paperback) 1994.

Jones, John Bush *W S Gilbert: a century of scholarship & commentary,* New York, New York University Press,1970.

Jump, Harriet Devine *Women's Writing of the Victorian Period,* London, St. Martin's Press, 1999.

Kermode, Frank *Pleasure and Change: the Aesthetics of Canon,* Oxford University Press, 2004.

Kincaid, James (Editor) *Soaring with the Dodo; Essays on Lewis Carroll's Life and Art,* Charlottesville, University Press of Virginia, 1982.

Knoepflmacher, Ulrich C. *Ventures into Childland: Victorians, fairy tales and femininity,* University of Chicago Press,1998.

Lambert, Richard S. *The Railway King,* London, Allen & Unwin,1934.

Lamborne, Lionel *Victorian Painting,*London, Phaidon,1999.

Leach, Karoline *In The Shadow of the Dream Child,* London, Peter Owen, 1999.

Lear, Edward, *Nonsense Songs and Stories,* London, Frederick Warne & Co, Ltd, 1894.

Lear, Edward, *The Complete Nonsense of Edward Lear.* Editor, Holbrook Jackson, London, Faber & Faber, lst edition, 1947, 18th impression, 1989.

Lear, Edward, *The Complete Nonsense and Other Vers*e, Editor, Vivien Noakes, London, Allen Lane, Penguin Books, 2001.

Lehmann, John, *Edward Lear and His World,* London, Thames & Hudson, 1977.

Lehmann, John, *Lewis Carroll and the Spirit of Nonsense.* Nottingham Byron Lecture, 1972.

Lerner, Laurence, (Editor) *The Victorians; The Context of English Literature,* London, Methuen, 1978.

Levi, Peter *Edward Lear,* London, Macmillan, 1995.

Little, Judy *Comedy and the Woman Writer: Woolf, Spark and Feminism,* Lincoln, Nebraska University Press, 1983.

Lecercle, Jean- Jacques *The Philosophy of Nonsense,* London & New York, Routledge, 1994.

Lucas, F.L *Ten Victorian Poets,* Cambridge University Press, 1940.

MacCarthy, Fiona *Byron: Life and Legend,* London, John Murray, 2002.

McKee, Patricia 'Public and Private: Gender and Class in the British Novel 1764-1878', YWES 78 (1997)572-644

McKellar, Peter *Imagination and Thinking,* London, Cohen & West, 1957.

Malcolm, Noel *The Origins of English Nonsense,* London, Fontana, 1998.

Mangan, J.A. *Athleticism in the Victorian and Edwardian Public School,* Cambridge University Press, 1981.

Mason, Philip *The English Gentleman, His rise and fall,* New York, William Morrow, 1992.

Menninghaus, Winifried *In Praise of Nonsense,* Stanford University Press, 1999.

Merleau-Ponty, Maurice *Sens et Non-Sens,* North Western University Press, 1964.

Messkoub, Hannah 'Theories on Left Handedness and Laterality'. www.serendip.brynmawr.edu/bb/neuro Accessed 6/6/008

Miftari, Virginia Clinical Director, Cottonwood de Tucson, 17, Wimpole St, London WI. Psychotherapist; consulted in relationship to Edward Lear.

Milne, A.A. *Now We Are Six,* London, Methuen,1927.

Nettle, Daniel *Strong Imagination: Madness, Creativity and Human Nature,* Oxford University Press, 2001.

Nichols, Ashton 'Romantic Rhinos and Victorian Vipers'. www.dickinson.edu/~nicholsa Accessed 6/6/2008

Nickel, Douglas *Dreaming in Pictures,* Yale University Press, 2002.

Nicolson, Harold *The English Sense of Humour and other Essays,* London, Constable, from the limited edition by The Dropmore Press, London.1946.

Noakes, Vivien, *Life of a Wanderer: Edward Lear,* London, William Collins & Co., 1968. Revised paperback edition, London, Fontana, 1979.

Noakes, Vivien, *Edward Lear: His Life and Letters,* Oxford, Clarendon Press, 1988.

Noakes, Vivien, *Edward Lear,* London, Royal Academy in association with Weidenfeld & Nicolson, 1985.

Nowottny, Winifred *The Language Poets Use,* London, Athlone Press, 1966.

Olson, Kirby *Comedy after Postmodernism: re-reading comedy from Lear to Willeford,* Texas Technical University Press, 2001.

Orwell, George *Funny But Not Vulgar: Collected Essays and Journalism,* London, Secker & Warburg, 1968.

Pearson, Hesketh *Gilbert and Sullivan,* London, Hamish Hamilton, 1935. *Gilbert, His Life and Strife,* London, Methuen, 1957.

Pollard, Arthur (Editor) *The Victorians: Sphere History of Literature in the English Language,* Volume 6, London, Sphere Books, 1970.

Porter, Roy *Myths of the English,* Cambridge, Polity Press, 1992.

Powell, Kerry *Women and the Victorian Theatre,* Cambridge University Press, 1997.

Press, John *The Fire and the Fountain,* Oxford, OUP, 1955.

Price, Cecil 'The Victorian Theatre', *From Sphere History of Literature in the English Language,* Volume 6, London, Sphere Books, 1970, pp386-401

Priestley, J. B. *English Humour,* London, Longmans, 1930. *Victoria's Heyday.* London, Heinemann, 1977.

Quiller-Couch, Arthur (Editor) *Oxford Book of English Verse.* Oxford, Clarendon Press, 1931.

Radin, Paul, *The Trickster: A study in American/Indian Mythology.* New York, Schocken Books, 1956.

Rainbow, Bernarr,   'The Rise of Popular Music Education in 19th century England', VPR.30(1986) 25-49

Ranson-Polizzotti, Sadi '42 Seconds Underground: The Photography of Lewis Carroll', www.tantmieux.squarespace.com Accessed 6/6/008

Read, Herbert, *Phases of English Poetry,* London, Hogarth Press, 1928.

Reike, Alison, *The Senses of Nonsense,* University of Iowa Press, 1992.

Reynolds, Ernest, *Early Victorian Drama*, Cambridge, W. Hefler & Sons,1932.

Revels *History of Drama on the English Stage.* London Methuen, 1975.

Richardson, Joanna, *Edward Lear,* London, Longmans, 1965.

Romani, Roberto, *National Character and Public Spirit in Britain and France,*

1750–1914, Cambridge University Press. 2002.

Rose, Jonathan, *Intellectual Life of the British Working Classes,* Yale University Press. 2001

Rowell, George, *The Victorian Theatre,* Cambridge University Press, 1978.

Ruskin, John, *Sesame and Lilies: Two Paths: The King of the Golden River.* London, Dent Edition,1907, reprinted 1970.

Ruskin, John, *The Stones of Venice,* New edited & abridged edition, London, Penguin, 2001.

Sala, Michele, 'Lear's Nonsense Beyond Children's Literature.' www.nonsenselit.org/Lear Accessed 6/6/008

Samuel, Raphael Editor, *Patriotism: The Making and Unmaking of British National Identity,* London, Routledge,1989.

Sanders, Valerie (Editor.) *Records of Girlhood: an anthology of 19th century women's childhood.* London, Ashgate Press, 2000.

Schmidt, Oscar *Essays on English Social Life and Politics,* London, Jarrolds, 1926.

Schonfield.Hugh J. *The Train,* London, Denis Archer, 1932.

Schramm, Jan Melissa, 'The Anatomy of a Barrister's Tongue: Rhetoric, Satire and the Bar in Victorian England', VLC (2004) 285-303

Scott, Derek, *The Singing Bourgeois,* Milton Keynes, Open University Press, 1989.

Sellar, W.C. & Yeatman, R.J. *1066 And All That.* London, Methuen, 1930.

Sewell, Elizabeth, *The Structure of Poetry,* London, Routledge & Kegan Paul, 1951.

Sewell, Elizabeth, *The Field of Nonsense,* London, Chatto & Windus, 1952.

Sewell, Elizabeth, *The Orphic Voice,* London, Routledge & Kegan Paul, 1961.

Shabermann, R.B. *Under the Quizzing Glass: A Carroll Miscellany,* London, Magpie Press, 1972.

Shakespeare, William *Twelfth Night. Julius Caesar.*

Shattock, Joanne (Editor) *Women and Literature in Britain 1800–1900,*

Cambridge University Press, 2001.

Sheridan, Louisa Henrietta 'Comic Offerings of the 1830's: Gender and Humour in the Early Victorian Era', VPR 29(1996) 95 - 115

Sitwell, Edith *Facade,* First published 1918: now from London, Duckworths & Co, 1950/1957.

Smith, Lindsay, *Victorian Photography, Painting and Poetry: the Enigma of Visibility in Ruskin, Morris and the PreRaphaelites*, Cambridge Studies in Literature and Culture 6, Cambridge University Press, 1995.

Stedman, Jane W. *W.S. Gilbert – A Classic Victorian and his Theatre,* Oxford University Press, 1966.

Stephens, John Russell, *The Profession of the Playright,* Cambridge University Press, 1992.

Strachey, Edward *Introduction to Nonsense Songs and Stories by Edward Lear.* London, Frederick Warne & Co, 1894.

Strachey, Lady Constance, (Editor) *Letters of Edward Lear,* Vols 1 & 2. London, T. Fisher Unwin, 1907.

Strange, Carol G *Secret Peoples: Fairies and Victorian Consciousness,* Oxford University Press, 1998.

Sussman, Herbert *Victorian Masculinities,* Cambridge University Press,1995.

Sutton, Max Keith *WSG,* Boston, Massachussets, Twayne, 1975.

Taylor, George *Players and Performance in Victorian Theatre,* Manchester University Press, 1989.

Temperley, Nicholas *The Lost Chord,* Bloomington, Indiana University Press, 1989.

Tennyson, Lord Alfred *Poems,* 1842.

Tennyson, Charles *Alfred Tennyson,* London, Macmillan, 1950.

Thackeray, W.M. *History of Pendennis,* First serialised in London, 1848 - 1850.

Thomas, Donald L*ewis Carroll: a portrait with background,* London, John Murray, 1996.

Tigges, Wm. *An Anatomy of Literary Nonsense,* Amsterdam, Rodopi, 1988.

Thomas, Annie, *Only Herself,* London, Chapman & Hall, 1870.

Thomas, Annie, *Played Out*, Leipzig, Tauchnitz, 1870.

Trollope, Anthony, *The Way We Live Now,* London, 1875. Edition consulted, Wordsworth Classics, 1995.

Vance, Norman, *The Sinews of the Spirit: The ideal of manliness in Victorian Literature and Religious Thought,* Cambridge University Press, 1985.

Vemon Lord, John, *Illustrating Lear,* Published Inaugural Lecture for Brighton Polytechnic, Asa Briggs Hall, Falmer, Brighton. 1991.

Vemon Lord, John, *Afterward to Illustrating the Hunting of the Snark,* Artists Edition, 2006.

Wagner-Lawlor, Jennifer (Editor) *The Victorian Comic Spirit,* London, New Perspectives, Ashgate Press, 2000.

Ward, Sir A.R. (Editor) *Cambridge History of English Literature*, Cambridge University Press, 1932.

Whicher, Stephen 'Books and Records', College English, 22(1960)49-54

Wilson, A.N. *The Victorians,* London, Hutchinson, 2002.

Wolfe, Humbert *English Verse Satire,* London, Hogarth Press, 1929.

Woolf, Virginia *The Moment and Other Essays*. New York, Harcourt Brace, 1948.

Wullschläger, Jackie *Inventing Wonderland,* London, Methuen, 1995.

Young, Arlene, *Culture, Class and Gender in the Victorian Novel: Gentlemen, Gents and Working Women,* New York St. Martin's Press, 1999.